cal Histo
n on Tel

ALSO BY CHRISTOPHER P. LEHMAN

*American Animated Cartoons of the Vietnam Era:
A Study of Social Commentary in Films
and Television Programs, 1961–1973*
(McFarland, 2006)

A Critical History of
Soul Train on Television

CHRISTOPHER P. LEHMAN

McFarland & Company, Inc., Publishers
Jefferson, North Carolina, and London

LIBRARY OF CONGRESS CATALOGUING-IN-PUBLICATION DATA

Lehman, Christopher P.
   A critical history of Soul train on television /
Christopher P. Lehman.
      p.   cm.
   Includes bibliographical references and index.

   ISBN 978-0-7864-3669-9
   softcover : 50# alkaline paper

   1. Soul train (Television program)   2. Cornelius, Don, 1936–
I. Title.
PN1992.77.S664L44   2008
791.45'72 — dc22   2008010538

British Library cataloguing data are available

Cover art ©2008 Shutterstock

Manufactured in the United States of America

*McFarland & Company, Inc., Publishers
  Box 611, Jefferson, North Carolina 28640
   www.mcfarlandpub.com*

Acknowledgments

For their help in facilitating interviews, I thank Jake Austen, Bridget Goins of WVON radio, Barbara Kensey, Dan Land, Lisa D. McGill, Stefanie Mielke of the Chicago Blues Museum, and Joe Vannelli.

For interviews and correspondence by letter, I thank Garrick Anders, Ron Bauchman, former *Soul Train* host Mystro Clark, Lorenzo Clemons, Lucky Cordell, Theresa Davis, the Dells, Dr. Vera Dunwoody, Delwen Fields, Mic Gillette, Bobby Hutton, Bill Jackson of WFLD, Clarice Kavanaugh, Christa Lee, Mike McGill, Bruce W. Miller, George O'Hare, Gregg Parker of the Chicago Blues Museum, Howard Shapiro of WCIU, Marshall Thompson of the Chi-Lites, Gino Vannelli, Joe Vannelli, Crescendo Ward, and Art West.

I thank Conrad Hansen of Moore and Hansen for advice about the book. I appreciate all of the help given by Ayana Haaruun of the *Chicago Defender* in locating relevant articles.

I am extremely grateful for the love and support of my family. My mother, father, and brother have encouraged me as long as I can remember. My children Imani and Erik are tremendous sources of inspiration. My wife Yolanda has stood by me through all the time it took to write the manuscript and motivated me when I felt most exhausted. Without her, especially, this book would not exist.

Table of Contents

Preface

This book discusses television producer Don Cornelius' role in the evolution of his groundbreaking dance series *Soul Train* from a small, all-black show in Chicago in 1970 to a lucrative brand name applying not only to the program but also to awards and various merchandise in the present day, and Cornelius' promotion of African American issues over the lifetime of the series. It also explores the various genres, artists and record labels involved with the show throughout its run. Changes in the music and television industries also receive attention, whether *Soul Train* caused them or adapted to them.

A Critical History of Soul Train *on Television* is written as an unauthorized chronological narrative. The first two chapters focus on Cornelius' years in Chicago and his launching of *Soul Train* there. The next two chapters explore how his nationally televised, California-based version of the show steadily rose both in popularity and cultural influence among African American viewers. Cornelius is also examined as a rising celebrity during that period. The final chapters illustrate his efforts to branch out beyond his dance show through various music-related business ventures, his redefinition of the series amid cultural changes beyond his control, and the decline of the program's relevance to young African Americans as he increasingly touted the show's history during its final years of production.

Articles from periodicals, which comprise most of the primary sources, reveal the periods of greatest interest by the media in the series. Although reporters have discussed the program throughout its existence, most of the coverage of *Soul Train* appeared from 1972 to 1974. In this period, only African Americans starred on the show and performed the songs that were played there. Since then, occasional surges in the number of articles have corresponded with milestones in the show's history such as the retirement of Don Cornelius as host in 1993.

Interviews with former cast members and guests are other important sources. Several interviewees participated in the Chicago-based series and discussed its impact on their lives and on African American adolescent socialization. Dancers from the nationally syndicated show described *Soul Train* as a fun means of receiving media exposure. Musical guests recalled their enjoyment of their performances on the program. One of them, Gino Vannelli, also told of his experience as the first white guest star on the show.

A chronology of the series appears as Appendix C of the book. It features important dates in the professional life of Don Cornelius, and it notes significant developments in *Soul Train*, both in Chicago and in syndicated television. The projects on which Cornelius worked in addition to *Soul Train*, and television series and networks that became formidable competition for *Soul Train* are also included in the chronology.

Very few books examine television shows created and produced by African Americans. Situation comedies such as *The Cosby Show* receive more coverage than music-oriented programs. Authors of monographs on televised music tend to discuss *Soul Train* only within the context of Dick Clark's competing dance show *American Bandstand*. However, such analyses ignore the impact of *Soul Train* on African Americans and the television industry. This book seeks to illustrate the historical importance of the series in relation to televised images of African American expression and opportunities for African Americans in television production.

Introduction

"The Exciting World of Soul"?
The 2007 Soul Train Music Awards

In early 2007, Don Cornelius celebrated the longevity of his *Soul Train* franchise, which he had created in 1970, by airing episodes that had last appeared on television in the early 1970s, and he planned the year's Soul Train Music Awards, which had begun exactly two decades earlier. Even the announcing of the nominees for the awards had an air of familiarity, for Cornelius staged the corresponding press conference in the same place where past conferences for the awards had taken place: the ritzy Beverly Hills restaurant Spago.

Routines, however, soon gave way to unfortunate events. Publicity for the twenty-first annual Soul Train Music Awards ominously began on February 6, 2007. Although Don Cornelius Productions (DCP) announced the nominees of the prizes for ten different categories of African American musical performance, Cornelius himself was too ill to attend the conference. The media received word that he had suffered a case of food poisoning but promised to recover within the next two days.

On March 10, the Soul Train Music Awards proceeded to honor modern music stars and pay homage to *Soul Train*'s history, just as previous ceremonies had done. Contemporary rhythm & blues (R&B) singers LeToya Luckett and Omarion Grandberry hosted the event. Veteran entertainer Ronald Isley, whose professional music career stretched five decades, paid tribute in song to the recently deceased "soul" singer James Brown, who had developed a career of similar longevity.

The awards also acknowledged *Soul Train*'s durability by interspersing clips from old episodes throughout the telecast of the ceremony. The images of James Brown and the S.O.S. Band on the *Soul Train* stage reminded viewers of the singers that the series showcased when no other programs on television did. The ceremony, however, did not connect any contemporary singers to the dance show with any clips of their appearances as guest artists. As a result, *Soul Train* appeared to cater solely to fans of "oldies" music, despite its continued weekly syndication.

Winners of only two of the ten categories bothered to attend. The absent victors were Mary J. Blige, John Legend, Gnarls Barkley, and Beyonce Knowles. If Knowles had appeared to receive her best single (female) award for the song "Irreplaceable," she would have faced an awkward reunion with Luckett, a former bandmate from the group Destiny's Child. Luckett was fired from the group seven years earlier, and she sued for breach-of-contract and defamation.

The low turnout gave the Soul Train Music Awards an image of irrelevance to the R&B industry — an image inconsistent with the franchise's history. *Soul Train*, after all, had once been a celebrity magnet. Thirty years ago few artists refused Cornelius' invitations to appear on the program. The show had a loyal following among African Americans, especially adolescents. Prominent African American entertainers and politicians boarding the "train" became part of a hip program, generating publicity unavailable through many other television series and selling themselves to the most likely of music consumers.

Even the winners who did appear at the 2007 awards ceremony without complaint faced their own scandals. Isley, who received the best album (group) award for "Baby Makin' Music," awaited the start of a three-year federal prison term for tax evasion. Six months earlier a U.S. District Court had ordered him to pay the Internal Revenue Service $3.1 million in back taxes.

The other present award recipients, Webstar and Young B, had caused a stir with the video to their song "Chicken Noodle Soup." Critics complained that the dancers in the video made gestures that resembled the gyrations of nineteenth-century blackface minstrels. The popularity of the song, however, transcended the controversy of the video's outdated image of African Americans. "Chicken Noodle Soup" won the dance cut prize at the awards.

Like the low attendance, Webstar's win clashed with *Soul Train*'s heritage. When the dance show first appeared on nationwide television in 1971, part of its appeal to viewers came from the unique steps of the show's dancers. The series was the first to televise popular moves such as "pops" and "locks" as well as the dance craze the "Robot." The program created what later became a tradition at African American teenagers' parties: the *Soul Train* line. Now, nearly four decades later, as the video for "Chicken Noodle Soup" featured moves that pre-dated *Soul Train* by a century, the dance show disregarded its own legacies by validating Webstar's clownish shuffling with an award.

Although most newspaper reports of the ceremony merely listed the night's winners, a few articles focused on the absent celebrities. Journalists began asking if the awards show was in trouble. Soon afterward, reports surfaced regarding Academy Award winner Jennifer Hudson's alleged attempt at breaking her commitment to personally receive the Entertainer of the Year prize. She reportedly told Cornelius that she would not appear, at which point he called Clive Davis of Arista Records to complain. Reluctant or not, she attended the ceremony, graciously received her award and sang a song from her recent movie *Dreamgirls*.

The chaos surrounding the Soul Train Music Awards underscored how far the event had strayed from the roots of the show that spawned it — the dance series *Soul Train*. Newspapers that had not covered the series in years now asked how the awards could have suffered a low turnout of honorees. After all, the show had introduced some of the most successful R&B acts to television audiences. The hip clothes and moves of the program's dancers created national trends among young African Americans. Now, especially as the stories about Hudson circulated, reporters began assessing the current show and did not print much that was favorable.

The negative press about the ceremony marked only the latest comments from a small number of journalists and celebrities about the decline of the *Soul Train* franchise. For almost two decades, isolated critics of the dance show listed uninspired dances and underdressed women among its faults. In addition, when Cornelius produced anniversary specials for *Soul Train* over the years, his failure to include many segments of old episodes also drew criticism. Still, so few people had taken Cornelius to task over the years that when the 2007 awards were over, most journalists covering the festivities made no connection between the ceremony's problems and criticisms from the recent past. They reported the absences of the awardees as an unexpected phenomenon.

Most remarkable, however, is that Cornelius' empire had stood the test of time for so long. Rarely do television programs last for thirty-seven years, and that only one man was at the helm of the series for that length of time is even more rare. Then again, Cornelius had always beaten the odds when keeping his franchise afloat. After all, a Midwest-based dance show hosted by an African American former police officer with little broadcasting experience was not a likely recipe for success.

5

1

"Here's Your Host"

Don Cornelius and "Soul Train" Before Soul Train

The fascination of Americans with African American dance and musician-ship — a fascination upon which Don Cornelius built his empire in the enter-tainment industry — predated his birth in Chicago on September 27, 1936, by at least one century. As early as the 1830s, white stage performers entertained audiences by approximating African American speech and dance. Several troupes promoted themselves by advertising their accurate performance of actual African American cultural practices. The performers wore burnt cork on their faces to look like blacks, and many of their songs glamorized slavery. One of the first popular dances from these blackface minstrels came from the song "Jim Crow," which referred to a comical black characterization: the rural, slow-witted slave.

At the time of Cornelius' birth, Americans' enjoyment of African Amer-ican song and dance had spread beyond the stage to the medium of film. Blackface minstrels initially provided such performances in movies, most notably the first sound feature *The Jazz Singer* (1927). Movie studios eventu-ally hired African American performers for musical roles, although most of them featured such racially stereotypical settings as southern cotton fields. Other movies provided one or two scenes in which an African American sang or danced. A black orchestra in a film scene usually played in a box isolated from white dancers, but Bill "Bojangles" Robinson had tap dance duets with child star Shirley Temple in her starring features.

Soul Train had an even more direct ancestor in the all-black musical fea-ture films. They provided rare employment to African Americans in the film industry. Also, backed by major distributors, the movies served as precedents of Hollywood investing heavily in African American performance. *Cabin in the Sky* and *Stormy Weather* were among the most successful of those movies.

Another predecessor of *Soul Train* was the all-black musical short. African American musicians and dancers performed their hit songs in live-action films running usually between five and ten minutes. Blues singer Bessie Smith sang "St. Louis Blues" in one such film. The genre became popular enough for animators to borrow from it from the 1930s to the 1950s. As early as 1931, Walt Disney had his flagship character Mickey Mouse sing and scat to "St. Louis Blues." They produced musical cartoons that usually set African American music to racial stereotypes. Producer Max Fleischer had resisted the trend in his animated tributes to singer Cab Calloway's hits but depicted Louis Armstrong as a cannibal. Leon Schlesinger populated his African American animated musicals with gambling and drunk characters, and Walter Lantz's figures included plantation laborers, big-lipped cats, and bigger-lipped ghosts.

Long before Chicago's African American children appeared on television sets citywide via *Soul Train*, both a radio program and a book offered American citizens two dramatically different illustrations of African American life in the Windy City. One was fictional while the other resulted from scholarly research. One came from a pair of white men, and an African American pair produced the other. One caused a media frenzy — as *Soul Train* later did, to a lesser extent — and perpetuated racial stereotypes, but the other did not.

The radio show *Amos 'n' Andy* began in Chicago on the station WGN as *Sam 'n' Henry* in 1926. The creators — two white men named Freeman Gosden and Charles Correll — voiced in stereotypical dialect two fictional black characters who had recently migrated from the South to Chicago's South Side. When the series went national in 1929, Gosden and Correll changed the show's setting to Harlem. However, the actors continued to produce their show in the Windy City. After Cornelius was born, *Amos 'n' Andy* still broadcasted from Chicago for an additional year.

The series did not flatter black Chicago. Gosden and Correll claimed to have surrounded themselves with local African Americans in order to give accurate portrayals of their characters. As a result, their interpretations of African American Chicagoans informed audiences as to the thoughts, sayings and behaviors of urban African Americans, for many listeners did not have contact with African American city dwellers and, therefore, had no frame of reference about them beyond the radio show. Andy was more gullible than Amos, constantly falling prey to "get rich quick" schemes from another black character, named Kingfish. Both characters, however, frequently mismanaged their money. In addition, Gosden and Correll demonstrated their roots in blackface minstrelsy by having their characters utter malapropisms that became national catchphrases, such as "I'se regusted."

As World War II ended, St. Clair Drake and Horace R. Cayton's book *Black Metropolis* offered a much different portrait of African American Chicago than *Amos 'n' Andy* had. The African American authors wrote a sociological study of the city's black community. They argued that African American Chicago, which they dubbed the "Black Metropolis," mirrored the Windy City itself. On the other hand, the residents of the Black Metropolis were socially and economically removed from white Chicagoans.

In the Black Metropolis of Cornelius' youth, ample opportunity existed for people to see African American entrepreneurs. Although blacks noticed the businesspeople, the potential customers instead supported white-run establishments. In the 1930s local African American businesses numbered close to 3,000. The most numerous black-owned enterprises — beauty parlors, barbershops, and clothing businesses — concerned personal appearance. Many food-related businesses such as grocery stores and restaurants also had African Americans in charge. On the other hand, ninety percent of money spent by local blacks went to white businesses. Entrepreneurs usually started their businesses because they were tired of working for someone else, but they struggled to satisfactorily address customers' complaints of high prices, no credit, and inferior service. Race-based appeals to "buy black" and to boycott facilities that did not employ African Americans did not significantly help attract customers.[1]

Education was separate and unequal in Chicago as in the rest of the nation. The black schools had disproportionately more inexperienced teachers than the white schools had. In addition, as residential areas were ethnically divided via de facto segregation, so were many of the city's schools. The high schools, however, were not. In the 1950s the all-black high school Englewood had four all-white feeder elementary schools. The students comprising all-black Carver came directly from a public housing project. The city districted Du Sable as an African American high school, although white schools surrounded it in every direction.[2]

Raised on the south side of Chicago, Cornelius attended Du Sable High School, where he gained early experience in producing art for the media. He was an art student there, and one of his extracurricular activities was as a cartoonist for the school newspaper. His work foreshadowed his first jobs in the field of entertainment in the 1960s. At Du Sable he made print cartoons for an African American audience at an African American institution. When he later went into radio and television, he worked at stations that produced programming for African Americans and that hired African American employees.[3]

His work as a cartoonist was also notable because it was an unlikely position for African Americans outside of African American media. To be sure, many black-owned newspapers printed comic strips written and drawn by African Americans. In the 1950s, however, no African American had a nationally syndicated comic strip in mainstream newspapers; the first one — Morrie Turner's *Wee Pals*— did not start until 1965. Film cartooning was just as segregated, for no African Americans worked as animators on Hollywood cartoon films until 1954. Moreover, during Cornelius' high school years, cartoon images of African Americans strongly displayed roots of blackface minstrelsy. Metro-Goldwyn-Mayer's "Tom and Jerry" cartoons starred a frumpy, shuffling "mammy" caricature until Cornelius' sophomore year, and the following spring the Warner Brothers character Bugs Bunny dressed up in blackface to imitate a slave in *Southern Fried Rabbit.*

Du Sable was the perfect school for someone whose future lay in the business of rhythm and blues music. The school produced some noteworthy African American graduates who later had phenomenal music careers. Even before Cornelius started high school there, alumnus Nat "King" Cole had already started a long run of hit songs. Singer Sam Cooke did not attend Du Sable but another high school for Chicago's African American children. Still, when his group the Soul Stirrers performed throughout the city, one venue they played at least once a year was Du Sable. Moreover, quite a few times during Cornelius' high school years, the group provided an annual Mother's Day program there.[4]

The Soul Stirrers' annual Du Sable shows also influenced young musicians who helped bring Chicago "soul music" national popularity in the 1950s and 1960s. As teenagers, Jerry Butler and Curtis Mayfield watched the Soul Stirrers perform at the school. They later formed their own group, the Impressions, and subsequently launched successful solo careers. Their music, especially as members of the Impressions, featured several gospel references, not unlike the Soul Stirrers' numbers. The group, for example, produced a crossover "pop" hit in 1965 by adapting the gospel standard "Amen" to R&B.[5]

Du Sable gained notoriety in sports as well as music while Cornelius studied there. In 1954, the year that he graduated from Du Sable, the school's basketball team lost the state championship game. The team would have been the first African American team to win a state high school tournament. "The kids took pride in the fact that they were black and had a black coach," noted Du Sable's basketball coach Jim Brown. "They knew about being the first all-black state champion." Many people believed that the referees caused Du Sable to lose by having three team members fouled out. "The game was taken away from us," Coach Brown declared.[6]

Although black Chicagoans missed an opportunity for a racial victory, an even more important victory for African Americans nationwide took place as Cornelius graduated that spring. The Supreme Court unanimously decided in *Brown v. Board of Education* that segregation in public schools was unconstitutional. The victory motivated civil rights activists already working towards racial equality. They figured that if segregation could be made illegal in schools, then it could disappear everywhere else. However, new groups forming to resist desegregation — White Citizens' Councils and Mississippi's taxpayer-funded State Sovereignty Commission — formed within two years of the *Brown v. Board* decision in order to keep businesses and institutions racially segregated.

Cornelius enlisted in the Marines and served eighteen months on an air force base in South Korea. The Korean Conflict had recently ended after two years (1951–53) and 33,000 U.S. casualties. It was the first conflict in which the armed forces were racially integrated; years earlier President Harry Truman had ordered their desegregation. Despite the war's recent conclusion, U.S. forces maintained a significant military presence in Korea. Also, as Cornelius joined the Marines in 1954, the Geneva Conference had just failed to resolve disputes between North and South Korea. His stint, however, was relatively tranquil. He served as an aviator crash crewman, keeping watch for any military plane crashes; but no serious crashes happened during his tour.[7]

When Cornelius returned to the United States after his military service ended, he held a variety of jobs over the next decade. He reportedly had no fewer than fifteen jobs between the ages of twenty and thirty. He drove a taxicab and sold tires, automobiles, and insurance.[8]

Cornelius made an especially good living selling insurance. He worked as an agent for the Golden State Mutual Life Company and earned $250 per week. Moreover, he had found work in a field in which many local African Americans thrived. Insurance companies in Chicago were historically the most successful African American business ventures in competition with similar white-owned businesses for much of the early twentieth century. African American insurance agents thrived by noting to African American customers that white agents charged them higher premiums than they charged white customers.[9]

Cornelius' ultimate goal, however, was to be his own boss. "I had difficulty working for other people," he admitted. A meaningful life lesson about labor came from his hard-working father, whom he admired. "My father taught me you needed to work with your brain and not your back," he remembered. "I've made that a passion. When I have a job to do, time means nothing. I lose patience with people who work on a clock." Thus, being self-employed would allow him to work at his own pace.[10]

By the mid–1960s, Cornelius had started to work for the city in an unexpectedly high-profile municipal position: a police officer. At the time the Chicago Police Department (CPD) had made national headlines because of African American unrest. Part of the national attention resulted from the long-term presence of the Rev. Dr. Martin Luther King, Jr. and his civil rights organization in Chicago. For months the group had conducted demonstrations against poor housing conditions for African American residents.

Other incidents during Cornelius' tenure in the CPD demonstrated the need for African American children to have recreational resources in Chicago. On July 12, 1966, a riot ensued after police had shut off fire hydrants that black youngsters opened on that hot day. As rioters smashed windows and robbed stores, the police arrested twenty-four people, and ten others were injured. The next day snipers and Molotov cocktails were added to the disturbance. Then, on July 14, two people died when police and snipers shot at each other in black neighborhoods. Local and national civil rights leaders worried that, at worst, the police would use excessive force and hurt or incarcerate people.[11]

The CPD ironically generated some rare positive press about police officers assigned to civil rights demonstrations. The coverage was symbolic of the civil rights movement's difficulty in portraying Chicago government as villainous — a tactic that had previously worked in other locations. Throughout the 1950s and 1960s, movement activists across the nation staged nonviolent protests, and they counted on generating sympathy from the nation after reporters displayed film of police officers arresting the demonstrators, if not beating them, attacking them with police dogs, or spraying them with fire hoses. On the other hand, in Chicago, the police officers protected the marchers from violent bystanders armed with bricks and rocks in the summer of 1966. Fighting violence with violence, the policemen assaulted unruly white mobs with nightsticks and consequently saved the marchers from injury.

Similarly, whenever Mayor Richard Daley received a complaint from the movement about an inner city problem such as the lack of sanitation service at a tenement, he at least addressed it with short-term action like an immediate garbage collection at that tenement instead of wholly ignoring the cries of African Americans, which southern city and county governments tended to do at the time.[12]

Meanwhile, Chicago's African American officers had their own specific problems as a result of the department's conduct as a whole. CPD officers frequently engaged in police brutality upon African Americans. They treated African American traveling after dark as prostitutes. The officers also made public spectacles out of stop-and-search procedures with African American ministers and businessmen, treating them as if they were career criminals. Consequently, members of the city's African American community started to openly question African American officers about why they worked for the department. What did the CPD mean to them? Did they consider themselves an occupying force? As a black CPD officer, Cornelius was among the officers challenged by black Chicagoans. Small wonder that he later seized upon a chance opportunity to find a different line of work.[13]

One day in the mid–1960s, he made a fateful traffic stop — one that significantly altered the course of his life. He pulled over Roy Wood, the news director of local radio station WVON, to cite him for an infraction. As Cornelius spoke, his deep voice caught Wood's attention. The driver then asked the officer if he had ever thought about going into radio. Before Wood and Cornelius parted ways, the news director invited the policeman to WVON to discuss a possible job at the station.[14]

Cornelius accepted Wood's invitation. General Manager Lucky Cordell met him and found him to be a very personable and affable man with whom people got along easily. Wood visited with Cornelius again and hired him. During his tenure there, Cornelius established himself as a consummate professional on and off the air. Cordell later could not recall Cornelius ever having disagreed with any of his colleagues at the radio station. The new employee initially enjoyed his work. "It was the first job I'd wanted to do," he said. "I'd never had a job that I liked before."[15]

Shortly before starting work at WVON in 1967, Cornelius enrolled in a three-month broadcasting course. He wanted to create his own music program that met the needs of African Americans. "I knew that in order to make anything happen, I had to get some training in the business, and I basically knew nothing about show business," he later remarked to reporter Jae-Ha Kim with a laugh. The class was a costly investment; at $400, it comprised two-fifths of Cornelius' monthly wages. Still, the course provided him both professional and personal dividends. "The class helped me understand the technical side [of show business] a lot better — not that I'm an expert, by any means. Even more important, it gave me the confidence that I could do it and not just dream about it."[16]

Cornelius, however, needed more than confidence to land a job in radio. The broadcasting school cautioned students that Chicago stations were unlikely starting places. Cornelius landed his job at WVON through networking. "My best buddy was thrown out of broadcasting school. He was so bad they didn't feel right about taking his money," he stated. His friend immediately found work at WVON and hired Cornelius to read the news after he completed the course.[17]

At WVON Cornelius held a variety of jobs. He initially answered the telephone for the station's talk show host Wesley South — one of very few African American talk show hosts at the time. Cornelius later began reading the news on the air. "I fell in love with working in media, starting as a radio newsman," he later recalled. His work at WVON fulfilled a lifelong dream. "Getting into broadcasting was something that I'd wanted to do even as a kid, but it had seemed unrealistic at the time so I didn't pursue it."[18]

However, he soon discovered what he truly wanted to do in broadcasting by filling in for disc jockeys at the station whenever possible. He enjoyed it so much that he began to hope that one employee for whom he substituted would remain absent in order for the temporary gig as disc jockey to become more permanent. "I found it frustrating," he complained, "because they [WVON] couldn't give me a show of my own." He started to plan a career playing records full-time. "Music was always in the back of [my] head," he remembered.[19]

At times he expressed his unhappiness at the station to coworkers. The friend who helped him get the job at WVON listened patiently to the complaints for a while. He finally advised Cornelius, "I don't know why you're complaining, because you're really going to do all right in this business." To Cornelius the prediction seemed highly unlikely. "This was the dumbest guy that ever attended the school I went to, and he wound up owning that radio station in Chicago," he recalled. However, he learned an important lesson: "The point is, if we work at it, as he did, and as I did and still do, we all have a shot."[20]

Cornelius found a mentor in WVON disc jockey E. Rodney Jones. Jones had been at the station ever since 1963, when Leonard Chess of Chess Records bought it and hired Jones as program director. In addition to playing records, he promoted concerts and helped launch the careers of several R&B artists. Marvin Gaye, Wilson Pickett, and the Supremes were among his friends. He mostly played blues records, however — sixteen hours per day. Dubbing himself the "Bluesologist," he explained, "Muddy Waters, Howlin' Wolf, Little Walter, Sonny Boy Williamson, I knew them all and worked with them all." He played blues records on the air at a time when stations rarely broadcasted that music. In addition, he introduced records shipped by Berry Gordy from Motown Records, and WVON consequently helped many of the label's artists become gold-record stars. Eventually Cornelius also established connections in the African American music industry, but Jones had done so first and very well. Former record promoter Paul Gallis declared, "Rodney knew more about R&B and black music than even the guys that were singing it."[21]

Another important legacy of Jones that Cornelius later followed was establishing a career by promoting African American culture. Jones considered blues his bread and butter. "All the radio stations in the Chicago area were moving in a different direction," he noted. "But here was a chance for me to excel without trying to compete with these people." He excelled indeed, winning radio industry awards as disc jockey of the year and music director of the year.[22]

Cornelius further emulated Jones by using his stature in entertainment as a platform for activism. Long before Cornelius complained to interviewers about the lack of African American culture on television, Jones dramatically changed the radio industry by organizing its employees. He founded and led an African American radio union. As a result, he formed relationships with disc jockeys nationwide. He made political connections by promoting the Rev. Jesse Jackson's "Operation Breadbasket" campaign. The similarities between Jones and Cornelius were not lost on radio star Guy Brody, who remarked, "Here's a guy [Cornelius] who patterned himself after E. Rodney Jones and he's a multi-millionaire. E. Rodney's nowhere near a multi-millionaire. It doesn't even seem fair."[23]

Jones and Cornelius were among WVON employees who were influential in popularizing soul music. They were known collectively as the "VON Good Guys." The top "guy" was Pervis Spann "the Blues Man," who ran the station. Herb Kent "the Cool Gent," Ed "Nassau Daddy" Cook, Bill "Doc" Lee, and Bill "Butterball" Crain were popular on-air personalities. Many of them spent the majority of their broadcasting careers at WVON.[24]

During Cornelius' stint at WVON, he witnessed the enthusiasm of African American listeners towards African American music and the neglect they felt from the mass media. The "VON" in WVON stood for "Voice of the Negro," and the station committed itself to addressing relevant issues in the Black Metropolis and playing the music embraced by that community. The community's support was important, for popular music was largely segregated. Despite the crossover appeal of African American rock and roll in the 1950s, white artists successfully adapted R&B to popular music trends in the following decade. Very few African American artists outside of Detroit's Motown label saw their music receive exposure outside of radio airplay and concerts. Chicago artists may have had access to television programs aimed at teenagers like *American Bandstand* (1957–1989) and *Hullabaloo* (1965–1966) but rarely to coveted and higher-rated prime time series like *The Ed Sullivan Show* (1948–1971).[25]

Cornelius broke into radio at a most opportune moment. African American radio stations had never been in better economic shape. One advertiser claimed that no black stations anywhere were losing money. Most of them featured community-focused news and programming that addressed African American interests. Also, with recent African American economic growth, the stations dropped advertisements for products and businesses that had typically supported them — cure-all drugs, easy-credit stores, and shady used car dealerships.[26]

Events in Chicago outside of the music industry, however, were not as pleasant. WVON was licensed in Cicero, Illinois — a town where African Americans worked but did not reside. The station's listeners were concentrated not in Cicero but rather on Chicago's South Side and West Side. Before the mid–1960s, anyone attempting to integrate a neighborhood in Cicero met with violent intimidation. Cicero had just been the setting for one of the most violent civil rights movement demonstrations of the '60s. Just as the Rev. Dr. Martin Luther King, Jr. of the Southern Christian Leadership Conference (SCLC) had drawn the nation's attention to southern segregation and voting disenfranchisement through marches and speeches earlier in the decade, King attempted to use the same tactics to dramatize segregated housing in Chicago in the summer of 1966. Although King and his organization did not march into Cicero, 250 others did that September and were met by a mob of three thousand residents pitching rocks. Breaking from King's tactic of nonviolent protest, the marchers threw the rocks back at the mob. So oppressive was Cicero that at least one demonstrator considered the return of anyone in the march to Chicago alive a major victory.[27]

WVON offered its support of King and the SCLC. Whenever the Chicago branch took its "Operation Breadbasket" program to local churches in order to address urban poverty and hunger, the station broadcast each event live. SCLC had a radical reputation in Chicago as a result of the organization's summer 1966 activities there, and King's public anti–Vietnam War stance the following April resulted in a significant loss of civil rights allies throughout the nation. Thus, WVON's airings of the Breadbasket shows were no small accomplishment. A majority of the city's churches, whose pastors supported Mayor Richard Daley, refused to host the SCLC. Those who hosted the group ran into trouble building parishes.[28]

The station lent its support to political activists with even more radical stances than King's. Herb Kent noted that the "Good Guys" raised money for H. Rap Brown and Angela Davis, among others. Both personalities had gained unsavory reputations among mainstream Americans because of their politics. Although Brown led the Student Nonviolent Coordinating Committee in the late 1960s, he openly advocated violence as self-defense and observed that violence "is as American as cherry pie." Davis, meanwhile, achieved notoriety for her public embrace of communism, which led the University of California Board of Regents to fire her from her position as a philosophy professor. Much of Chicago's African American community, however, admired WVON for aligning with Brown and Davis. "We were heroes," Kent declared, "and people hung on to our every word."[29]

WVON's activism went through a severe test during Cornelius' tenure when the city's West Side rioted upon the assassination of King in April 1968. The station received a flood of calls from all over Chicago. People of all racial groups sought the advice of the "Good Guys." "We were a reference point," Herb Kent remembered. "We told people to go back to their homes, to stop. We said, 'You're not getting anywhere by continuing to burn, break and pillage. Cool out.'" Witnessing the riots firsthand, the disc jockeys risked their lives trying to calm down violent, distraught mourners. "Somebody took a shot at Rodney but just missed him," Kent recalled. "I stood on a corner and watched the West Side go up in flames — blocks and blocks of these flames. There was nothing anybody could do."[30]

While at WVON, Roy Wood invited Don Cornelius to moonlight with him at television station WCIU, Channel 26. It was a fitting transition for them, for both stations targeted ethnic minority audiences. WCIU broadcasted experimental ethnic programming, such as the daily newscasts *A Black's View of the News* and *Spanish News*, a polka show, and telecasts about Asian

American issues. Starting in 1968, after only one year of radio broadcasting experience, Cornelius landed his first on-camera job as the sports anchor on *A Black's View of the News*—a position that Wood had secured for him. One of the new anchor's mandates from the station, however, was more creative; WCIU directed him to think of series that fit with the station's commitment to diverse ethnic programming.[31]

As he developed *Soul Train* at WCIU, he kept the project a secret from some of the WVON staff. Cordell did not recall discussing the development of the show with Cornelius. As a result, when it first aired, his radio colleagues were surprised. It had just emerged from nowhere, as far as they were concerned.[32]

One person in whom Cornelius confided was George O'Hare, a manager of Sears-Roebuck in the Chicago area. Cornelius told him, "I'm gonna have a TV show someday." O'Hare was not as confident, responding that the popular African American singer Nat "King" Cole did not have his own show for very long. O'Hare certainly had good reason for his skepticism. Since the cancellation of Cole's variety series on the National Broadcasting Company (NBC) in December 1957 after only thirteen months, the only other variety show with an African American host — *The Sammy Davis, Jr. Show*—lasted less than one-fourth of Cole's run in 1966.[33]

Cornelius and O'Hare had met inadvertently because of the civil rights movement. O'Hare was a recent convert to the movement, having previously held anti-black views and having considered King a radical and a communist. Meeting African American comedian Dick Gregory and attending one of King's speeches gave O'Hare a change of heart. He soon started working with Operation Breadbasket. One evening, during the SCLC's summer 1966 protests, the organization asked him to escort King to WVON for an interview with the station's evening talk show host Wesley South. At the time King temporarily lived in a run-down building in Chicago to demonstrate the city's poverty, and his campaign inspired South to invite him on the show *Hotline*. While at the station, O'Hare met Cornelius, who asked if he was King's lawyer. After they introduced themselves and spoke for a while, Cornelius invited him to drinks on Chicago's South Side. Thus started a lifelong friendship between them.[34]

A few times over the next few years, Cornelius met with O'Hare in the latter's office to discuss *Soul Train*. Cornelius once came in the room with his wife, asking for funding for the project, but O'Hare responded that he did not have the money. Another time he and Wesley South, his boss at WVON, approached O'Hare with a signed contract from WCIU for the series, but O'Hare still lacked the money. He also informed Cornelius that Sears-Roebuck simply did not advertise R&B.[35]

Finally O'Hare decided to contact the company's national record buyer named Dick Mabbet. The buyer then spoke to Cornelius. Oblivious to the other end of the conversation, O'Hare heard Cornelius struggle to explain the show's title: "Soul is soul. We'll just put the word 'train' after it." He promised that the viewers would understand what "soul" was. In a short while, however, the buyer told him that no money was available.[36]

Having hung up with Mabbet, Cornelius began to leave the building with O'Hare for a drink. Then, O'Hare's secretary chased them down the hall to tell Cornelius that the buyer had called for him. He miraculously found financial backing but from Detroit instead of Chicago. He told Cornelius that the Motown record label had just called Mabbet and mentioned wanting to do "something soulful" in Chicago. As a result, Cornelius received money for thirteen weeks of episodes. In exchange for *Soul Train*'s airing of three Sears-Roebuck commercials per episode, the company paid Cornelius $100 per weekday broadcast.[37]

The title of the series came from road shows that Cornelius had produced. For each show he booked several dancers and musicians and took them from high school to high school in Chicago to perform after final classes were dismissed for the day. It was not unlike a caravan or train. The road shows were the direct ancestor of *Soul Train* not only in title but also in that they gave Cornelius experience in marketing music and dance to African American teenagers.

The phrase "Soul Train," however, had existed for several years before Cornelius' road shows had begun. It was the title of several songs performed by a variety of artists. Each song gave the phrase a different meaning. By the time most of the singers had recorded their interpretations of "Soul Train," their careers had already peaked. As a result, the phrase did not resonate with record buyers as much as with the performers. Mary Wells, one of the Motown label's earliest stars, released her rendition long after she had left the label and stopped generating hits. Two more "Soul Train" songs ironically came from early rock 'n' roll artists: singer Little Richard in 1968 and guitarist Bo Diddley the following year.

One interpretation of "Soul Train" came from a little-known group in Phoenix, Arizona. The local band Soulsetters recorded the song in the 1960s. Their version is upbeat and emphasizes the saxophone. It is a dance song with a fast tempo, similar to the tempo of Wilson Pickett's 1966 hit song "Land of 1,000 Dances." Like Pickett, the lead vocalist for the Soulsetters screamed a series of directions for the listener wanting to dance. The song's commands like "shake it" and "get on board" were rather generic, however.

White recording groups also performed "Soul Train" songs. Dennis Yost and the Classics IV had already struck gold with hits "Spooky," "Stormy," and "Traces" by the time they made "Soul Train" in 1969. The song, written by band producer Buddy Buie and guitarist James Cobb, illustrates the train as a couple's act of heavy petting while listening to R&B records on a stereo. In the lyrics the protagonist encourages his female partner to embrace him and forget her troubles. Thus, for the Classics IV, "Soul Train" meant sexual escapism.

Another early "Soul Train" came from pioneering Native American guitarist Link Wray. He had developed "rumble" and "fuzz" sounds for the instrument in the 1950s and early '60s. The latter is prominent in his "Soul Train" song from the mid–1960s for Swan Records. The song details the protagonist's travels across the country and the dances observed such as New York City's "Nitty Gritty." As a result, Wray's version of "Soul Train" focuses more on the musical aspect of soul than the Classics IV. Also, Wray noted the importance of different locations of train stops, whereas the Classics IV specifically stated that the couple in their song had no destination.

The phrase "Soul Train" was an outgrowth of a movement among musicians of the 1960s to popularize the concept of "soul" music — an R&B style that prioritized passionate, stylized singing instead of the playing of guitars and drums, as in most of the day's white rock-and-roll songs. "Soul" music initially had religious connotations, as in the group the Soul Stirrers. In the 1960s the word "soul" became synonymous with African American self-empowerment; when singer Sam Cooke started radio stations for African American communities to operate among themselves, he called them "soul stations."[38]

Over the next decade, people promoting "soul" described it as either a sense of "coolness" or a synonym for Afro-centricity or both. The group the Impressions scored one of the first popular songs with the word in the title — "Woman's Got Soul." Motown created a label subsidiary, aptly named "Soul," for this type of music and signed groups Junior Walker and the All-Stars and Gladys Knight and the Pips to it. This concept of soul soon extended beyond the music industry into politics. The Rev. Jesse Jackson of the SCLC changed the popular Afro-centric empowerment chant "Black Power" to "Soul Power" when leading a demonstration for the Poor People's Campaign in the summer of 1968.

"Soul" music had such a strong reputation as African American music that no one but an African American singing in that style was accepted as a "soul singer." The genre's peak of popularity among white artists took place between 1964 and 1966. Their songs were dubbed "blue-eyed soul" by the trade press. Such a distinction either went to rock 'n' roll balladeers with booming voices like the Righteous Brothers and Tom Jones or to wailing, shouting hark rockers like the Animals. In addition, several white performers like the Beatles and Johnny Rivers covered R&B songs. In 1967, however, blue-eyed soul waned as psychedelic music became a more popular trend, especially after the publicity surrounding that year's "Summer of Love" in San Francisco. The Animals immediately switched to slow, mellow, quiet grooves and never wailed or shouted on another single. "Soul" music returned to the exclusive property of African Americans, with rare exceptions.

As the development of *Soul Train* for WCIU became a greater priority for Cornelius, his employment at WVON grew tenuous. Station owner Leonard Chess intended to fire him but never did before dying in October 1969. Ten months later, on August 17, 1970, when the television station first aired *Soul Train*, Cornelius quit his job at the radio station after three years. "To make a success out of [*Soul Train*], I had to quit the other job at WVON," he reasoned.[39]

By the time Cornelius left WVON, the station had grown. General Manager Robert Bell cited supportive advertisers, the on-air station talent, and the station's African American community involvement as reasons why audiences were increasing. From Monday through Saturday, WVON played R&B. On Sundays the station played gospel music. Other programming included eight issue-oriented editorials per day, a sixty-minute daily telephone call-in show, a live show hosted by the Rev. Jesse Jackson, and the weekly drama *Black History*. Forty-three of the forty-six employees were African American.[40]

Despite Chess's feelings regarding Cornelius' imminent departure from WVON, the *Soul Train* creator still had plenty of allies at the station after beginning full-time work at WCIU. He personally and professionally remained in contact with many of them for years. By keeping these relationships and fostering new ones, he was able to put *Soul Train* on the air at the television station. His old radio contacts helped provide the necessary musical resources — top-selling records to play and artists to make appearances.

Meanwhile, his new acquaintances in television and advertising introduced him to the day-to-day realities of television production.

As with his success with the broadcasting course he took in 1966, however, the former insurance salesman and police officer proved that he was a quick study. After all, the switch from disc jockey to television show host was one more career change to add to his list. Whether at thirty-three years old he was making his final job transition remained to be seen and depended on his success in one of the most fickle businesses in the country — television entertainment.

2

"Welcome Aboard"

Soul Train *in Chicago*

The development of *Soul Train* was a project for which success seemed unlikely. The developer had only two years of television experience, which overlapped with his three years of radio broadcasting. One of his early supporters was a former anti-black racist. In addition, an African American supporter had never financed a regular television series. Finally, Cornelius had no idea how to manage a dance show.[1]

When Don Cornelius made the decision to start *Soul Train*, he had to make drastic sacrifices. Having left WVON, he worked without pay on the production of *Soul Train* for the first two or three months. In addition, he had a slim budget with which to fund the show, having only four hundred dollars in his bank account when he began production of the series.[2]

A decade earlier an R&B dance program had greater potential for success. In the 1960s the Windy City was the African American dance center of the nation. Chicagoans created and popularized such moves as the Bird, the Barracuda, the Monkey, and the Watusi. These dances spread throughout the nation and eventually appeared on network television series like *American Bandstand, Shindig*, and *Hullabaloo*, each of which featured a mostly white dancing troupe.

By 1970, however, soul singers nationwide had long traded dance crazes for social messages. For years Curtis Mayfield had tried to do both; he wrote "message songs" for his group the Impressions but composed dance hits for other artists like Major Lance ("Monkey Time"). As the 1970s dawned, he left the group for a solo career and composed no more dance songs for anyone. Meanwhile, the only new dances in soul songs that attained popularity in 1970 came not from Chicago-based artists but rather from Memphis-based singer Rufus Thomas, who introduced the "Push and Pull" and the "Funky Chicken."

Although no longer a dance metropolis, Chicago still had a strong music industry. As a result Cornelius had a large pool of artistic talent from which to draw for guest spots on his program. Durable labels Chess, Brunswick, and Mercury were in the Windy City, along with Mayfield's own new label Curtom. Chess was the home of Etta James, the Dells, and Chuck Berry. Brunswick had the Chi-Lites and Tyrone Davis. Mercury had Jerry Butler, another former member of the Impressions. Meanwhile, both Mayfield and the Impressions recorded for the new label Curtom, which Mayfield himself created and Buddah Records distributed.

One person who contributed to Chicago's dance reputation was African American choreographer Clinton Ghent, who worked with Cornelius on the launching of *Soul Train*. In 1963 Ghent and dance partner Jean Dawkins won a "Monkey-dancing" contest at the popular local R&B nightclub Budland; singer Major Lance, whose song "Monkey Time" popularized the dance, presented the award to the couple. By the late 1960s, Ghent had become a choreography teacher with the Chicago Park District. He also served as a choreographer for some of Chicago's biggest R&B singing groups. "He worked with everybody," recalled Marshall Thompson of the Chi-Lites.[3]

Even before Ghent became an important figure in Chicago soul music, he and Cornelius had crossed paths. They both came from the same Windy City neighborhood of 51st and King Drive — nicknamed "The Valley." They gave each other nicknames. Cornelius called Ghent "Clinton Baby," and Cornelius was dubbed "Donald Duck" because of his skill at drawing pictures.[4]

As the 1970s began, Ghent and Cornelius unexpectedly reunited for the first time in years at one of the many popular nightclubs in Chicago's South Side. From there, a fortuitous relationship restarted and led to the development of *Soul Train*. "He heard I knew how to choreograph kids," Ghent recalled of his old friend, "and he was putting together a television pilot. That's how we hooked up."[5]

Cornelius pitched the idea of *Soul Train* to WCIU's manager, who was one of the owners of the station. The show was a perfect fit for the station, which broadcasted several original shows aimed at minority audiences. Thus, the manager responded, "Sure, we'll try that, too." Station owners Bill O'Connor and Howard Shapiro — "two of the most important guys I've ever met," according to Cornelius — did not demand ownership of *Soul Train* when they gave Cornelius their approval to air it. Shapiro later confirmed that WCIU essentially gave the program to him.[6]

The show was filmed at the top of the Chicago Board of Trade Building.

The facilities barely fit the dancers and crew. The size of the studio did not surpass that of a living room in a house. The lack of space necessitated sparse camera work. "It was a one-camera shoot—maybe two," remembered former dancer Crescendo Ward. If the camera was not on the host, then it was on the dancers. Lorenzo Clemons, whose group the Mandells appeared on the show during its first year, similarly recalled with amusement, "It was funny to see the dancers being shifted from side to side so the cameras could move, and it made [the studio] look like a large ballroom."[7]

Soul Train had other technical shortcomings. Although network television had aired all-color programming since 1967, WCIU filmed all of its programs

The Chicago Board of Trade building, where WCIU filmed *Soul Train.* Courtesy Chicago Board of Trade.

The Chicago-based group the Mandells. Left to right, top row: Bobby, Milton, Lorenzo; left to right, bottom row: William, Lil' June, Robert. Courtesy Lorenzo Clemons.

in black-and-white. *Soul Train* was no exception. Color television, however, was still a novelty. As late as the 1970–71 season, each color-filmed program began with an announcement that the show was produced in color. In addition, sales of color television sets would not outnumber those of black-and-white ones for the first time until 1972. That same year the periodical *TV Guide* switched from specifying shows filmed in color to noting which programs — usually reruns of defunct series — appeared in black-and-white. Thus, while new shows were rarely without color, black-and-white programming was still commonplace when *Soul Train* made its debut in 1970.

An after-school show, *Soul Train* aired weekdays for an hour, starting at 4:30 P.M. The time slot was perfect for several reasons. It allowed teenagers enough time to commute home from school without missing any of the show. Because each broadcast ended at 5:30, the series did not overlap with network news broadcasts for the parents. When the show first aired, competing stations did not have any 4:30 offerings that targeted teenage viewers, especially African American ones.

From the beginning, *Soul Train* employed a format based on Cornelius' fondness for radio. "I really put it together as a radio show, and the pacing has remained the same ever since," he said. That formula consisted of Cornelius announcing songs, introducing and interviewing acts, and mentioning advertisers. Chicago-based singer Bobby Hutton, who appeared several times on the local show, considered each episode "thrown together rather quickly," but he also acknowledged, "Don had a basic format which held things together. All he had to do was fill in the empty spots. What I mean is the entertainer who [was] available, and what dancer can come to the studio."[8]

One of the means by which he connected his radio roots to the program was through its theme song. Cornelius opened the show with a recording of "Hot Potatoes" by King Curtis, just as he had done for his radio broadcasts. "Hot Potatoes," however, did more than establish a musical transition from radio to television. The song also symbolized the show's embrace of "soul." Curtis was one of the most respected bandleaders of that music genre, and as a talented saxophone player, he worked with several professional jazz and rock musicians — black and white — for nearly two decades. Many of his recordings had "soul" in the title: "Memphis Soul Stew," "King Size Soul," and "Sweet Soul." Thus, a song by Curtis was fitting for a television program that professed to have "soul."[9]

Soul Train was one of two series to introduce Curtis's music to television viewers on a regular basis. Because the saxophonist played on some of R&B's biggest hits by other artists, television audiences heard several of his solo parts over the years but saw only the lead singers on the soundstages. Thanks to *Soul Train*, music credited solely to Curtis played five days a week in Chicago. Within two months of the show's premiere, the African American variety series *Soul* made its debut on public television and used another tune by Curtis — "Soulful 13" — for the theme. The song fit, for in New York, where *Soul* originated, the show aired on Channel 13. When *Soul Train* later went national, Curtis had the distinction of having two different songs as national television program themes — a rarity for an African American musician in the early 1970s. Only Quincy Jones was as prolific at the time.[10]

Before *Soul Train*, television stations and networks had offered programming that either promoted R&B music for African American audiences or offered Afro-centric entertainment by African Americans. In the 1950s and 1960s, white television host Buddy Deane provided occasional episodes of his dance show in which African American teenagers could dance on stage by themselves; on most days white adolescents ruled the dance floor. In 1964 Deane cancelled the show instead of bowing to racial integration. Four years later the producers of the comedy variety show *Rowan & Martin's Laugh-In* developed an African American counterpart called *Soul!*, but the show aired only once. At the time viewers were not ready for a regularly scheduled program featuring entertainment strictly from an African American perspective.

Rarely did African Americans themselves host or produce R&B series at that time. In North Carolina, disc jockey J.D. Lewis served in both capacities for the local dance show *Teenage Frolics*, which aired on Saturdays from 1959 to 1983. Local educator E.B. Palmer remarked that Lewis contributed to the maturation and socialization of teenagers. "When he hosted *Teenage Frolics*, he really had the teenage community doing wholesome and positive things, getting a chance to express themselves," Palmer said. Back in Chicago, WCIU had aired another African American music series before *Soul Train*. Starting in 1967, local disc jockey Big Bill Hill hosted the dance program *Red Hot and Blues*. But young viewer Crescendo Ward felt the show did not appeal to people his age. The cast of dancers was definitely younger than the teenagers on *Soul Train*; WCIU permitted no one above fourteen years of age on Big Bill Hill's program. The series lasted for six years, but its focus on young demographics alienated older viewers who eventually started watching *Soul Train*. "No one really cool was on his show," Ward declared.[11]

Clinton Ghent almost became the host of *Soul Train*. However, he experienced difficulty in adjusting to the medium of television. "I had no technical training in television, and it was real rough on me in terms of diction and presence." Cornelius soon became the host, and Ghent served as the choreographer for the teenagers. Garrick Anders, a *Soul Train* dancer in the fall of 1970, recalled, "Clinton Ghent was like the stage manager. He kept us in line — told us where to stand during the commercials. He directed us." Lorenzo Clemons considered him "Don's assistant, sort of an associate producer."[12]

In addition to Cornelius and Ghent, choreographer Ronald Paul Johnson became a fixture on the show. Before *Soul Train* he and Ghent had given performances at the Chicago nightclub Budland — the same club where Ghent had won the "Monkey" dance contest years earlier. On a nightly basis, they choreographed and pantomimed songs there. In addition to club work, they developed dances as a team in the artist's development department of Perv's Music — a local music company that published songs and managed groups.

Johnson and Ghent worked with local singing groups like the Chi-Lites and the Emotions. Theresa Davis, a former member of the latter group, considered Ghent and Johnson "a good team," and noted, "they worked well together, yet their styles were somewhat different." Johnson choreographed the moves for the Emotions' ballads, because his movements were "fluid." Ghent, in contrast, had a "snappier" and "sassier" dancing style. As a result, he created steps for the faster songs. Despite their complementary specialties, they were not confined to them but could alternate dance styles as well. "They were both versatile and easy to work with," Davis said. "They made it fun."[13]

Johnson, especially, became a surrogate brother to the all-female Emotions. Davis described him as both gentlemanly and "streetwise." He listened to the concerns of the group members and offered sound advice. "He was always looking out for us," she remembered. After complimenting her for refusing to fall prey to a financial scam, he told her, "An honest person can't be scammed, because it's only those who want something for nothing that can be." Thus, in addition to his choreography skills, his wisdom and his personable demeanor made him an invaluable part of the WCIU *Soul Train* team.[14]

As choreographers, Ghent and Johnson knew how and where to find dancing talent. They scouted for dancers at Chicago nightclubs. Clarice Kavanaugh recalled either Ghent or Johnson approaching her at the club Guys and Gals. Having seen her moves, one of them asked her to go to the Board of Trade. Once there, she was invited into the studio for taping and became one of the show's first regulars.[15]

Soul Train staff went to local high schools to recruit dancers. "You had to be in high school," Ward said. Alston and Proviso East were among the inner-city high schools represented in the show. "They'd have a 'cattle call,'" former dancer Gregg Parker remembered. A representative for the show passed out flyers advertising it and inviting dancers. According to Parker, the advertisements had little aesthetic appeal; he likened the strange green color of the paper flyers to the color of vomit. In addition, the representatives promoted the show as a "black *American Bandstand*." This comparison appealed to African American youth, not so much because of the reference to Dick Clark's show but rather due to the use of the word "black." Among African American youth, the racial identifier "Negro" had lost appeal ever since civil rights activists began calling for "black power" in 1966.[16]

Soul Train at WCIU greatly resembled *American Bandstand* when Clark's series was in Philadelphia from 1957 to 1964. Both shows aired on weekday afternoons and recruited local high school talent. Popular local and national performers appeared on both series, and the local music industries benefited from the exposure of their acts on the shows. Dance contests took place. In addition, the dancers on both programs gained loyal followers. Certain couples became "teen idols."

The dance shows differ, however, in terms of racial identification and formality. Clark's program tended to draw from the schools in closest proximity to the studio, which were mostly white Catholic schools. On the other hand, Chicago teenagers went to school too far away from the Board of Trade to walk conveniently to the show. As a result, no particular schools dominated *Soul Train*. In contrast to the working-class and middle-class dancers on *American Bandstand*, many of *Soul Train*'s adolescents commuted from the inner city.

In addition, WCIU employed a less strict dress code than *American Bandstand*'s mandatory coat-and-tie for male dancers. Studio staff told some teenagers to wear "decent" clothes, which meant casual dress. Parker noted that people danced in their street clothes. Another dancer, Garrick Anders, remembered wearing a Brooks Brothers shirt and a pair of jeans to his taping. While he was at the studio that day, he noticed most of the male dancers wearing jeans. He did not see anyone wearing suits.[17]

Soul Train promoted itself in the most populist of terms in the program's early weeks. An advertisement in the *Chicago Defender* promoted the accessibility of the series to a wide range of people. It boasted, "'The Soul Train' has become a hit with teens and young adults of all races." Focusing specifically on minorities, the pitch continued, "And, we dare you to find a single Black or Spanish person under 30 who is not watching the program if he is home at that time." The show had some standards, but students found ways around them. Dancers had to be at least sixteen years old. They did not, however, experience strict checks of their background. As a result, some high school students benefited from looking older than they actually were. Teenagers as young as fourteen years old entered the Board of Trade facility. The print advertisement promised, "Even though your age does not meet the requirements, we'll make an exception upon receipt of your applications."[18]

Not every aspect of *Soul Train*'s production was informal. The staging of each dance sequence was systematic. Once the students arrived to dance on the show, the staff determined the pairings of dancers. Thus, the restricting of admittance to couples guaranteed that, after the rearranging of couples, no dancer would be without a partner. The assigning of couples had an aesthetic quality. "Somebody would come in with a partner," Ghent recalled. "You would play some Ohio Players and watch them dance together. Well, they might not fit that partner. So we'd exchange partners until we got it coordinated, until it looked right. It was like working a puzzle."[19]

The dancers also developed their own rituals in relation to the show. Ward described, "At 3:00, when school was out, you'd jump on the 'L' [train], go to the Board of Trade, and go up to the [top] floor." Once on that floor, "you had to stand in this long line." Dancers also had to have partners before receiving permission to enter the studio. WCIU did not prohibit any particular boy-girl pairings. While some courting couples appeared, on one occasion a pair of cousins went on the show together.[20]

The filming of *Soul Train* became a well-oiled machine. In a typical episode the host stood off to the side as the dancers stood in their own space. The host introduced a song. Then, an off-camera staff member pointed to the teenagers, and they started dancing. In addition, the filming took place in segments, and the staff called people to the studio only when taping their specific parts on the show. Clarice Kavanaugh, who occasionally danced on the program between 1970 and 1972, recalled coming to the Board of Trade to film "the dance portion of the show" only after having been summoned by the staff.[21]

The Chicago program had guest stars, not all of whom were musicians. At times the choices in guests had political significance. The Rev. Jesse Jackson regularly appeared as a guest. Between 1965 and 1971, he had served as a member of the Southern Christian Leadership Conference (SCLC) — the civil rights organization led by the Rev. Dr. Martin Luther King, Jr. before his assassination in 1968. Jackson had made the first public calls for the SCLC to march through Cicero. By the time he started showing up on *Soul Train*, he had become the head of SCLC's Chicago branch. He did not, however, use the show as a political platform. Rather, he made a couple of brief cameo appearances in the early days. The minister also appeared with his children on a Christmas episode of the program. According to Theresa Davis, whose group the Emotions also boarded the "train" that day, Jackson gave a special message "stressing the importance of family unity, in the spirit of the holiday season and always."[22]

The Rev. Jackson's appearances on the show partly resulted from Cornelius' stint at WVON. At the radio station, the two were coworkers. During and after Cornelius' tenure there, talk show host Wesley South shared his nighttime program *Hotline* with Jackson every Friday. The minister often called into the show from out-of-town to promote upcoming Operation Breadbasket meetings. Thus, King's death did not stop WVON from supporting the SCLC. Similarly, Cornelius' departure from radio did not end his encouragement of Jackson. Just as WVON provided Jackson initial radio exposure, through Cornelius, WCIU granted the activist his first television forum.[23]

Jackson, however, was not the only local African American clergyman with appeal to young urbanites to appear on *Soul Train*. Moreover, when Father George Clements of the Holy Angels Catholic Church participated in a January 1972 episode, he gave it a decidedly political slant. The *Chicago Defender* billed the episode as a chronicle of "St. Martin Luther King." Here, *Soul Train* broke new ground, for at the time very few television programs — especially variety shows — commemorated King's life. In addition, four years after his death, he was thirteen years away from becoming a national holiday figure. Only six years had passed since his demonstrations in Chicago angered whites to the point of stoning him. Meanwhile, the Nixon administration frequently spoke out against demonstrators of civil disobedience, which was a tactic of the civil rights movement. Through Clements' tribute, *Soul Train* symbolically supported civil disobedience by supporting King's work.[24]

No stranger to controversy, Clements was an appropriate facilitator of the tribute to King. He supported Chicago's branch of the Black Panther Party and admired the determination of the group to have public officials pay attention to its concerns. The Chicago priest had eulogized Fred Hampton, a local leader of the Black Panther Party whom the Chicago Police Force had assassinated in 1969. At the time J. Edgar Hoover, director of the Federal Bureau of Investigation, had dubbed the Panthers the number-one threat to the internal security of the United States. A well-known Chicago figure by 1972, Clements' appearance on *Soul Train* made the second page of the *Chicago Defender*.[25]

Clements put his guest spot on *Soul Train* to great and innovative use. He capitalized on the show's appeal to African American teenagers by recruiting sixth-grade students from Holy Angels' school to take part in his presentation. In addition, he was able to potentially reach a large African American adolescent audience — a demographic that many churches have historically struggled to recruit. Rarely had religious figures used music television, especially shows devoted to rock-and-roll or R&B, to reach out to young viewers. Certainly the likes of Jackson and Clements had not been on *American Bandstand* or *The Flip Wilson Show*, although gospel singer Clara Ward and her choir appeared on the latter program.

In addition to racism, poverty, and social justice, the Vietnam War became an issue examined on *Soul Train*. The musical group referring to the conflict, however, offered a patriotic message to soldiers instead of an anti-war song. In March 1973, as all remaining U.S. troops prepared to leave South Vietnam at the end of the month, the local group the Auditions went on the show to promote their aptly titled recording "Returning Home from Vietnam." The group's record label pitched the song as a "political and social statement in music about the long war in Vietnam and the return of our G.I.'s," and the singers dedicated the song to the returning soldiers and prisoners of war.[26]

Even in its infancy, *Soul Train* evolved into a television force recognized in Hollywood. A cast member of the hit television series *Julia* appeared in July 1971, months after the cancellation of the series. At nine years old, actor Marc Copage was one of the youngest performers on *Soul Train*. His appearance also demonstrated the appeal of the dance show with young viewers. He sang "Will It Be Me," his single which had begun rising on WVON's airplay chart.[27]

Another actor's guest spot was considerably less likely. Actor Gene Hackman appeared on the show to promote his new movie *The French Connection*, which Twentieth Century–Fox released to theaters in the fall of 1971. *Soul Train* was an odd choice for advertisement of the film, for it lacked overt relevance to the dance show's young viewers. *The French Connection* did not have a large African American cast. Despite *Soul Train*'s advertisements as diverse and welcoming, the main character of *The French Connection*, a white Irish American alcoholic detective trying to stop an international heroin shipment, was a bigot.[28]

Soul Train also set high standards for guest musicians. They appeared by invitation only, and, according to Lorenzo Clemons, "You had to have a record on the radio play list to get the invite." His group the Mandells received considerable airplay at the time of their episode, and they also knew most of the "VON Good Guys." On the show the group either sang "Think Back" or "Now I Know," both of which were popular records then. Clarice Kavanaugh, meanwhile, was present for appearances by well-known performers Garland Green and the Chi-Lites.[29]

Local group the Chi-Lites, who had several hits on the charts throughout the 1970s, made frequent stops on the Chicago *Train*. "We was always on the show," said founding member Marshall Thompson. He remembered the program's facilities as having left much to be desired. He lamented that the

series had a low budget, which made for a small space for performing and "less things to work with."[30]

Other talented entertainers landed a gig on *Soul Train* through networking. The Chicago-based group the Emotions first encountered Cornelius while rehearsing in the back of their manager's office. The manager — Pervis Staples of the gospel-singing family the Staple Singers — was a friend

Top: The Chicago-based group the Mandells. Lorenzo Clemons is leaning on the drums. The other band members are unidentified. Courtesy Lorenzo Clemons. *Bottom*: The single "Now I Know" by the Chicago-based group the Mandells. Courtesy Lorenzo Clemons.

of Cornelius. At the time the Emotions met Cornelius, he was still working at WVON. He remembered them, however, and they appeared on the show at least three times between 1970 and 1974. One of their episodes was a Christmas show, and the group accordingly performed the song "Black Christmas."[31]

Staples especially helped make the Emotions memorable to Cornelius. The act was one of his first successes shortly after he had left the Staple Singers in 1969 to start Perv's Music. He complemented the Emotions' voices by hiring a seven-piece band to accompany the group. Whenever the members were in town, they worked daily with Ghent and Johnson. While running Perv's Music, he also worked as the Chicago representative of the renowned R&B label Stax/Volt Records. He sent recordings of any Chicago-based act with potential for success to the label's headquarters in Memphis. The Emotions were among the Windy City acts contracted with the southern label.[32]

Soul Train was one of many gigs the Emotions played at the time. Having sung together since their ages had ranged between three and six years old, the members had developed a strong following. They were, however, dedicated artists who cared about their craft, as demonstrated by their daily dance lessons and their longevity in the music business. Their camaraderie as sisters provided a familial support network. In addition, their father served as the Emotions's guitarist. By 1969 the group had played at New York's Apollo Theater for a week and at the National Association of Television and Radio Announcers convention.[33]

Through *Soul Train*, viewers were able to see multiple groups in individual episodes. Lorenzo Clemons said that the Mandells appeared on an episode with the group The Whispers. Moreover, the program attracted entertainers of considerable stature. One episode in particular starred the Chi-Lites, Tyrone Davis, the Dells, and the Staple Singers. All four acts had already achieved massive chart success within the past two or three years, and they all still had major crossover appeal with songs among the top forty slots of *Billboard* magazine's "Hot 100" charts.[34]

What the artists did not have, however, was consistent major television exposure. The Chi-Lites, for example, had not previously appeared on a nationally televised musical variety show before going on *Soul Train*. Soul singing often involved improvisational sounds like grunts and moans, and artists unskilled at pantomiming had difficulty in convincingly moving their lips to their recordings. When performing live, singers forced to rely on television studio bands instead of their own musicians crooned over significantly less "funky" instrumentation, which watered down the soul of the songs. Still another problem was that the (white) hosts of the day rarely conversed with African American artists before or after their songs. Thus, the groups took advantage of the rare opportunity of promoting themselves and their music to African Americans on television, and *Soul Train* benefited from having the presence of major "soul" stars on its stage.[35]

The musicians also lacked their own designated area for performing separately from the dancers. Unlike most dance shows, which provided platforms or risers on which the performers could entertain, guests on *Soul Train* shared the floor with the dancers. "The studio was too small for a platform, because they had the old-fashioned cameras that had to move to set up separate shots," Clemons explained. "The platform would have caused [too] much movement."[36]

In this regard *Soul Train* had more in common with defunct dance shows *Shindig* (1964–66) and *Hullabaloo* (1965–66) than with *American Bandstand*. In Clark's series the guest performers sang on stage by themselves; the host and the dancers sat together offstage and off-camera and watched the guests. In contrast, *Shindig* and *Hullabaloo* featured dancers performing their routines while the guest musicians sang their hits. Similarly, *Soul Train* placed its dancers with the guests. Cornelius, however, did not sexualize his dancers, whereas *Hullabaloo* had featured go-go dancing women writhing in cages.

Soul Train in Chicago instantly became a hit show. Early promotion of the series centered on famous guests. The *Chicago Defender* contributed to the success by focusing its coverage of the debut episode on guest musician Jerry Butler. The article provided more information about Butler's recent musical success than about Cornelius, but the host's picture appeared in the article.[37]

The first two weeks of the show provided a strong start. In addition to Butler, the first week featured local talent the Emotions, the Chi-Lites, Lost Generation, and the Five Stairsteps. In the following week, the show featured soloists, Gene Chandler, Sly Johnson, and Otis Leavell; as well as groups, the Sequins. Despite the newspaper's focus on Butler, the Five Stairsteps and Gene Chandler had current mainstream hits and performed them on the program. The former sang "Ooh Child," and the latter sang "Groovy Situation."[38]

Competing local stations scrambled to find programs to schedule against *Soul Train* during the 1970–71 season, but the dance show remained strong in its 4:30 P.M. time slot. In the spring of 1971, WGN, Channel Nine, tried replacing its reruns of the cartoon *The Flintstones* with the durable live-action children's show *Garfield Goose and Friends*. By the fall, however, *The Flintstones* had returned to its usual 4:30 P.M. airings. All of this tinkering was to no avail for WGN, for a study by local college students revealed that *Soul Train* had beaten *The Flintstones* in the ratings. The defeat of the popular cartoon show was unlikely, because at the time of *Soul Train*'s premiere, *The Flintstones* had just entered syndication after nine years on network television. The cartoon had appeared in prime-time network television for six seasons (1960–66) and on Saturday mornings for three seasons (1967–70). Thus, the ratings victory of a local program over a nationally established one was no small accomplishment.[39]

Meanwhile, on WFLD, Channel 32, the last thirty minutes of the hour-long, live-action show *Cartoon Town* aired against *Soul Train*'s first half-hour. In early 1971 the station moved the two-year-old series to a 3:30–4:30 P.M. period and aired reruns of the cartoon series *Speed Racer* from 4:30 to 5:00 P.M. By fall, *Cartoon Town* was back in its 4:00–5:00 P.M. berth. Throughout these changes, reruns of the live-action situation comedy *The Flying Nun* aired from 5:00 to 5:30 P.M., against *Soul Train*'s last thirty minutes.

One of the gimmicks of WCIU's *Soul Train* was its weekly dance contest. The Friday broadcasts revealed the winners. Local businesses offered prizes to the victors. Some establishments offered dinners, others donated free concert attendance, and still others gave clothing and accessories. At least one of the female champions won platform shoes that came from a Chicago store operated by Chaka Khan.

Thanks to the success of *Soul Train*, WCIU had a lock on teenage viewers for an hour in the afternoons. Because programming for minors barely lasted two hours between the time children returned home from school and the start of evening news telecasts, having no competition for a particular minor age bracket for sixty minutes was especially significant. Bill Jackson, the host of *Cartoon Town*, viewed *Garfield Goose and Friends* as more of a competitor than *Soul Train*. He explained, "*Soul Train* was very popular but was not considered a direct ratings competitor because of the older age of viewers making up the bulk of its audience." On the other hand, with *Garfield Goose and Friends*, WGN targeted the same age demographics — six-to-eleven-year olds — that WFLD did.[40]

WCIU itself experimented with its schedule in order to capitalize on the success of *Soul Train*. Before late 1971, the program *Black's Preschool Fun* aired in the time slot directly preceding *Soul Train*. The station eventually decided not to place two shows with two completely different age demographics in the same hour. *A Black's View of the News*, previously a 10 P.M. offering, replaced *Black's Preschool Fun* by the end of the year.

Eventually Cornelius and Ghent did not have to beg local teenagers to dance on *Soul Train*. The show was especially popular among the city's African American viewers and dancers. According to WCIU executive Howard Shapiro, "the show was so popular that in order for a kid to get on [the show], he had to write ahead." Dancers also received an invitation on the show by telephone after having called WCIU first. On the other hand, Garrick Anders was a last-minute substitute for a girl whose partner suddenly could not attend; she had already acquired tickets and gave one to Anders. "We jumped on the bus, and that was that," he remarked about his ease in getting on the show.[41]

The size of the crowd on *Soul Train* reflected the popularity of the show among Chicago's African American teenagers. For most episodes approximately thirty kids came on the show to dance, but the number of dancers ranged from fifteen to twenty couples. Chicago television offered very little exclusively for African American adolescents. The program not only played the music of their tastes but also provided a means for the teenagers to see people just like themselves on television.[42]

Soul Train's success in offering entertainment to teenagers and young adults in Chicago came on the heels of years of negative press regarding police brutality against youth, especially African American youth. In 1970 only two years had passed since Mayor Richard Daley's order to "shoot to kill" rioters mourning the assassination of the Rev. Dr. Martin Luther King, Jr., and since the clubbing and gassing of young demonstrators at the Democratic National Convention. When the show premiered, only eight months had elapsed since policemen had riddled the bodies of two local Black Panther Party leaders with bullets. Father Clements believed that Mayor Richard Daley was too powerful for African Americans to successfully organize and act for substantial change in their community.[43]

The exclusively African American cast of *Soul Train* was problematic for Cornelius when the ratings climbed. Word of mouth about the show eventually spread beyond African American teenagers to their white counterparts. As a result, white teenagers started heading to the Board of Trade to stand in line for a chance to board the "train." Cornelius had difficulty keeping the program all African American but managed to do so — to the disappointment of the young white hopefuls. Adding insult to injury, Chicago's only dance show for white children, WCIU's *Kiddie a-Go-Go*, ended the same year that *Soul Train* began, leaving white audiences with no alternative local program showcasing mainstream pop music. On the other hand, young devotees of

R&B were able to watch *Red, Hot, and Blues* and *Soul Train* on WCIU until the former's demise in 1973.[44]

As a result of the show's rising popularity, a slight struggle arose over control of the series. Cornelius received a visit from a representative of the owners of WCIU. O'Connor and Shapiro sent him to tell Cornelius the perspective they had on the program. "You know, that *Soul Train* show — it's really *ours*, you know," the representative declared on their behalf.

"No, it isn't," Cornelius replied. "And if you want to fight about it, I'm going to call my friend Jesse Jackson."

At that moment, the matter was dropped. Cornelius kept the ownership of *Soul Train* without dispute from that point onward. Meanwhile, he remained an anchor on *A Black's View of the News* until May 1971, when he no longer wanted to host both a "bubblegum" show and a "serious" show at the same time, as he told the *Chicago Tribune*.[45]

The corporation Sears-Roebuck — an early sponsor of the show — greatly benefited from *Soul Train*'s success. George O'Hare, the merchandising and advertising manager for the company in Chicago, remembered advertising sales of hit singles on the show. As a result, record purchases skyrocketed. "We couldn't keep up with the records," he declared. "They weren't being printed fast enough." His friend, entertainer Dick Gregory, had to help him secure African American record distributors; the white distributors no longer provided sufficient numbers of copies of records.[46]

The host himself gained clout in the music industry. He suggested to O'Hare that Sears promote a Chi-Lites album instead of selling 45 rpm singles for forty-five cents. Cornelius further convinced him to advertise the album not only on *Soul Train* but also on radio stations besides WVON. O'Hare, in turn, persuaded Chicago's top disc jockey to play it. The response was overwhelmingly positive, and one of the album's songs — "Have You Seen Her" — became a hit.[47]

"Hot Potatoes" — the adopted theme song for *Soul Train* — also became a popular song in Chicago as a result of exposure on the show. Within a short time after the premiere of the program, other local television programs started using King Curtis' tune. All three of the city's major television stations incorporated the theme into their newscasts. The increased exposure of "Hot Potatoes" illustrated that *Soul Train* now had some mainstream appeal. African American teenagers, musicians and disc jockeys were not the only people paying attention to the show.[48]

Curtis, however, did not live to see his song receive national television exposure. Two months before the premiere of the syndicated series, he was murdered in New York City. While fighting two men who were blocking access into his home, he received a fatal stab wound. He died on August 14, 1971. He had such a large following that when disc jockeys received word of his murder, they immediately began playing his music in his memory.

Cornelius continued to use "Hot Potatoes" as *Soul Train*'s theme after Curtis' death. After all, not only was Curtis an icon of "soul music," but he also had many commonalities with the *Soul Train* host. Having worked with numerous musicians over the years, Curtis had developed important connections in the music industry and played at respected music festivals. Meanwhile, in three years Cornelius had effectively networked among people to graduate from radio to television, and within two months of Curtis' passing, the host started establishing more relationships in the R&B music industry for his nationally syndicated version of the series. In addition, Curtis was a contemporary of Cornelius. Dying at age thirty-seven, the saxophonist was only two years older than Cornelius.[49]

During *Soul Train*'s first season on WCIU, Cornelius found a kindred spirit in a fellow savvy, Chicago-based African American entrepreneur: George E. Johnson, the founder and owner of hair-care product company Johnson Products. He and his wife Joan started the business in 1957. Like Cornelius, they catered specifically to African Americans. In addition, both Cornelius and Johnson offered diverse variations of their products in order to attract as many African Americans as possible. A typical episode of *Soul Train* offered music for the whole family: ballads, "message songs," and funk or disco songs with minimal lyrics. Similarly, Johnson's merchandise transcended black cultural politics. At first Johnson Products sold hair-straightening products Ultra Wave and Ultra Sheen. By the start of the 1970s, however, the company also capitalized on the growing Afro-centric "Black Is Beautiful" ideology of the period by offering Afro Sheen to customers preferring "natural" hairstyles.[50]

Johnson's fortunes significantly rose at the same time as those of Cornelius. Over the decade, money from annual sales by Johnson Products had nearly tripled. From 1965 to 1970, earnings per share skyrocketed from eight cents to one dollar. Then, on January 14, 1971, Johnson Products became the first black-run and black-owned company to appear on a major stock exchange list — the American Stock Exchange. The company's entrance into the national exchange dovetailed with Cornelius' plans to make *Soul Train* a national series.[51]

Johnson reached out to African Americans by other means than his products. His years of dealing with banks that did not support his vision for the company were "one reason that when the opportunity came in 1964 to organize a black bank, I took it." Since its founding, the Independence Bank of Chicago had increased its assets ($800,000 to $16 million) by 1970. His success in financial endeavors promoting black pride prompted *Time* magazine to quip, "Pride pays."[52]

Cornelius happened to launch his series at the same time that Johnson actively sought African Americans to advertise his products. In the early 1970s, Johnson spent nearly all of his $2 million advertising budget on African American print media, radio, and sporadic television programs aimed at minorities. He reasoned, "You must emphasize self-pride with blacks, something that other people have not paid attention to." As the 1970–71 television season drew to a close, Johnson decided to send some of his advertising dollars to Cornelius for *Soul Train*. Thus began a business relationship between two Chicago-based, African American entrepreneurs that lasted for over two decades.[53]

Johnson's decision to sponsor *Soul Train* influenced African American culture beyond the televising of R&B music. Through the promotion of his merchandise, he contributed to the increasing acceptance of "naturals" among African Americans in the 1970s. The hairstyle still had radical connotations in 1970, for Angela Davis — an African American communist accused of murder — was arguably the most televised woman wearing an "Afro" that year on the news. Johnson Products, however, promoted the hairstyle as beautiful and offered its merchandise as means to accentuate its beauty. No commercial had previously validated the attractiveness of the "natural." The style's endorsement from corporate America helped make it more mainstream.[54]

Cornelius, in contrast, took pride in having a popular show that was not in the mainstream. He boasted that *Soul Train* was "the only black entertainment program on the air." Black comedians Flip Wilson and Bill Cosby had network series, but to Cornelius they did not count; their material did not specifically address African American concerns. Cornelius critiqued, "Flip is black, but his show is not." On the other hand, he considered Redd Foxx a comedian who excelled in African American humor.[55]

Having successfully launched *Soul Train*, Cornelius began to decrease his involvement in his own series. Although the "official" host, Cornelius was frequently absent from *Soul Train*. He eventually began traveling to California periodically to search for a national distributor for the show. By 1971 he had established Don Cornelius Productions in Hollywood. Whenever absent, however, he made provision for temporary replacements by bringing aboard local disc jockeys to host Cornelius-less episodes. The growing popularity of the series despite the invisibility of its creator demonstrated that the dancers and the entertainers themselves significantly contributed to the program's appeal.[56]

Cornelius sometimes relied on his former colleagues — the "Good Guys" at WVON — to substitute for him. As popular disc jockeys in Chicago, they had a built-in following for their particular *Soul Train* episodes. For his radio show, guest host Herb Kent had developed on-air alter egos like the "Gym Shoe Creeper" and the "Wahoo Man." Some WVON personalities did not need the work but still hosted the show. Pervis Spann, the station's nightshift personality, made money outside WVON by promoting and producing concerts. *Soul Train* gave him not only television exposure but also access to an audience during the daytime.[57]

Cornelius' colleagues at WCIU "conducted" *Soul Train*, too. Big Bill Hill of *Red, Hot, and Blues* was another practical choice. He already had experience as a host of a televised music program. As both a television star and a radio disc jockey, he brought his fans from both media to *Soul Train* whenever he hosted. In addition, he shared some physical features with Cornelius; both men, for example, were very tall African Americans.[58]

When Cornelius decided to take *Soul Train* into nationwide syndication in 1971, he made a very savvy choice of which Chicago episode to pitch to broadcasters. He took to California the episode that featured the Dells, the Staple Singers, Tyrone Davis, and the Chi-Lites. At the time all four acts were very popular on urban radio. Moreover, three of them had crossover hits in the 1970–71 season. The Chi-Lites' "(For God's Sake) Give More Power to the People" was among the top thirty songs for at least one week. The Staple Singers scored with "Heavy Makes You Happy (Sha Na Boom Boom)." Davis had the biggest hit with "Turn Back the Hands of Time." Cornelius contacted all the group leaders to inform them of his decision to use their appearances in order to try to sell the show on the West Coast. The host and producer eventually found a distributor for the series, and he started production on a nationally syndicated version of *Soul Train* in Los Angeles in the middle of 1971.[59]

Mike McGill of the Dells did not recall the Staple Singers boarding that particular episode of *Soul Train*. He did, however, note that fellow Chicagoan Jerry Butler made the pilot with them and the Chi-Lites. Butler also would have been a wise choice as a guest for the episode. Throughout 1971 he landed four songs in *Billboard*'s "Top 100 Singles" charts.[60]

The Dells. Left to right, top row: John Carter, Charles Barksdale and Michael McGill; left to right, bottom row: Verne Allison and Marvin Junior. Courtesy the Dells.

Although California's *Soul Train* became a syndicated hit series within a year of its debut, WCIU had no opportunity bask in the national version's glory. Almost immediately Chicago's *Soul Train* became an obscure footnote to the syndicated show. Many reporters outside of the Windy City either referred to WCIU's version in the past tense, failing to note the continued production and airing of the series, or noted the national show's Chicago roots without mentioning the continued existence of the WCIU series.[61]

The local press treated the local show only slightly better than the national press did. The *Chicago Defender* continued to promote WCIU's version, informing viewers as to scheduled appearances of prominent guests. It also provided photographs of national celebrities posing with the host after an appearance on the local show already had taken place. The newspaper, however, only focused on the syndicated series when covering it. Nobody mentioned the local series in the context of the syndicated one, except when reporters provided brief biographical sketches of Cornelius' career in articles.

On the other hand, the Los Angeles–based *Soul Train* had little to do with WCIU's version. Rather, both shows became separate entities. The weekday show remained a combination of a dance show and a public affairs program,

The Dells. Left to right: John Carter, Verne Allison, Marvin Junior, Michael McGill and Charles Barksdale. Courtesy the Dells.

but the new weekend series focused on dance. The national show did not promote the local one, and guests who had previously appeared on the Chicago version were rarely introduced on the national show as previous local guests. Cornelius developed a more expensive, flashier show for syndication, but WCIU did not do the same for the local market. Then again, the station did not have to do so, for the Chicago show — as viewers had known it since 1970 — remained a phenomenally successful *local* program. WCIU saw no need to tamper with a popular show.

Ronald Paul Johnson departed from *Soul Train* at this time. He became the choreographer and road manager for the R&B group the Dells. His loss was especially significant to the show, because he helped make the show enough of a success for Cornelius to take it to syndication. Whereas Cornelius gave the series personality with his hosting talent, Johnson had chosen some of the dancers, whose moves subsequently attracted numerous teenagers to the program.[62]

Cornelius initially did not completely sever his ties from WCIU after developing the syndicated version in 1971. He told the press that the Chicago-based show was not good because of its low budget and hasty daily production. For two additional years, however, he hosted both the local and national shows. Reporter Leah Davis of *Soul* magazine was one of very few journalists outside of Chicago to note during the first syndicated season that "Cornelius ... still hosts a local Chicago TV show daily with the same format as the national show." The host initially spent one weekend per month in California filming for the syndicated series. Then, he began receiving and accepting offers to play small roles in films and to host episodes of other California-based television programs. Still, as late as March 1973, the *Chicago Defender* continued to identify him as the host of WCIU's *Soul Train*, and six months later the newspaper listed him among guests at a Chicago event as "Don Cornelius, *Soul Train*, Chicago and Los Angeles."[63]

By that fall, however, Clinton Ghent had effectively taken over the hosting duties from Cornelius. Reflecting the growing lack of coverage the WCIU series received in the press after the national version began, the local press did not treat the personnel change with great fanfare. No newspaper specified when Cornelius left and Ghent began. Also, unlike the first articles about the program, in which brief biographical sketches of Cornelius appeared, the paper provided no information about Ghent's career before *Soul Train*. The first time the *Chicago Defender* referred to Ghent as the host of the show was in a photograph caption on August 4, 1973. He had posed next to local singer Denise LaSalle on the set of the program after the completion of her performance of "What It Takes to Get a Good Woman." The new host's name did not appear again until three months later, when the periodical noted the appearance of singer Annette Snell on *Soul Train* after enjoying success with her song "You Ought-ta Be Here with Me." The newspaper article stated that she was "Clenton Gent's [sic] guest on the Chicago edition of *Soul Train*." Afterwards, the press covered Ghent and *Soul Train* even less frequently than before.[64]

The series, however, aesthetically stayed the same. It remained in black-and-white and retained its weekday afternoon time slot of 4:30 P.M. It continued production atop the Chicago Board of Trade building. And, most importantly, African American adolescents continued to flock to the facilities after school each weekday.

Clinton Ghent received mostly positive reviews as host from *Soul Train's* participants. Marshall Thompson remembered him as a "great personality" who handled the show as a "stone professional." Dancer Crescendo Ward said, "Clinton was just cool." Ward elaborated, "He was just smooth. Nothing upset him." Clarice Kavanaugh described him as "very dapper" as well as "very talented, had a gift of gab, and a very sharp dancer." The public took to Ghent well, and he became a local celebrity after becoming the host.[65]

Ghent provided several visual contrasts to Cornelius. The new host had frenetic energy, which Cornelius lacked. In contrast to the former host's reserved demeanor, Ghent was very "animated," according to Theresa Davis of the group the Emotions, and occasionally danced with the teenagers on the dance floor. Ghent also was significantly shorter than Cornelius. Dancer Delwen Fields described him as "a thin, short guy" who was "dark-skinned."[66]

The dancers themselves also became local celebrities. Ghent responded to audience members' written and telephoned requests not only to play certain songs but also to feature prominently certain adolescents. Crescendo Ward recalled, "If you were a good dancer, you could be a celebrity." He noted that the dancers with the most appeal had the most time on screen: "When you became the favorite, the camera was always on you." He also remembered that the most popular girls did not have to wait in line to get on stage.[67]

Ward credited his fame from *Soul Train* with saving his life on more than one occasion. He once had to take home a girlfriend who lived in the Cabrini Green projects, which the Vice Lords gang claimed as their territory. After he had parted from her, some of the gang members approached him and demanded, "Represent!"

He responded, "No love," which meant that he did not belong to a gang.

They proceeded to pat him down and take his money until one of them yelled, "Yo, wait a minute — that's that *Soul Train* motherfucker!" As the others recognized him, they stopped the mugging and began taking a collection for his bus fare home.[68]

The show also launched Ward's dancing career. He and other teenagers from the show formed their own dance group the Puppets. They did "locking" moves not unlike the Los Angeles–based troupe the Lockers. The Puppets opened for musicians in Chicago and frequented Perv's House — a club run by Cornelius' friend Pervis Staples — for gigs. As their local fame grew, they no longer had to wait in line at the Board of Trade but could instead go right into the *Soul Train* stage area. When television personality Wolfman Jack went to Chicago seeking local talent for an episode of the music variety show *The Midnight Special*, he at first thought the Puppets were the Lockers. Still, the Puppets got the television gig because the Lockers wanted too much money, according to Ward. He and the other Puppets eventually left *Soul Train* to tour with Wolfman Jack, but he continues to credit the program for having started him successfully in the entertainment business.[69]

After the first year of the show had caused a stir among WCIU's competitors, local programming temporarily became more stable. For the 1971–72 season, only WFLD slightly shifted its programming against *Soul Train*. The station overhauled the format of *Cartoon Town*, changing the title to *B.J. and Dirty Dragon*. Bill Jackson continued as host.

Then in the 1972–73 season, both WGN and WFLD implemented significant changes to compete against the dance show. WGN replaced *The Flintstones* with repeats of the live-action series *Lost in Space* in the fall of 1972, but a few months later, *The Flintstones* returned. By early 1973 WFLD had replaced *The Flying Nun* with reruns of the live-action adventure series *Lassie*. That summer *Soul Train*'s most formidable competition, *B.J. and Dirty Dragon*, finally went off the air. At the time Jackson had been on local children's television for eight years. *Soul Train*, however, did not drive him off the air. Rather, he said, "The reason for *Cartoon Town*'s demise was because Kaiser Broadcasting, a chain based out of Detroit, bought WFLD-TV and instigated a policy of airing syndicated programming rather than creating its own — a trend followed by most of the industry."[70]

In the meantime WCIU had developed a schedule of shows starring African Americans to complement *Soul Train*. In late 1972 the station gave former pro-football player Gale Sayers his own half-hour series, which aired in the time slot directly preceding Cornelius' program. After *Soul Train*, at 5:30 P.M., was *A Black's View of the News*. Then in early 1973 WCIU replaced Sayers with a ninety-minute show called *Harambee*. The *Harambee-Soul Train-A Black's View of the News* block gave Chicagoans three consecutive hours of local African American programming until late 1974.

In the 1973–74 season, the other stations continued to struggle against *Soul Train*. The year started for WFLD, now under new management, with

The Soul Train Puppets

The Chicago-based dance group the Puppets. Left to right: Maurice Christian, Melvin Shrumpert, Samuel Feltz, Anthony Fairchild, Wayne C. Ward. Courtesy Crescendo Ward.

syndicated reruns of *The Little Rascals* replacing *B.J. and Dirty Dragon* at 4:30 P.M. Then in early 1974, another syndicated live-action program, *Batman*, took *Lassie*'s 5:00 P.M. slot. WGN aired local news at 5:00 in the fall of 1973 but switched to repeats of the live-action show *I Dream of Jeannie*.

That same season a new program that did not compete with *Soul Train* offered another image of life for young African American residents of Chicago. In February 1974, the CBS network began airing *Good Times*—a situation comedy about African Americans in a Windy City ghetto. The program featured a family headed by a former maid from another CBS show, *Maude*, which was a spinoff of the network's top-rated *All in the Family*. Although filmed in Hollywood, *Good Times* opened and closed with shots of Chicago tenements. Like *Soul Train*, this new series offered entertainment and (at least three) cast members in their teenage years or early adulthood. *Soul Train*, however, was pure escapism, while *Good Times* tackled topical issues like the underground drug trade, urban gangs, and poverty, albeit with humor. Despite its topicality, *Good Times* never made references to WCIU's *Soul*

Train, despite its immense following among local African American teenagers. Nevertheless, for over five years, both shows presented relevant images of young black Chicagoans to receptive audiences.

In early 1975 *Soul Train* suffered from programming changes at WCIU. The station launched a fifteen-minute show, *For or Against*, and placed it in a 4:00–4:15 P.M. time slot. Meanwhile, *A Black's View of the News* moved to 5:00 P.M. In between the two series was *Soul Train*, not only starting at a new time but also reduced from a sixty-minute show to forty-five minutes instead.

The cut in episode length did not lessen the quality of WCIU's *Soul Train* in its later years. A year into Ghent's hosting duties, the show demonstrated that it was still a top-notch television venue in R&B by welcoming the guest performance of an R&B group that had a nationwide chart-topping R&B and pop hit. When the Hues Corporation, scoring with the song "Rock the Boat" in the summer of 1974, appeared in Chicago that August to perform at the Mill Run Theatre, the act caused a sensation in the local African American media. The RCA Victor record label threw a "Rock the Boat" party for the members, and the local black press covered it, from newspaper *Chicago Defender* to radio stations WJPC and WBMX. Meanwhile, WCIU celebrated the group's arrival by holding a "Rock the Boat" contest on *Soul Train*. The first-prize winners received dinner and a show at the theatre. In addition, the *Chicago Defender* photographed them with the group, Clinton Ghent, and RCA employee Leroy Phillips.[71]

No other guest act on *Soul Train* during Ghent's tenure as host generated as much media coverage as the Hues Corporation. However, Crescendo Ward, who danced on the show from 1974 to 1976, stated that the show still provided popular R&B groups as guests. All of them pantomimed their songs. During his tenure he saw Blue Magic, Brighter Side of Darkness, the Staple Singers, and the Chi-Lites, among others. He especially remembered the latter group appearing frequently during his tenure on the program.[72]

Space, however, remained a problem at WCIU's Board of Trade facilities. Delwen Fields, who danced on the show sometime between 1975 and 1976, remembered the set as "very small," even with only six couples in attendance on the day he filmed his episode. He recalled that the dance studio was about twenty-five feet long and as many feet deep. All the adolescents danced in one area for technological reasons. If anyone stepped out of the area, which the staff delineated with tape on the floor, the television camera's focus on him or her would become blurred. Fields noted that his episode was produced live, leaving no possibility for the director to re-shoot a sequence if a teen-ager crossed the tape.[73]

Soul Train also continued to showcase popular dances among teenage African Americans. The moves constituted a mixture of contemporary and older dances. Kavanaugh remembered performing the "spank" and "the football" in the early 1970s. In addition to the latter dance, Ward listed the "bump," the "push and pull," the "robot," and the "Errol Flynn" among the dances he saw and performed in the middle part of the decade. Rufus Thomas had introduced the "push and pull" in 1970, and the Jackson Five had unveiled the "robot" in 1973. The dances, however, still found favor with Chicago teenagers.[74]

One change in the show after Cornelius' departure was the dress code of the dancers. By the time Ghent began hosting, dancers had started to wear more formal clothes to tapings. A major contributor to this change was the popularity of the motion picture *Superfly* (1972) with young African American audiences. The central character, a pimp named Priest (played by Ron O'Neal), wears extravagant suits and straightens his hair — a far cry from the ethnocentric dashikis and "Afros" that had until recently characterized popular African American fashion. Kavanaugh called the new style of dress "definitely what we would call 'fly' — like in *Superfly*! Dress to kill, the sharper the better."[75]

On the other hand, a certain degree of informality still existed on the show. Teenagers did not have to wear formal attire to be invited to participate in tapings. When Delwen Fields and his female cousin were invited to dance as a couple, he recalled, "[The staff] told us to wear decent clothes." Having connections helped people get on the show. His cousin had already appeared in previous episodes. "My cousin was really popular," he remembered. "She was trying to be a model." All he had to do was call the station, and he eventually heard from WCIU. "They called and told us where to be," he said.[76]

In 1976 the station finally replaced *Soul Train* on Monday through Thursday with another dance series: *Soul of the City*. The Chicago *Soul Train* had never fully recovered from the changes of the previous year. With the Friday, June 11, 1976 broadcast, Chicago's *Soul Train* ceased to be a weekday series. The series replacing it the following Monday effectively capitalized on the popularity of *Soul Train* by borrowing the word "soul" from the title of its predecessor. The show was produced in Baltimore and hosted by that city's popular R&B disc jockey "Moon Man." Meanwhile, on June 18, WCIU began airing *Soul Train* on Fridays only.[77]

Soon afterward, WCIU once again expanded its broadcasting of *Soul Train*. The station packaged repeat episodes of the local program as *The Best of Soul Train* and aired them on Saturdays during the 1976–77 season. The move was financially savvy for two reasons. The airing of repeats allowed WCIU to capitalize on the popularity of Cornelius' show twice per week. In addition, reruns were cost-effective, because the station was not paying for the production of new episodes. To maximize its audience potential, WCIU scheduled an airing of *The Best of Soul Train* in the early afternoon and another in the early evening, and neither broadcast conflicted with Cornelius' more popular show on Channel 2.

Meanwhile, WCIU's *Soul Train* kept chugging along but in an increasingly diminished capacity. By 1978 the station had whittled the program down from forty-five minutes to thirty, airing it from 4:00 to 4:30 P.M. The show ironically outlasted its replacement, *Soul of the City*, which ended that year. However, another Baltimore-based dance show from "Moon Man," aptly titled *Moon Man Connection*, became *Soul Train*'s new Monday-through-Thursday counterpart. The new series had a spaceship set, and "Moon Man" himself referred to it on-camera as the *Moon Man Space Connection*. The host sat in a chair beside a mock control center when addressing the audience.

Finally, on July 27, 1979, Chicago's *Soul Train* completely derailed. Its time had long passed. As if to underscore that images of urban teenagers from Chicago no longer comprised compelling entertainment, the show's situation comedy counterpart *Good Times* aired for the last time on CBS five days later. The most frequent images of African Americans on television networks at the time — black children adopted by a rich white man on *Diff'rent Strokes* (1978–86), a butler on *Soap* (1977–81), a bartender on *The Love Boat* (1977–86) — were no more promising. More importantly, they had little relation to the teenage figures with whom *Soul Train*'s and *Good Times*'s viewers had connected over the past few years.

Still, *Soul Train* left WCIU just in time, in terms of changes in local musical taste. Two weeks earlier the Windy City had made national headlines for a violent disco backlash that had taken place at a Chicago White Sox baseball doubleheader. After the first of two scheduled games on July 12, a local disc jockey blew up disco records in the center of the field at Comiskey Park. By doing so he visually and violently expressed the frustration that some people felt about disco's media oversaturation. Anti-disco attendees then swarmed towards the baseball diamond and vandalized the park. The second game was forfeited. Chicago no longer had the racial climate to welcome *Soul Train* or the music promoted on that show.

Chicago's R&B groups lost an important television forum when the WCIU show ended. Only a few of the musical guests remained affiliated with Cornelius for years, performing on the California-based *Soul Train*. But even they were soon left out in the cold. Cornelius relied frequently on Chicago-based guests in the first national year; but *Soul Train* then became a hit, and the host looked increasingly to singers from Los Angeles and Philadelphia. Only the biggest of the Windy City stars such as Jerry Butler, the Chi-Lites, and Tyrone Davis still appeared on the program as the 1970s ended. Most of the WCIU guests, however, never boarded the syndicated "train." When the local series concluded, Chicago R&B permanently faded from television screens.

By 1979 the local R&B industry itself was nearing disintegration. The Chess label had folded. Curtis Mayfield's label Curtom ceased operations in 1980, and Brunswick followed suit in 1981. Meanwhile, Mercury Records relocated its base out of Chicago. To be sure, WCIU's cancellation of *Soul Train* did not cause the labels to falter. However, with the current backlash against disco and the resumed segregation of popular music, the loss of the local show left the few Chicago labels remaining with hardly any options for televised promotion of their artists.

Cornelius did not burn bridges by leaving Chicago. On the contrary, he continued his professional relationships after moving to California. He and Shapiro remained in contact with each other through the years. Years after Cornelius departed WCIU, he asked his former boss to hire his son, Tony Cornelius. Shapiro complied, and Tony worked at the station for three years. In addition, Cornelius still periodically speaks to George O'Hare.[78]

Now a touring motivational speaker on racial issues, O'Hare is proud to have contributed to the development of *Soul Train*. It was part of his work in improving the lives of urban African Americans from the 1960s onward. His allies over the years included not only Don Cornelius but also the Rev. Dr. Martin Luther King, Jr., comedian and activist Dick Gregory, and Father George Clements. O'Hare's work, moreover, received recognition from his colleagues. In April 1972, Clements' Holy Angels Church named O'Hare the "Black of the Month" for his labors. Acknowledging the recipient's white racial identity, the pastor quipped, "Blackness is a way of life, not merely skin color."[79]

As for WCIU, the station still exists and remains independent as of this writing. Shapiro still owns WCIU. The unique local programs have since been cancelled. The station broadcasts all of its shows in color. It has come a long way from its days of mostly minority, all black-and-white programming. The current employees, however, have not forgotten the station's roots. To this day, WCIU proudly boasts on its Internet web page that it was the birthplace of *Soul Train*.

3

"People All Over the World"

Soul Train *Enters Syndication*

In order to transform *Soul Train* from a local to national hit show, Cornelius decided to set up production in Los Angeles to produce the kind of show that would attract a national audience. WCIU's version of the show required too many changes for the show to find an interested distributor, and the station did not have the resources to bring the adjustments to fruition. Some of the problems were of a technical nature. He elected to have a technologically sophisticated, fancily lighted set and more advanced cinematography than the two or three camera operators who took turns filming scenes in Chicago. Also, in contrast to WCIU's black-and-white, the national show was to be filmed in color.[1]

When Cornelius and Ghent first started producing the show in California in the summer of 1971, people in the film industry made the Chicago transplants feel like outsiders not only to the state but also to the film industry itself. Ghent remembered, "When we [Cornelius and Ghent] went to Los Angeles, all the cameramen were white. They were just shooting. I'd go out there, and we'd try to tell them how to shoot to make the show interesting." The crew, however, did not appreciate Ghent's assistance. "They'd start cussing us out, saying we were telling them how to do their job."[2]

The differences between Chicago dances and Los Angeles dances also prompted Cornelius to relocate the show. "In Chicago the criterion is how cool, how smooth you can be," the host explained. "In Los Angeles it's all about how wild you can be and, of course, that's much more interesting to watch." Dancer Garrick Anders of Chicago's *Soul Train* confirmed, "We didn't do much dancing in those days [1970]. Most of it was boppin' and steppin.'" No elaborate freestyle dancing took place. Because Cornelius was initially not able to consistently bring nationally famous musicians to his program, the dancers' moves were especially important in relation to entertaining viewers.

As a result, the dancing on the show had to be extroverted and draw in audiences instead of keeping them at a distance.[3]

Cornelius and Ghent arranged to have young dancers audition for the program whenever the two commuted from Chicago to Los Angeles to tape four shows in one weekend each month. The host and his assistant visited several youth groups and organizations, where adolescents tried to impress the pair enough to become dancers on the show. Leah Davis, one of the first journalists to discuss the syndicated *Soul Train*, considered the casting call an "easy matter" for the potential cast members as well as for Cornelius and Ghent. She remarked that the youngsters "merely dance and display their ability to party and have a good time."[4]

The *Soul Train* staff followed the WCIU format by recruiting high school students. Show coordinator Pamela Brown traveled to various clubs all over Los Angeles to seek teenagers for the program. Whenever she saw people she wanted, she handed her business card to them and invited them to the show. At least twelve of the dancers from the first syndicated season attended Los Angeles High School during their tenure on *Soul Train*. Among them were Ron Bauchman, Steve Lott, and Damita Jo Freeman.[5]

Los Angeles High School unwittingly became a symbol of conflicting images of young African Americans — somewhat like the images of Chicago's black teenagers from both WCIU's *Soul Train* and *Good Times*. Instead, ABC's situation comedy *Room 222* (1969–74) contrasted with the syndicated *Soul Train*. The former series used the actual high school as a backdrop for the fictional Walt Whitman High School, and the entire cast — teacher and student characters — consisted of black and white actors. On the other hand, the latter show cast only African American students from the actual high school. At the time both *Room 222* and *The Flip Wilson Show* featured multiethnic guest rosters, and other network offerings with African American leads before the 1973–74 season contained white actors. As network programs they had to appeal to as many viewers as possible. Meanwhile, *Soul Train*, as a syndicated show catering specifically to urban markets, could afford to be Afrocentric.

Cornelius' timing in entering *Soul Train* into syndication was fortuitous. In 1971 the Federal Communications Commission (FCC) ordered networks to give their affiliates the 7:30–8:00 P.M. time period of Monday through Saturday and the 7:00–7:30 P.M. slot of Sunday. Before the ruling, television stations had long complained that the networks owned too many hours of prime time programming. Although the FCC tried to encourage the stations to produce local programming, they usually filled the half-hour with inexpensive syndicated shows. As a result, local stations were hungry for syndicated programs in 1971.[6]

On the other hand, the stations were not as enthusiastic about broadcasting series that catered to ethnic demographics besides European Americans. That same year *The Barbara McNair Show*, a syndicated musical variety show starring a versatile African American performer, was cancelled after two years. Another syndicated music show, *Upbeat,* also left the airwaves after five years of frequently showcasing African American musical talent. Although *Soul Train* now stood to become the only African American–oriented syndicated program for the 1971–72 season, stations did not anxiously seek to replace *Barbara McNair* or *Upbeat* with Cornelius' show.[7]

The host heard only curt dismissals from would-be distributors. "There was just 'We don't want it. We pass,'" he later told the press. Some stations acknowledged the good production quality of the show but lamented that they had no open slots in their schedules available. The executives never mentioned the African American target audience or show content as reasons for refusing to carry the series. "No one was blatant enough to say that," he remembered. He eventually found a distributor when the advertisement firm Bozell and Jacobs, which represented businesses catering to African American markets, helped to syndicate the show.[8]

Cornelius expressed discontent for his show to be alone in African American syndicated programming. He complained about the absence of sponsors for ethnic programming, saying, "You can't convince advertisers to sponsor a program geared toward the black viewer. And even if blacks make up 30 per cent of their total market, they only spend about 1 per cent of their advertising budget in black media." Thus, no matter how black a city was, if the majority was still white, then stations prioritized white audiences. "This means that they're giving me, an urban black, a *Hee Haw*, on Sunday evening," noted Cornelius.[9]

The *Soul Train* producer sought twenty-five markets for his initial year in syndication but only received eight. Still, they were large markets with sizable African American populations. They spanned the continental United States: the South, the Midwest, and both coasts. Seven of the markets—Atlanta, Cleveland, Detroit, Houston, Los Angeles, Philadelphia, and San Francisco—aired the debut on October 2, 1971. Many of these cities were progressive on the issue of race, and three of them—Atlanta, Detroit, and Los Angeles—elected African American mayors over the next two years.

Meanwhile, Cleveland's own African American mayor, Carl Stokes, had already retired by 1971.

Chicago, ironically, was one of the cities that did not carry the premiere episode with the aforementioned seven markets in early October. Rather, the debut aired twenty-eight days later, on October 30. The local CBS affiliate, WBBM-TV Channel 2, did not seem to put much stock into the success of the series. The station introduced the West Coast *Soul Train* to the "Windy City," scheduling it at 2:30 P.M. The slot was undesirable for producers and advertisers seeking young viewers. The show started over two hours after Saturday morning cartoons ended, and the affiliate did not broadcast anything to hold the attention of adolescents. Adding insult to injury, the *Chicago Tribune* misspelled the name of one of the groups performing on the show, promoting the "Honeycomb" instead of the Honey Cone.

Soul Train's main competition among syndicated series consisted of more familiar and mainstream programs. Some of the most durable syndicated shows in 1971 included Mike Douglas' talk show and the game shows *What's My Line* (1968–74) and *To Tell the Truth* (1969–77). New shows that appeared in several markets that fall included three popular series recently cancelled by CBS — the adventure show *Lassie* (1954–71), the dance hour *The Lawrence Welk Show* (1955–71), and the comedy variety hour *Hee Haw* (1969–71). At the time the network underwent a major overhaul of programming to target urban and young adult demographics, and some series with high ratings like *Hee Haw* and the situation comedy *Mayberry R.F.D.* (1968–71) still disappeared that year merely because they had rural settings. In syndication, however, *Lassie* enjoyed a three-season run, while Welk's program ran to 1982 and *Hee Haw* for an additional decade beyond Welk.

Syndicated television did not have a rich African American history beyond *Barbara McNair* and *Upbeat* in 1971. Before *Soul Train*'s long run, the only show featuring African American principals to last in syndication longer than one decade was *Amos 'n' Andy*. A situation comedy with roots in blackface minstrelsy, *Amos 'n' Andy* only appeared on CBS from 1951 to 1953, but the network syndicated the program for thirteen years beyond its network cancellation. After years of protests from civil rights activists, CBS finally withdrew the show from the stations. Network television at the time, however, only offered one series with an African American lead —*I Spy* (1965–68), starring Bill Cosby.

Cornelius was also at a disadvantage, because *Soul Train* was cheaper to produce than the more expensively made syndicated shows funded by major corporations. Businesses ranging from Chevrolet to Colgate poured lots of money into syndicated series but offered them to stations at low fees in exchange for free advertising. These corporately funded programs aired in many markets attracted to the brand names that accompanied the shows. Johnson Products simply did not have as much name recognition among local broadcasters as Chevrolet.[10]

George Johnson, however, remained supportive of *Soul Train* and sponsored it on the national level. "It took a George Johnson who had both the money and the foresight to get the show started," Cornelius noted. Even after the show had gained more markets, he predicted that "if Johnson pulled out, there would not be anyone willing to fill his spot." As a result, *Soul Train* needed Johnson more than Johnson needed the program. Still, he benefited from supporting it. He received distinction among his business peers, for no African American businessperson had ever previously sponsored a national network television program.[11]

Moreover, Johnson was the only Chicago-based entrepreneur to finance *Soul Train*. The head of the advertising department at Sears-Roebuck had high hopes for the series. He called all his friends in the advertising business to invite them to a restaurant for the showing of the pilot episode. Both he and George O'Hare figured that someone would support the show after seeing the pilot. All of the attendees, however, refused to have anything to do with the program. One guest, openly concerned about African Americans producing a show of quality, stereotypically remarked, "These people don't have any money." Johnson saw potential that his business colleagues missed and informed O'Hare, "I wanna take the show."[12]

In addition to funding the show, Johnson became a spokesperson for it. This role demonstrated Cornelius' trust in the businessman, for no one besides Cornelius usually spoke on his behalf about *Soul Train*. For at least the first two syndicated seasons, articles from the *Chicago Defender* about the series often featured quotes from Johnson but none from Cornelius. Moreover, Johnson was not talking about the products he advertised but rather about the show's success and potential. Referring to the upcoming 1972–73 season, he told the newspaper that he expected *Soul Train* to pick up additional markets.[13]

In addition, at least in the Chicago area if not elsewhere, Johnson was unofficially the first host of the syndicated *Soul Train*. When the series premiered in Chicago, the first face that viewers saw was his. Introducing the program, he boasted, "We're very excited about this show and think it's the finest of its kind." After his brief welcome, the debut commenced with Cornelius as the host. Johnson's appearance on camera was unusual, for by 1971 sponsors of national television shows rarely placed their advertisements or products within the show. Such product placement had not appeared on national television frequently since the 1950s, when such series titles as *The Colgate Comedy Hour* (1950–55) and *The Dinah Shore Chevy Show* (1956–63) were common. On the other hand, the practice was standard with local shows, especially cartoon programs hosted by local personalities; cartoon hosts advertised products between films until the FCC banned commercials within children's programming after New Year's Eve 1972. Many local shows subsequently ceased production after the FCC ruling, but *Soul Train* was not a "children's program" and, therefore, not subject to the mandate.[14]

Johnson's appearance was also strange, because an entrepreneur of hair care products was vouching for the quality of a "soul music" series. Despite his success with Johnson Products, he had as little experience in network broadcasting as Cornelius, and he certainly lacked Cornelius' knowledge of the R&B music industry. In contrast, over fifteen years earlier, CBS used a well-known actor of "Western" movies (John Wayne) to introduce the debut of the Western series *Gunsmoke* (1955–75). Still, Johnson had some credibility in relation to *Soul Train*'s quality, for if he had not believed in the project, he would not have funded it.

Johnson and Cornelius jointly pioneered African American television advertising. The former made commercials starring African Americans, and the latter aired them during commercial breaks. In addition, Cornelius supplied many of the actors in the advertisements. Dancers on *Soul Train* did not receive financial compensation for performing on the program. Johnson, however, cast several of them for his commercials and paid them for their work.[15]

The relocation of the show from Chicago did not keep Cornelius from promoting the Windy City's soul music. In the first year of syndication, Chicago-based artists performed on the show. Their songs received heavy airplay on urban radio at the time. The Dells, The Independents, The Five Stairsteps, the Chi-Lites, Laura Lee, Jerry Butler, the Impressions, and Curtis Mayfield made appearances. During the first two syndicated seasons, a Chicago-based soloist or group often appeared on three or four episodes in a row. Marshall Thompson, whose group the Chi-Lites sang on both the WCIU and the syndicated programs, considered the West Coast *Soul Train* a vast improvement over the Chicago version. He referred to the Los Angeles facilities as an "upgrade." He likened the advancements to a change in automobile ownership "from Cadillac to a Rolls Royce." Singer Bobby Hutton of Chicago concurred, "The Chicago show couldn't be compared to the Hollywood show. The Hollywood show was at the top of the hill, Chicago levels below."[16]

Cornelius promoted musicians signed to a wide variety of labels from Chicago. A few artists from Chess Records boarded the "train," but Chess had fallen upon difficult times by 1971. More acts on the show came from sturdier labels like Mercury and Brunswick. *Soul Train*, however, also championed singers from small recording operations. The Independents, who appeared several times between 1971 and 1974, were signed to Chuck Jackson and Marvin Yancy Productions. The appearance of the group Brighter Side of Darkness in early 1973 marked the peak of success for the performers. Personnel changes in the group took place after the group misbehaved on the trip from Chicago to California to sing their hit "Love Jones" on the show.[17]

Of all the Chicago-based artists, no one received more exposure as the syndicated debut premiered than Bobby Hutton. Between 1970 and 1971, he had become a popular new act in the city, with at least three songs in the region's top-ten charts. Cornelius demonstrated great faith in Hutton's career by promoting his music on the local and national programs. In September 1971, shortly before the syndicated *Soul Train* began, Hutton sang his latest single "You're My Only Reason" on WCIU's *Soul Train*. Then he performed it for the national debut. In fact, he was the only musical guest from Chicago in that episode and, therefore, the first artist to appear on both versions of *Soul Train*. "I believe because of my popularity, I was chosen for the first show," Hutton proudly remembered. "Some say the record company had a lot to do with my appearance. Either way it's part of *Soul Train* history or history, period."[18]

Hutton was so popular that he inadvertently overshadowed Cornelius on the day of *Soul Train*'s initial telecast in Chicago. The *Chicago Defender* had promoted the premiere as it approached in Chicago. Other cities had previously televised the episode, and the newspaper gave a favorable advanced review of it. In that article, although Cornelius was mentioned, Gladys Knight and the Pips were the only people photographed. Then, on the day of the premiere's Chicago broadcast, the corresponding article not only featured Hutton alone in the photograph but also mentioned only him in the headline, "Bobby Hutton Featured on 'Soul Train.'" The report also noted his upcoming show at a local hotel and his honor as one of the "best dressed men of 1971" for an event at the Holy Angels Catholic Church. Moreover, the article devoted four paragraphs to him but only two to Cornelius. Thus, the *Defender* promoted the singer — not the host — as the "local man makes good" as a result of *Soul Train*.[19]

Hutton's professional relationship with Cornelius went into a sharp decline as the Chicago press covered the national debut of *Soul Train*. Hutton attributed the breakdown in communication to his promotion in the media over Cornelius. Before the debut the singer had appeared many times on the WCIU series. After Chicago's telecast of the syndicated debut, Hutton never received another invitation from Cornelius for either the local program or the national version. Moreover, he has not heard from Cornelius since 1971. "Don is a nice person. I have to put myself in his shoes," Hutton said philosophically. "If it were my show, I would feel [slighted] as well, but I probably would have handled it differently."[20]

Other cities had greater musical exposure than Chicago on *Soul Train* because of their artists' popular recordings in the 1971–72 season. As Berry Gordy prepared to relocate Motown from Detroit to Los Angeles, the Motor City had a last hurrah of televised musical representation. Throughout the season, viewers saw label-mates the Four Tops, Edwin Starr, Jr. Walker and the All-Stars, G. C. Cameron, the Undisputed Truth, and Martha Reeves and the Vandellas. The premiere episode featured not only Chicagoan Bobby Hutton but also Motown colleagues Eddie Kendricks — freshly divorced from the Temptations — and Gladys Knight and the Pips. All of the guests got along well with one another; Hutton and Kendricks especially bonded, because they had previously crossed paths while performing in Chicago and New York.[21]

After Motown relocated, however, *Soul Train*'s episodes of the 1970s recorded the company in disarray. Some of the label's performers in the program's 1971–72 season made their final televised appearances as Motown artists on *Soul Train*, for they decided not to move with the label. Meanwhile, new acts like G. C. Cameron became frequent guests, and some of the veterans like the Temptations continued to support the show. Nevertheless, *Soul Train* was not *The Ed Sullivan Show*, in which a song promotion maximized chances for a crossover hit. As a result, major Motown acts singing on *Soul Train*— the Temptations, the Jackson Five, and Stevie Wonder — promoted their hits on other shows. *The Flip Wilson Show* and *The Sonny and Cher Comedy Hour* (1971–74), for example, welcomed the performers. Meanwhile, the label's biggest female star, former Supremes member Diana Ross, only made a cameo on *Soul Train* in early 1973 and never appeared as a guest performer.

Still, the support from Motown for *Soul Train* was especially significant, because it marked one of the first times that the label publicly associated its top groups with a television program marketed specifically to African Americans. In the 1960s Gordy worked hard for his African American roster of singers to have not just R&B success but crossover success. To that end he avoided placing their pictures on covers of singles and instead used either cartoons or white models. Even with the Jackson Five in the 1970s, he told the group not to the address any questions from the press about being African American. He mostly provided artists of the "Soul" subsidiary to *Soul Train*, because the "soul" music they performed best fit the show. Jr. Walker and Gladys Knight were among the "Soul" entertainers on the program.[22]

In addition to Motown, Memphis-based Stax Records also provided guest stars for Cornelius. Rufus Thomas, his daughter Carla, the Staple Singers, Jean Knight, the Bar-Kays, and Al Green graced the stage during the show's first and second years in California. In 1972 both the record company and the show mutually benefited from their professional relationship. *Soul Train* further established itself as a force in music-based television by attracting successful acts. Al Green especially hit with crossover audiences with "Let's Stay Together" and "I'm Still in Love with You" in 1972. Meanwhile, Stax used the program to promote its artists, many of whom starred in *Wattstax*— a feature-length motion picture documentary of a concert developed in Los Angeles by the label itself. The Bar-Kays sang their "blaxploitation"-inspired "Son of Shaft" in both the movie and their *Soul Train* guest appearance.

A factor helping *Soul Train*'s marketability was its variety of R&B offerings. In addition to the different cities represented by the music labels of the artists, the series offered a wide but cohesive range of "soul" music styles. Songs on the show consisted of funk songs backed by sparse instrumentation, lushly orchestrated ballads, and pop-influenced R&B. Even show tunes from the Broadway musical *Pippin* received airplay, for they received Motown's "soul" treatment. The Jackson Five sang "Corner of the Sky" in 1972, and Michael Jackson performed his solo number "Morning Glow" the following year.

The Jacksons' variations of *Pippin* songs comprised the latest attempt by Motown to attract mainstream buyers to its artists. Venues for the performers included exclusive clubs like the Copacabana in New York and assorted hotels in Las Vegas. Also, ever since the mid–1960s, the label had produced albums and television specials in which its singers sang Broadway hits. On television the Temptations sang "The Impossible Dream" from *Man of La Mancha*, and the Supremes teamed with Ethel Merman for a number. On vinyl the latter group released an album full of songs from the musical *Funny Girl* in 1968. *Soul Train's* televising of *Pippin* material represented the program's endorsement of Motown's "Broadway tactic," which was ironic considering the Afro-centricity of the series.[23]

Through *Soul Train* the guest musicians took advantage of the novel opportunity to sing on a national television stage to an exclusively African American audience. In contrast, white people were the overwhelming majority of studio audience members attending the filming of network television variety shows as late as 1971. Even Flip Wilson played to a nearly all-white crowd for the first two seasons of his series (1970–72). *American Bandstand* featured some African American dancers, but most of the cast was white. Thus, for the entertainers who had their pick of network guest spots, an appearance on *Soul Train* suggested the desire of the entertainers to have an Afro-centric television experience. For the singers whose careers did not last into the era of the cable television channel Black Entertainment Television in the 1980s, their *Soul Train* performances were their only means of reaching out specifically to African Americans through television.

The first two syndicated seasons were the peak years of *Soul Train's* televising of female R&B artists. Women appeared regularly on the show; the first eight episodes of the 1971–72 season featured either female soloists or groups with female vocalists as members. In addition, the songs women performed on the show covered a wide variety of topics. Some artists sang ballads, but others delivered songs with overtly feminist lyrics. Lyn Collins, a protégé of James Brown's, informed her listeners in "Think" that "the sisters" were not going to tolerate the infidelity of their men. Laura Lee, a deep-voiced Chicago native with roots in gospel music, boarded the "train" with even blunter songs "Women's Love Rights" and "Wedlock Is Deadlock." Many of Lee's recordings of this period contained long spoken parts or "raps"— a technique that frequent female *Soul Train* guests Millie Jackson and Betty Wright later employed in their work.[24]

The feminist tones in the songs from Collins and Lee resulted in unusual television in the early 1970s. Few African American women starred in television series at the time, and their roles were so small that their characterizations were largely undeveloped. The shows in which they appeared did not cover Afro-centric issues, let alone black feminist ones. The only programs with "liberated women" as lead characters — *The Mary Tyler Moore Show* (1970–77) and *The Doris Day Show* (1968–73) — had white casts. As a result, *Soul Train* was the only series to give African American feminism a regular forum for television.

The feminism in the music artistically captured ideas that African American women had only recently begun to discuss to receptive audiences. As the 1970s began, the feminist organization Third World Women's Alliance grew out of the Student Nonviolent Coordinating Committee. The activist group addressed hardships that came with being both African American and female — a topic that organizations of the African American civil rights movement failed to mention. In addition, in 1972 Congresswoman Shirley Chisholm ran for president of the United States on the claim of being "unbought and unbossed," but her campaign stalled as she experienced difficulty in receiving support from white feminists and African American (male) civil rights movement leaders. The rhetoric in songs by Collins and Lee, which center upon independence from men and discussion of rights, vaguely resemble speeches and articles given by the activists.[25]

The great difficulty for Cornelius concerning artists related to *Soul Train*'s hectic monthly taping schedule of four episodes in two consecutive days. Because most episodes featured three guest acts, he struggled to arrange for twelve different acts to be available to perform on the show in the same weekend. Moreover, he continued the standards of the Chicago version of *Soul Train* by only booking acts with popular songs. As a result his ability to consistently deliver established, successful entertainers to viewers every week was no small accomplishment.[26]

Many of the artists appearing on *Soul Train* in the 1971–72 and 1972–73 seasons sang hits from years earlier. In some cases the artists had obtained few television venues to perform their signature songs before *Soul Train* came along. Such singers usually introduced a new release and promoted an "oldie but goodie" in the same episode. In early 1973 Aretha Franklin belted four songs, only one of which — "Master of Eyes (The Deepness of His Eyes" — was a current single. Some entertainers, however, only crooned their standards. A few weeks before Franklin's episode, James Brown had boarded the "train" to wail several of his songs, all of which were at least a year old and at most one decade old.

In the early years of the national show, the guests and the dancers often exhibited mutual admiration. The latter always cheered respectfully if not loudly before and after each song, whether a recording or a live performance.

Similarly, the singers occasionally danced with the teenagers on the dance floor and sang among them on the floor instead of the center riser above them. In addition, some of the veteran entertainers graciously invited dancers on the riser. Dancer Damita Jo Freeman, an early standout who joined the show in its third weekend taping session of the 1971–72 season, demonstrated the "Mechanical Man" dance during James Brown's live rendition of the song "Super Bad" in his February 1973 episode.[27]

The Motown group the Jackson Five were among the entertainers best able to relate to the dancers on *Soul Train* during this period. Ranging in ages from fourteen to twenty-one when they first appeared on the program in October 1972, the Jackson brothers were as old as the dancers. The musicians enthusiastically answered questions from the cast. Departing from the usual Motown formality of tuxedos for male groups, the Jackson Five wore colorful, psychedelic costumes, which resembled the wardrobe of the dancers. The group even socialized with the show's adolescents beyond the *Soul Train* set, wanting to study their moves. Freeman later told the *Sentinel* newspaper, "Michael Jackson was so impressed with us, he had us over to his house, and we showed him some steps."[28]

Soul Train not only offered political music but also a political stance. The songs still had good dancing beats for the Soul Train Gang, but their lyrics consisted of pointed social commentary. More than a few called for the end of the Vietnam War, in which American involvement had reached its sixth year in 1971. Over 100,000 American servicemen remained in South Vietnam in December. Ten months later racial unrest erupted aboard the carrier *USS Kitty Hawk*, which was in Southeast Asian waters at the time. Meanwhile, between late 1971 and late 1972, during *Soul Train*'s first season, Freda Payne crooned "Bring the Boys Home," Edwin Starr delivered the chart-topping anti-war anthem "War," and Curtis Mayfield pleaded, "We Got to Have Peace." Co-opting the slogan of the Black Panther Party, the Chi-Lites performed their hit, "(For God's Sake) Give More Power to the People." The show further suggested a political bias by not presenting pro–Vietnam War songs.

By the end of 1973, "message songs" against the Vietnam War had run their course on *Soul Train*. In the middle of the 1972–73 season, all American troops left South Vietnam after twelve years of fighting. The only remotely anti-war song from a guest performer that season was "We Need Order" by the Chi-Lites. Then in a November 1973 appearance, fellow Chicagoan Curtis Mayfield performed "Back to the World," which told of an African American

Vietnam veteran returning from the conflict to urban problems at home. Singing the line "the war was never won," he brought *Soul Train*'s antiwar era to a sobering and bitter conclusion. The series never took an anti-war stance — musically or otherwise — with another military conflict.

While most guest artists sang ballads or played dance music, Mayfield pantomimed a "message song" in almost every episode in which he appeared. When he sang with the group the Impressions throughout the 1960s, he had composed songs containing hopeful, religious imagery such as "Amen" and "People Get Ready." But ever since going solo in 1970, his music became increasingly moody and critical. By then, however, few "message artists" in R&B sang uplifting tunes in the context of the assassination of Rev. Dr. Martin Luther King, Jr. in 1968 or the uprisings in inner cities throughout the late 1960s. Boarding the "train" at least once a year in the first four syndicated seasons, Mayfield bellowed pessimistic lyrics about urban communities. He provided the soundtrack for *Superfly* (1972) — a movie featuring a stylish African American drug "pusher" as the protagonist. In an episode in which he sang about urban poverty, drug sales, and soaring food prices in "Future Shock," Cornelius appropriately introduced him as "the master storyteller."

Soul Train expressed political stances through other means besides music. By the 1972–73 season, each episode of the series promoted Rev. Jesse Jackson's organization Operation PUSH (People United to Save Humanity) before signing off. The references collectively marked the show's closest approximation of the WCIU version's promotion of public affairs. He had begun the group in December 1971, after leaving the Southern Christian Leadership Conference. PUSH sought to improve African American economic conditions via boycotts, picketing, placing pressure on businesses to hire and promote African Americans, and encouraging support of African American businesses and banks. The group was also political. In September 1972 Jackson told a Chicago audience about the Vietnam War, "PUSH got $100-million to save the children, the military got $100-billion to kill the children." Stressing radical activism, he declared at the group's founding, "We must picket, boycott, march, vote, and, when necessary, engage in civil disobedience."[29]

Cornelius, however, did not allow his political preferences to compromise the entertainment of the *Soul Train* viewers. Guests with significantly different political views from Jackson appeared on the show, but they did not have a forum for their opinions unlike Jackson's PUSH commercials. *Soul Train* was one of a few places in which African Americans welcomed James Brown without hostility during the 1972–73 season. He suffered criticism from African Americans when he endorsed the re-election of Richard Nixon as President of the United States in 1972. He explained at the time by quipping, "I'm not selling out, I'm selling in." Still, many African Americans believed the former and harassed him for the remainder of Nixon's presidency. While praising Brown as "soul brother No. 1," an editorial from Howard University's radio station chided him, "As a politician, he ain't doodlie squat worthless." Meanwhile, at a performance in Baltimore in October 1972, only 2,500 people attended Brown's concert at an arena that held 13,000 seats. Outside the facility about five hundred people became rowdy and smashed windows; fifteen people were arrested. Cornelius' charitable devotion of a single hour to Brown on an episode of *Soul Train* the following spring was a fluke, for also in early 1973, African Americans picketed Brown's concert at New York's Apollo Theater.[30]

Cornelius' embrace of Brown immediately after the Nixon endorsement was fitting, not only because the singer had a vast musical library to showcase on *Soul Train* but also because Cornelius had achieved similar accomplishments to Brown's. They were "soul music" versions of Horatio Alger's "rags-to-riches" concept. Cornelius and Brown came of age in the segregated 1930s and 1940s; the singer was only three years older than the host. Brown started as an R&B singer but later became a crossover star, and he used his clout to start a radio station and launch his own revue of stars. His protégés often appeared as guests with him on *Soul Train*. Meanwhile, Cornelius graduated from an R&B disc jockey to a national television personality. Moreover, both of them made their accomplishments without government aid, which appealed to Brown. Explaining his endorsement of Nixon, the singer stated, "I never got no Government grant, I never asked for one, don't want one."[31]

Moreover, the syndicated *Soul Train* did not engage in public affairs, unlike the WCIU version. No national episode broke from dancing to feature tributes to slain civil rights movement leaders. No black activist figures, whether Father Clements of Chicago or the Black Panthers of California, stopped the music to speak about black pride. Overall, the politics of the show did not extend beyond the "message music." As a result, Cornelius had more time to devote to promoting what would sell — music and the latest fashions and dance crazes.

The Afro-centric dynamic of the show extended to the director's chair. Cornelius had the clout to recruit Emmy Award–winning director Mark Warren to direct the first few episodes of *Soul Train*. He was a perfect choice, for he had experience with African American programs and music programs. He had directed *Soul!*— a special telecast in 1968 that combined African American humor with the visual style of the hip comedy series *Rowan & Martin's Laugh-In*. The next year he became the director of Rowan and Martin's show. At the time that he worked on *Soul Train*, he was in his last season on the comedy program. When the 1971–72 season ended, however, he worked not on *Soul Train* but on the feature film *Come Back, Charleston Blue*.[32]

Warren's style is most visible in the opening of the syndicated debut. After some footage of the cartoon train, the sequence immediately jumps to a close-up of Gladys Knight. Then the camera zooms out to reveal her dancing with the Soul Train Gang. After a close-up of the last guest introduced, the camera zooms out to the dancers before a sudden camera switch to a full-body shot of Cornelius. Finally, the camera zooms in during his opening monologue. The rapid camera transitions and zooms characterized his work on *Rowan & Martin's Laugh-In*. The cinematography in the opening of *Soul Train* resembled that of the recurring "cocktail party" sketches from Rowan and Martin's series. At the "parties" Warren switched cameras to various dancing cast members before stopping at one actor and zooming in as he or she told a joke.

Cornelius himself inadvertently made his show similar to *Rowan & Martin's Laugh-In* through his personality. The comedy series starred hosts Dan Rowan and Dick Martin as the calm, senior comedians anchoring the show full of young, extroverted humorists cracking jokes amid psychedelic camera trickery. Meanwhile, Cornelius hosted his program in a reserved manner, while the Soul Train Gang cavorted to songs suited well for Warren's frenetic style. Both shows almost had a deeper connection, for *Rowan & Martin's Laugh-In* wanted to lure away the male winner of the dance contest of *Soul Train's* syndicated debut episode. The winner, however, declined due to other commitments.[33]

By the 1972–73 season, B.J. Jackson had taken over the role of director on *Soul Train*, and he developed a more relaxed visual style for the series. Each show now began with a shot of the set's faux train destination cities and then slowly panned across the floor full of dancers. Brief clips of the guests cut into the dancing, but the clips were muted so as not to interrupt the "Hot Potatoes" theme. Finally, when Cornelius came on camera, there was no zooming — just an immediate cut to a close-up shot of him. In fact, Jackson rarely used zooming as a tool on the show, and his zooms were not as fast as those of Warren.

Other cinematic touches from Jackson were psychedelic. He frequently resorted to the chroma-key process, which allowed for a director to superimpose an image over the scene filmed at the time. In November 1973, when Michael Jackson sang "With a Child's Heart," at one point he pantomimed the song while pictures of himself popped up behind him. B.J. Jackson also blurred the focus of the camera in order to provide a smooth transition from Cornelius' introduction of a song to the performance itself. Jackson usually blurred the imaging of stage lighting before panning to the guest, especially if the song had a long instrumental opening.

The aesthetics of the first years of the syndicated *Soul Train* suggested very little of the show's new West Coast setting or of its Chicago roots. Rather, they implied a rural environment. The set resembled a rural train station. Railroad tracks were painted on the dance floor. A silhouette of a small station house and some signs bearing the names of major cities adorned the back wall. In addition, the animated cartoon sequence that opened each episode and served as a "bumper" for commercial breaks displayed an old, coal-powered train traveling across a sparse countryside.

In contrast, the people on the show provided some images of urbanity. The dancers often dressed in "street clothes," as in the Chicago version. They wore their hair in trendy styles — usually Afros and "corn rows." Cornelius, meanwhile, wore suits with wide ties and gave his hair an Afro style. In addition, male guest musicians often wore colorful tuxedos, and female singers appeared in fashionable mini-dresses, "hot pants," and gowns.

Soul Train developed a formula for each episode of the first two syndicated seasons. Every week the show opened with the aforementioned cartoon of the rickety train chugging. Then the camera panned across the sea of dancers on stage. Meanwhile, the "Hot Potatoes" theme blared as the announcer boomed, "*Soul Train*— the hippest trip in America; sixty nonstop minutes across the tracks of your mind into the exciting world of soul!" Finally, he announced the guests, the dancers (as the "Soul Train Gang"), and introduced Cornelius, at which point the music stopped and the host began his monologue. The cartoon that segued commercials resembled the opening except that the train sped away from the camera during a high-pitched shout of the show's title. Meanwhile, a recording of Chicago crooner Gene Chandler's song "Familiar Footsteps" played in the background.

The closing also became a routine. After thanking the guests and inviting the audience to tune in the following week, Cornelius promised, "And you can bet your last money, it's all gonna be a stone gas, honey." Then, he restated his name and signed off, "And as always, in parting, we wish you love, peace, and soul!" The credits finally rolled as the camera stayed exclusively on the dancers.

The show's catchphrases were simultaneously hip and outdated. The hip factor came from the series' announcer and host speaking slang — not just the musical guest. Cornelius' closing line, for example, was hipper than Dick Clark's "So long" or Sonny and Cher's "Good night." On the other hand, "love, peace, and soul" also had connotations of the waning 1960s counterculture. By the early 1970s, love-ins by hippies had virtually ceased, and the Vietnam War's length and extension into Cambodia discouraged any prospects of peace. Also, the drug trade had grown violent, prompting the *Los Angeles Times* to warn readers in December 1973, "The peace and love drug trip is over. Now it is money and guns and danger and death."[34]

The hosting style Cornelius eventually developed for the Los Angeles *Soul Train* did not immediately take shape. In the first syndicated episode, he addressed the viewers and introduced songs as a radio disc jockey instead of a television host. He did not provide smooth transitions from himself to either commercial breaks or the guests. Rather, he gave somewhat verbose monologues in rhyme. Before the opening segment ended for advertisements, he declared, "After a message from the Johnson Products Company, three of the most beautiful and talented sisters you've ever seen in your life are gonna be lookin' you dead in your eyes where your beauty lies." Similarly, when introducing those "sisters" — the group Honey Cone — he described, "Look out now for the fabulous Honey Cone, sho' 'nuff rockin' 'em back, and that ain't no fiction, baby. It's a natural fact."

By 1972, however, Cornelius' hosting had transformed into a more traditional style. He shortened the length of his monologues and introduced acts in the same manner that most hosts or announcers of television variety shows did. Whereas the last words of his opening in the debut mentioned the Honey Cone instead of the commercials that followed, he now closed his openings with "after these messages" or some variation. As a result his audience was more conditioned for the advertisements. In addition, he introduced guests by describing either their beginnings in music or their past hit songs and then telling the viewers to "give a hand for" the performer. Other phrases that became commonplace during guest introductions included "How about it, gang?" and "One more time." As a result of these changes, his speaking became more television-oriented than radio-oriented, although his monologues were now more formulaic.

What set Cornelius' speaking apart from that of other hosts was his rhetoric. He often spoke in alliteration when introducing songs and guests; he once referred to the Jackson Five as "most mighty." Also, when addressing teenagers on *American Bandstand*, Dick Clark sounded formal, using the phrase "ladies and gentlemen" before introducing an act. Cornelius, on the other hand, collectively referred to the dancers as the "gang" — a word often used in relation to a group of young people by the 1970s. When a person collectively addressed his or her circle of friends in children's television programs like the cartoons *Scooby-Doo, Where Are You* (1969–72) and *The Archie Show* (1968–78), he or she often called them by that word. Thus, a *Soul Train* "gang" fit well with Saturday morning television.

On the other hand, the use of "gang" instead of "ladies and gentlemen" also represented a hierarchy of sorts on *Soul Train*. When Dick Clark introduced his guests, he sat in an offstage seating section with his dancers. The phrase "ladies and gentlemen," moreover, suggested that he considered them as his social peers. After all, he was often billed as "America's oldest living teenager." Cornelius, meanwhile, introduced guests from his lectern, away from the dancers on the dance floor. In addition, he did not group himself with his dancers by identifying himself as one of the "gang." Rather, Sid McCoy always announced the host and the teenagers separately — as "Don Cornelius and the Soul Train Gang," not "Don Cornelius and the rest of the Soul Train Gang."

On *Soul Train* the host did not promote the teenagers beyond their dancing. He rarely solicited their opinions. Part of the reason had to do with practicality. What Clark lacked in opportunities for individuals to shine while dancing, he compensated by asking his dancers their views. When he sat with them, he often asked several of them to introduce themselves, and he engaged in small talk with them. More importantly, *American Bandstand* had a "Rate-a-Record" segment, in which he asked a dancing couple if a new song had potential to become a hit. The segment impacted record sales; for example, the Beatles did not appear on the show in the 1960s, because dancers had rated the group's debut single poorly. *American Bandstand*'s loss, thus, became *The Ed Sullivan Show*'s gain in 1964. Cornelius did not depend on dancers' likes or dislikes of music but instead played what urban disc jockeys noted were popular songs. As a result, he was less risky with his music choices than Clark. Cornelius did not have to waste valuable time and resources on a potential failure.

Moreover, his refusal to converse with his dancers at great length was a natural extension of his radio days. Disc jockeys did not call teenagers to ask them what they thought of songs. Rather, they gave monologues in between records, conducted interviews with scheduled guests, and announced commercials. As a television host, Cornelius rarely deviated from his radio duties.

The host's lack of communication with the Gang put the teenagers at a disadvantage concerning the pursuit of stardom. On the Line, the dancers did not introduce themselves as they took their steps. Only during dance contests and the Scramble did the adolescents say their names. Consequently, if a dancer appeared on the Scramble weeks before the Line, the viewer had to recall the name of that teenager during the Line. In contrast, if a dancer went on the Line first, then upon hearing the name during the Scramble, a viewer could then match the name with the dance the Gang member performed earlier on the Line.

Cornelius as a host was more similar to Flip Wilson and Ed Sullivan than to Clark. He shared Wilson's knack of using contemporary slang, which corresponded to the youth appeal of both hosts' series. Like Sullivan, however, Cornelius made awkward gestures. The former often stood wooden and expressionless and jerkily waved his straightened arm toward an act he introduced in a monotone voice. The latter frequently smiled but delivered his lines in a monotone voice, and he tended to jerk an extended finger or an open hand in the air when introducing performers. In addition, when saying "love, peace, and soul" at every closing, he rapidly pulled his right arm to his side while simultaneously forming his right hand into a fist at the mention of "soul."

His eccentric mannerisms, however, did not limit his appeal to viewers, nor was he a caricature of a host. Rather, his delivery of his lines won him critical appeal. He had struck a successful balance between "soulful" and "professional" hosting. The *Chicago Defender* complimented his conversations and interviews as "relevant, but intelligently projected." His words were "exceptionally articulated even to a crisp 't' and 's' in every word." In addition, he did not overdo the contemporary lingo. "There wasn't any jive talk on *Soul Train*," noted the article.[35]

Soul Train usually played music in a manner commonly heard on commercial radio, which made the show very similar to *American Bandstand*. Both series only aired songs for no longer than three minutes, just as disc jockeys did for A.M. radio stations. For Dick Clark, the time limit made sense, because he promoted A.M. radio pop hits. For Cornelius, however, the restriction was problematic. In the late 1960s, R&B artists began cutting longer tracks on their albums, many of which were either completely instrumental or had lengthy instrumental sections. In order to receive radio airplay as singles, labels divided the songs into two parts. Such songs usually had lyrics in the first part and the instrumental section in the second part, and disc jockeys tended to play the first part. In some songs the second part was longer than the first part. At discotheques disc jockeys played such songs in their entirety, to the enjoyment of the attending dancers. *Soul Train*, however, was no discotheque but rather a television show with time constraints. On many occasions *Soul Train* ended a song even before the first part ended. More importantly, by always leaving out "part two," the series did not allow the dancers opportunities to move to rhythmic, improvised piano solos or drum breaks.

Soul Train and *American Bandstand* also resembled one another by frequently booking crooners of "love songs." Cornelius, however, restricted the music of these guests only to their personal appearances on the show. The Soul Train Gang did not dance to slow, romantic ballads if the singers were not there to pantomime them. After all, the dancers could not do the latest dances — a major attraction of the program for African American adolescents — while they were wrapped in each other's arms and moving slowly and rigidly. Many balladeers made multiple appearances during a single season, not only because of their popularity on the radio but also in order take advantage of the only opportunities they had to hear their songs on the show. Both Jerry Butler and Lou Rawls boarded the "train" twice during the 1971–72 season. In contrast, *American Bandstand* often allowed couples to have "slow dances," promoting romantic tunes despite the absence of the singer from the show.

Cornelius differentiated the format of his show from both *American Bandstand* and the WCIU version of *Soul Train* by introducing two new segments. The first was the Soul Train Scramble, in which two dancers tried to unscramble the letters of a famous African American's name in under sixty seconds in order to win prizes. In the other segment, the Soul Train Line, the crew cleared the risers from the stage, and the dancers formed four columns — two on each side of the stage. Couples danced down the aisle between the columns and toward the camera in various freestyle manners. The host himself only participated in the Line once; in an episode from May 1973, he stepped down a column with each member of the Motown group the Supremes.

The Soul Train Scramble gave *Soul Train* a pro-social edge that *American Bandstand* lacked. Clark's signature feature — "Rate-a-Record" — allowed his dancers a forum to express their views about a new single. On the other hand, with the Scramble the dancers actually *learned* something. In addition, by making the Scramble Afro-centric, Cornelius became a pioneer in educating African Americans about themselves through television. His syndicated show began combining African American education and entertainment an entire year before comedian Bill Cosby's more celebrated series, *Fat Albert and the Cosby Kids*, started mixing lessons with jokes and music on Saturday mornings in September 1972.[36]

The work of the dancers in unscrambling the letters was central to Cornelius' promotion of Afro-centric education. In order to educate about the people whose names were the Scramble's answers, the dancers had to correctly unscramble the letters. As a result, before taping the Scramble segments, Cornelius told the participants the answer to the puzzle in advance. As a result, the dancers promoted Afro-centric knowledge by appearing knowledgeable of the names. Also, Cornelius' giving away of the answer helped to streamline the taping of the segment. On a tight schedule and a tighter budget, he could not afford to re-shoot a scene due to spelling errors.[37]

The Soul Train Line became key to *Soul Train*'s rise in viewers. As press coverage of the show accelerated midway through the first California season, reporters commented on the dances. The media attention, in turn, led to a rise in markets signing on to broadcast the series. The Line was so popular that the Chicago *Soul Train* began to feature it after its success on the California program. Crescendo Ward, a dancer for the Chicago series, recalled that the Board of Trade facilities for the Windy City's version of the show were too small for the thirty dancers to do the Line. Thus, the segment only occasionally took place. On the other hand, the Soul Train Scramble did not happen in Chicago, according to Ward.[38]

The Line went through an early developmental period before becoming formularized. In the first syndicated episodes, Warren sometimes showed all four columns of dancers at the same time. Later directors simply cut rapidly from one pair of columns to the other. Some dancers received more time on-screen than others on the Line, depending on the director's interest in the dance.

The episode in which the host and the Supremes danced with the Gang down the Line was an anomaly, for only the show's cast typically went on the Line. By May 1973 the Supremes' eight-year run of top-forty crossover hits had ended, and *Soul Train* was one of the few series in which the prototypical "girl group," at one time second only to the Beatles in record sales, appeared that year. Another opportunity for their presence on *Soul Train* was not immediately forthcoming, especially because the group was on hiatus from recording. Cornelius could not book them without any hits for them to promote. The Gang appreciated the novelty of the guests and the host in the Line by cheering more loudly than usual as they danced and by frequently blowing a dance whistle to show support for their moves.

The host, guests and dancers achieved a bond in that Line that never again took place on *Soul Train*. Neither Cornelius nor the singing group needed the exposure in the Line, for they already were famous entertainers. Their presence in the Line as celebrities was more significant than their dance steps. Confident in their fame, they danced conservatively, as opposed to the extroverted, flamboyant moves of the adolescents. On the other hand, the presence of the entertainers in the Line among the dancers momentarily eliminated any hierarchy on the show. No host or "special guests" existed; rather, *everyone* was a member of the Soul Train Gang.

Cornelius, however, appreciated the hierarchy of his series. He was, after all, at the top level of it. Moreover, he reminded his dancers of it at different opportunities. When the teenagers clapped more loudly for one couple in a dance contest than for others, Cornelius reprimanded the Gang, "Hey, no cheerin' y'all. When you cheer they can't hear me. And I'm the King, right?" The *Los Angeles Times* described his admonition as "cool" and "offhand," but did not say it was lighthearted or partially in jest. Small wonder that after the Supremes' May 1973 episode, Cornelius quickly reestablished the program's hierarchy.[39]

The syndicated show only resembled the Chicago version in terms of guest quality and staging. Both series attracted top musicians. Also, Cornelius staged the set similarly to the Chicago set. The host stood to the side, and the dancers had their own area. This look contrasted with *American Bandstand*, in which Dick Clark's lectern stood above the dancers at the halfway point of the rear of the dance floor. As a result, in camera shots of the entire dance floor, Clark appeared with his dancers in the middle of the screen; whereas Cornelius and the dancers did not share camera time unless he left the lectern to walk to the dance floor. In addition, *Soul Train*'s musical guests still shared the dance floor with the adolescents, although the musicians now towered over the teenagers by standing on a riser.

One of the most significant differences between *Soul Train* and *American Bandstand* was that guest acts on the former show performed live on a few occasions. *American Bandstand* featured pantomimed songs, and most of the time *Soul Train* did, too. After all, the use of recordings guaranteed that musicians did not make mistakes while playing or singing, nor did instruments unexpectedly malfunction; either scenario would have resulted in an expensive re-shooting of a sequence. On the other hand, guests with significant clout in R&B, especially acts with their own exclusive episodes, received Cornelius' permission to sing live. The up-and-coming act Tower of Power also won the privilege, but the leniency was practical because of the group's large size — a ten-piece band featuring a prominent horn section. Mic Gillette, a member of the group at the time, noted, "We refused to lip-synch and played live. It was worth it."[40]

In the early 1970s, only NBC's *The Flip Wilson Show* provided competition against *Soul Train* for top African American musicians. As a network show and the number-two series of the 1971–72 season, *The Flip Wilson Show* had a larger budget for guests than Cornelius did. Moreover, Wilson's success enabled him to woo African American artists who had frequently appeared on *The Ed Sullivan Show* before its demise at the end of the 1970–71 season. The Temptations and the Supremes, two of Sullivan's frequent Motown guests, turned up on Wilson's series more than once during the show's four-year run. As if acknowledging a "passing of the torch," Sullivan himself popped in on Wilson's show twice between 1971 and 1973.

Meanwhile, on *Soul Train* the Jackson Five and other established, popular acts received special treatment as opposed to less proven musicians. The famous Jackson brothers, Aretha Franklin, and Bill Withers were the only guests in their respective episodes. In contrast, episodes tended to have between two and four musical acts. *Soul Train* also showed respect for durable entertainers by changing the set for them. The hanging neon words "Soul" and "Train" were replaced by group names or, for solo acts, the artist's first name. Stevie Wonder and the Supremes were among the artists to sing in front of their names, and James Brown sang under the lighted banner "James Is No. 1." The personalization differentiated *Soul Train* from other musical variety shows like *The Flip Wilson Show* and *American Bandstand*, both of which did not change their sets to exhibit their guests' names.

Soul Train catered to teenagers, but the success of another Saturday morning program demonstrated that a juvenile audience existed for televised soul music. One month before the national debut of *Soul Train*, ABC introduced the animated half-hour series *The Jackson Five* to Saturday morning viewers. Airing for two seasons, the program featured the caricatures of the famous musicians and at least two of their songs in each episode. The cartoon had more sophisticated graphic visualizations of songs than the guest perform-ances on *Soul Train*, which often merely featured flashing colors for a few sec-onds. In addition, the animated show displayed only slightly better animation than the cartoon sequences of Cornelius' show. On the other hand, *Soul Train* offered more entertainers, a greater variety of dances, and more episodes dur-ing the 1971–72 season than *The Jackson Five*.

Some ABC affiliates carrying *Soul Train* gave the Jacksons significant exposure on the Saturday morning of October 21, 1972. The group appeared on *Soul Train* to sing six songs — only one of which the cartoon show had fea-tured ("I Want You Back"). Whereas *The Jackson Five* only aired for thirty minutes, *Soul Train* episodes lasted twice as long. As a result that fall morn-ing, ABC viewers were treated to three times the usual length of Jackson Five-related broadcasting.

A similar situation developed whenever fellow sibling group the Sylvers performed on *Soul Train*. Edmund Sylvers, a singer of the group, also pro-vided a speaking voice for one of the Jacksons on *The Jackson Five*; actors played all the brothers, but at least two actual recorded songs from the group graced each episode. In addition, during the 1971–73 run of the cartoon on ABC, the Sylvers appeared on *Soul Train* more often than the Jackson Five did. Thus, more Saturday mornings on ABC stations featured ninety min-utes of Edmund Sylvers than of the Jacksons. As the Sylvers' songs became more popular later in the decade, the voice artist abandoned cartoon work to concentrate more fully on his singing career.

As for the cartoon segments on *Soul Train*, they were simultaneously tra-ditional and unique. Since the early days of television, various genres of pro-grams had featured animated sequences, especially in the opening credits. The trend was on the wane by the time *Soul Train* premiered, but the show was not the only live-action series with an animated introduction; in the 1971–72 season, Screen Gems Productions' situation comedies *Bewitched* (1964–72) and *The Partridge Family* (1970–74) opened with cartoons. Dance shows, however, did not usually open with animation. Still, a cartoon was practical for *Soul Train*, because as a Saturday morning show, its opening ani-mation provided a prefect segue from the preceding animated series to *Soul Train*'s live-action dancing.

In its first two syndicated seasons, *Soul Train* had a cartoon motif, which reflected Cornelius' talent for cartooning. Moreover, both the animated sequence and the set resembled stylized animated cartoons of the 1950s. Back then, the animation studio United Productions of America (UPA) produced films of limited animation and sparse backgrounds as a response to the literalistic, detailed images in films by competing studios. *Soul Train*'s cartoon sequences also employed those aspects of UPA's cartoons. In addition, the set's silhouetted train station exemplified the stylization and lack of detail that characterized the backgrounds of UPA's films. During the first syndicated season, Anthony Sabatino became the show's art director, and he significantly contributed to the program's look over the next two decades.[41]

Despite the show's cartoon-like imagery, Cornelius gave "soul" music a serious context on *Soul Train*, which set him apart from the only other African American television producers of the early 1970s. When Bill Cosby produced his situation comedy *The Bill Cosby Show* and his comedy variety series *The New Bill Cosby Show*, he hired Quincy Jones to score the music for both programs. Cosby himself sang over Jones' track in the former show. Fellow comedian Flip Wilson often cast his "soul" guest artists in comedy sketches. Cornelius was, thus, an anomaly as an African American producer presenting R&B without jokes.

Dancers, meanwhile, were among the show's first defectors. After the first syndicated season, a few members of the Soul Train Gang left to form the dance troupe the Lockers. One of the members, Don Campbell, had just won second place with Damita Jo Freeman in one of the program's dance contests. Despite his departure, Freeman rebounded by the next season with another talented male dancer: Jimmy "Scooby Doo" Foster.[42]

By the end of the first syndicated season, *Soul Train*'s stock had risen. As of February 1972, fifty markets aired the series — more than six times the number of cities broadcasting it when it had premiered five months earlier. A few periodicals had reported on the program's success. In addition, the "soul" music genre that the show exploited reached an unprecedented level of popularity. For a week in May 1972, the top eight mainstream hit songs came from African American artists for the very first time in chart history. Such a development in the music industry was just the boost that *Soul Train* needed. As new viewers tuned in to hear the music, they returned week after week for the dancing. The program was on its way to becoming a phenomenon.[43]

4

"The Hippest Trip
in America"

Soul Train *as Cultural Phenomenon*

In the first four seasons of the syndicated *Soul Train*, the success of the series resulted in an extraordinary amount of press coverage and several means by which cast members could exploit their popularity with viewers. In the early 1970s, the amount of attention the show received in the media usually was reserved for network programs — not syndicated ones. In addition, few syndicated shows were popular enough to inspire stage adaptations and traveling shows, as *Soul Train* did. Some of the more recent stage variations of television series were of network programs like *Rowan & Martin's Laugh-In* (1968–73) and *The Brady Bunch* (1969–74).

Despite having a show similar to *American Bandstand*, Cornelius did not choose to become a "black Dick Clark." Rather, his career in entertainment sharply contrasted with that of Clark. The producer of *American Bandstand* parlayed his fame into a career as a producer of movies and television programs, and he hosted telecasts ranging from New Year's Eve parties to game shows. From 1972 to 1974, Cornelius was most willing to occasionally appear in films having nothing to do with *Soul Train*. Nevertheless, he primarily sought to maximize the popularity of his show instead of himself, and the press was largely supportive of his efforts.

Soul Train's initial press coverage was Afro-centric. *Soul* magazine treated the show as a welcome addition to the African American community. In the article's subtitle, "We've Got Our Own," the periodical claimed the program for African Americans. When providing background information on Cornelius, reporter Leah Davis referred to him as "a brother in Chicago." When discussing the show's distinguishing features, she considered the commercials for Johnson Products "pride inspiring." She concluded by celebrating the series as "great, timely entertainment, by Blacks, for Blacks."[1]

On the other hand, Davis tempered the Afro-centric content with congratulatory remarks about the mainstream appeal of the series. After all, in order for markets without a strong African American presence to broadcast *Soul Train*, the show needed to demonstrate its ability to reach beyond African American viewers. She identified the program as a "dream come true" not just for young African American viewers but also for "white ones who want to learn the newest dances and see the latest clothing styles." This sentence, however, implied that white people having never seen the series were not hip.[2]

More importantly, in the *Soul* article Cornelius made a rare disclosure about the racial construction of *Soul Train*. Despite the program's all-black guests and all-black dancers, the African American host acknowledged, "White youngsters are welcome." He reasoned that few of them bothered to audition, because the talent of African American dancers intimidated them. "They just don't seem to feel up to the competition, I guess," he theorized as if unsure himself of the reason for the absence of white people from the Soul Train Gang.[3]

"*Soul Train*: We've Got Our Own" perfectly illustrated the series in its infancy. At the time of the article's publication, dancers were not yet celebrities on *Soul Train*. Davis did not mention a single member of the Soul Train Gang by name. Rather, she listed the prominent African American musical guests from the first syndicated season. Moreover, she featured photographs of three of the guests — crooner Lou Rawls, blues guitarist B.B. King, and singer Patrice Holloway (a singing voice for the Saturday morning animated cartoon *Josie and the Pussycats*) — in their *Soul Train* episodes. By doing so, Davis promoted the show more on the merits of the guests Cornelius booked than on the merits of the show itself. She completely overlooked the unique dances by the Gang.[4]

On the other hand, *Soul* was a periodical that, like *Soul Train*, aimed at a young urban audience. The Soul Train Gang performed moves that African American teenagers across the country did. As a result, the article's readers would not have been surprised by a listing of the dances that their peers did. The point of the article was that the dances were now on television and that people could see the Soul Train Gang moving to beats in the presence of the very people making the music.

One means of attracting viewers to *Soul Train* was booking musical performers who contributed songs to popular urban-marketed movies. In the

1972–73 season, Cornelius invited several such acts to play on his program. As the market for theatrical feature films starring African Americans peaked during 1972 and 1973, *Soul Train* became an invaluable promotion tool of the soundtrack albums for both the movie studios and the record labels. Curtis Mayfield, who made the soundtrack to *Superfly*, performed songs from the film. Artists appearing in both *Soul Train* and the concert movie *Wattstax* included Luther Ingram, Johnnie Taylor, the Bar-Kays, and Chicago-based acts the Emotions and singing duo Mel and Tim. On the other hand, James Brown appeared on the show as *Black Caesar* arrived in theaters but did not sing any of his songs from the movie.

In the fall of 1972, Cornelius launched a new segment for *Soul Train* episodes. Nearly every week of the 1972–73 season, an African American entertainer from television, movies, or sports gave a cameo performance. These appearances gave Cornelius a great opportunity to capitalize on press attention to famous personalities in the 1971–72 season. Also, the host was able to demonstrate his new Hollywood connections to the nation and establish himself as a figure of West Coast media instead of a Chicago transplant. Meanwhile, the celebrity guests benefited from their cameos by associating themselves with a national hip, youthful show and receiving approval from the young dancers in attendance. The stars became more relevant, more "cool."[5]

Soul Train attracted many of Hollywood's African American elite. Several actors made cameo appearances. One of the first was Heshimu, who played a high school student on *Room 222*. As a result, *Soul Train* ironically juxtaposed an African American from a show filmed at Los Angeles High School with actual students from that same institution. In addition, singers not scheduled to perform showed up to dance. Soloist Smokey Robinson, for example, made a cameo on the same episode that his former group the Miracles performed. At the height of the cameos, an average of two such appearances per month took place in the 1972–73 season.

The show also became a vehicle for mainstream politics. Tom Bradley, the newly elected mayor of Los Angeles, made a brief appearance in the fall of 1973. One of very few elected officials appearing on the program, he spoke for about three minutes to an enthusiastic teenage audience about youth, promise, and enterprise. He visually contrasted with his surroundings on the set. He wore a gray suit and white shirt when addressing the dancers, who wore such items as Lurex pullovers and reggae shirts. A towering figure, his balding head emerged above the slicked and corn row-braided hair of the teenagers.[6]

The cameos, ironically, did not attract the press. Reporters gave more coverage to *Soul Train* in the 1972–73 season but for its own merits instead of its guest stars. The dances drew viewers, which drew the journalists to the dances and the dancers performing them. The host, meanwhile, became a celebrity in his own right. Many articles did not even mention the cameos, no matter how prominent the figure. Consequently, as Cornelius' stardom increased, he gradually decreased the frequency of the cameos from the fall of 1973 onward.

The nation's capital was the first city to admire the content of *Soul Train* and the charisma of its host. In December 1972, when Cornelius toured Washington, D.C., the *Washington Post* covered the event by discussing the host as a celebrity. People followed him wherever he went in the city. The *Post* article differed from the *Soul* article in that the nation's capital focused exclusively on Cornelius and did not rely on the star power of guests to promote the series. On the other hand, both reports had in common no acknowledgement of the dancers.

To the *Washington Post*, Cornelius was a visual curiosity. The article devoted a paragraph exclusively to his physical appearance. Such attention illustrates the difference in reporting between an African American periodical and a mainstream one. *Soul*, because it had an African American readership, assumed the readers' familiarity with *Soul Train* and did not elaborate on the host's hip apparel. On the other hand, the *Washington Post* wisely avoided covering the story as if its readers already knew about the show. The article mentioned Cornelius' height and described his suit, shirt, tie and shoes in terms of color and style.[7]

The host soon received confirmation of his national fame — via false rumors of his death. In the summer of 1972, Cornelius reran viewers' favorite episodes of *Soul Train*. Audiences, however, did not know why new episodes of a hit show had stopped; after all, ABC did not air reruns of *American Bandstand*. When the second national season began in September, the rumors died down. Then, in December, Cornelius aired two fan-favorite reruns as a Christmas treat for viewers, which revived the rumors of his passing. When invited onstage weeks later at a concert in Los Angeles, he made a point to say, "I just dropped by to let you know I'm not dead."[8]

Another new segment Cornelius introduced for each episode of the 1972–73 season was the "Create-a-Dance." By early 1973 the series had amassed a substantial repertoire of popular dances. They included the "Breakdown," the "P.A. Slaughter," the "Homosexual," the "Penguin," and the "Backbreaker."

Except for the "Breakdown," none of the dances were popular enough to warrant their own musical tributes, unlike Chubby Checker's "The Twist" of the past or Van McCoy's "The Hustle" in the near future. On the other hand, the new moves began to receive some notice, and the *New York Times* listed them by name and described them. The article continued the tradition of neglecting to introduce members of the Soul Train Gang to readers. Nevertheless, the listing of the dances revealed that at least the journalists were paying attention to the Gang. The *New York Times* succinctly declared the Gang's importance to *Soul Train*: "The kids *are* the show."[9]

Implementing new gimmicks for the second season was standard practice in syndicated programming. Most syndicated shows of the 1970s did not last beyond two years, and the majority of series surviving the first season underwent significant changes for the sophomore year. Producers eliminated aspects of shows that did not register with viewers and accentuated the successful parts. By doing so, they maximized the potential for sponsors and distributors to continue funding the series. Cornelius' emphasis on celebrities and the dances made practical sense, because they were the aspects of *Soul Train* most covered by the press.

The Soul Train Gang did not have to dance to visually entertain viewers. Several dancers developed unique looks or gimmicks that distinguished them from the rest. Damita Jo Freeman often wore her hair in "Afro puffs" while kicking her legs extraordinarily high on the Soul Train Line. Pat Davis put a flower in her hair, and her blouses often featured butterflies. In addition, she frequently used props while dancing — once sucking on a baby bottle while on the Line.

One of the most controversial trends the dancers promoted came from the blaxploitation movie *Superfly*. In the first two years following the film's 1972 release, many of the male members of the Soul Train Gang straightened their hair, grew it to their shoulders, and wore sharp suits, not unlike the film's protagonist — a drug-seller named Priest. At the time, *Superfly* divided African Americans. Some media observers celebrated the movie for its African American cast, director and soundtrack musician. Powerful African American organizations, however, protested the prevalence of "dope pushers, pimps, and prostitutes" in "blaxploitation" films. They lamented that the servile stereotype had given way to the "supernigger" image — an African American character with "vast physical powers but no cognitive skills." Ron O' Neal, who played Priest, defended his role: "The hustler is as much a part of the black community as the doctor, lawyer or preacher." Still, none of the *Soul*

Train dancers wore medical scrubs or clerical collars, which suggested that Priest's lifestyle had appeal to African American teenagers even if the means of attaining the lifestyle did not.[10]

Soul Train, however, balanced the "Priest look" with several performances of songs condemning the drug trade. Singing on the show in early 1973, Curtis Mayfield performed "Superfly" and "Pusher Man," about fictional drug dealers wanting to leave the business but seeing no other means of making a living. Later that year another act deliberately referred to a particular drug in order to discourage its use. When Tower of Power performed "What Is Hip" on *Soul Train*, one line that lead singer Lenny Williams sang on camera was about the song's main character smoking marijuana. The lyrics, however, focused on a fictional character failing to be hip despite using marijuana among other unsuccessful means.

The dancers were not the only ones to dazzle viewers with new dance crazes on *Soul Train*. Arguably the most popular dance to debut on the series was popularized by Michael Jackson. When the Motown group the Jackson Five appeared in November 1973 to sing "Dancing Machine," fifteen-year-old Michael used the song's break to imitate a mechanical man by moving his arms and legs stiffly while sliding across the floor. Some members of the Soul Train Gang had previously made those moves, most notably Damita Jo Freeman onstage with James Brown in the previous season. Also, in October 1971, during the first syndicated episode, Cornelius asked a couple to discuss popular dances, and one of the dances mentioned was the "Mechanical Man." The Jackson Five, however, were the first performers to borrow dance steps from the program's dancers, thus giving the Gang legitimacy as dancers.

More importantly, *Soul Train* helped the "Robot" become a *televised* popular dance. Within a year of their debut of the dance, the Jackson Five brought the moves to a wide variety of shows that appealed to demographics besides young African Americans. The brothers did the "Robot" on the syndicated morning talk show *The Mike Douglas Show* and the top-ten network hit series *The Sonny and Cher Comedy Hour* in early 1974. On each show Michael drew wild applause whenever he went into his spastic trance. *Soul Train*, however, was where he did it first. As a result, Cornelius was now on a par with Dick Clark, Ed Sullivan, and other variety show hosts for starting dance crazes through television.

On the other hand, the co-opting of *Soul Train* moves by the Jackson Five set a dangerous precedent for the series. Now that musicians could learn the dances of the Soul Train Gang and take them to other programs, *Soul*

Train stood to lose its television monopoly on original African American dance steps. As a result, the show had to stay fresh by developing new dance crazes. In addition, Cornelius became more protective of his program from predators.

Television was not the only industry noticing the program's ascent after the first national season. The music industry also paid a great deal of attention to Cornelius and *Soul Train*. Successful R&B groups visited the show, and several new R&B artists made their television debuts there. Cornelius received invitations to more concerts. In addition, *Soul Train* had become a favorite of the critics. The hip, well-respected rock music periodical *Rolling Stone* named the show the "best musical television series during 1972." It was no small accomplishment, for the competition included *American Bandstand* and *In Concert* (1972–81) on ABC, and *The Midnight Special* on NBC (1972–80).[11]

By this time *Soul Train* had amassed such a large audience that it threatened the show after which Cornelius had patterned his own. In many markets where *Soul Train* aired directly opposite Dick Clark's *American Bandstand*, Cornelius' series regularly trounced Clark's. By this time *Bandstand* played a wide variety of popular music, ranging from soul to bubblegum, whereas *Soul Train* remained focused on soul music. Even when both shows played the same music, *Soul Train* still attracted more viewers because of the unique moves of the dancers.[12]

The Soul Train Line especially influenced *American Bandstand*. Before the 1970s, Clark mandated that his dancers wear formal attire and forbade them from looking at the cameras filming them. *Soul Train*'s Line, in contrast, served to give couples extended camera time. The staff usually chose dancers with the flashiest clothes and the best dance routines for the Line. In addition, the camera operators positioned themselves at the end of the Line. Thus, the chosen dancers had no choice but to face the cameras when strutting down. Through fancy footwork and mugging for the camera, the adolescents made the most of their five to ten seconds in the spotlight. Playing off the camera gave *Soul Train* energy that *American Bandstand* lacked. Clark subsequently tried to beat Cornelius at his own game by copying *Soul Train*.

In March and April 1973, Dick Clark occasionally replaced *American Bandstand* with the series *Soul Unlimited* on ABC. It featured soul music and starred an African American host and African American dancers. Clark named the host — disc jockey Buster Jones of the Los Angeles radio station KGFJ — the executive producer and developed the production company Super Soul

Productions for the new series. *Soul Unlimited* immediately improved upon *American Bandstand*'s ratings and, according to an irate Rev. Jesse Jackson, dented *Soul Train*'s ratings in some markets while pre-empting it in others.[13]

Jackson and fellow Operation PUSH member Clarence Avant wrote letters of protest to the ABC network. They charged that ABC allowed Clark to capitalize on the success of *Soul Train* at Cornelius' expense. Moreover, they were concerned that the network and Clark stood to monopolize "soul" on television by the power of the purse. Jackson specifically illustrated the network as the "Goliath" to Cornelius' "David." The minister noted, "*Soul Unlimited* seriously endangers *Soul Train* not because it is a better show, but because ABC, as a power, is able to outspend *Soul Train* in promotion, production and talent recruitment."[14]

Clark initially was unmoved. Having received the Saturday afternoon time slot for *American Bandstand* from ABC since September 1963, he declared to reporter Ben Fong-Torres, "That's my time period," adding, "They [ABC] want to put a black *Bandstand* on, then I'll do it." Claiming to have met with both Jackson and Cornelius, he referred to their disagreement as a minor business matter. In addition, he curiously flavored his comments with class-based elitism by dismissing Cornelius' accusations of racism as a result of "the ghetto paranoia."[15]

The *Bandstand* host, however, took up the issue of racism in a disingenuous manner. Both he and *Bandstand* producer Judy Price criticized Cornelius for making *Soul Train* an all-black show. Price referred to it as "segregation." Such declarations glossed over *American Bandstand*'s own history as a nearly all-white show in Philadelphia from 1952 until its relocation to Los Angeles in 1964. When the program switched from big-band music to R&B in the mid–1950s, African Americans wanting to appear were kept off the series, because they did not already possess membership cards for admittance; and the staff rarely distributed new cards. When the racially homogenous *Bandstand* became a nationally televised series in 1957, few outside Philadelphia knew of the city's actual racial diversity in its population.[16]

The competition for domination of Saturday afternoon "soul" did not last long after the spring of 1973. ABC pulled the plug on the series before the summer began. Nevertheless, one legacy of the controversy that remained was that *Soul Train* dancers continued to appear on *American Bandstand*. Cornelius did not approve, but the Soul Train Gang members were not contractually bound to dance only on his show. Moreover, the moonlighting dancers were the most popular *Soul Train* cast members, and Cornelius could not afford to lose them.[17]

Clark then tried to stay competitive with *Soul Train* by increasing the soul music content on *American Bandstand*. In 1974 African Americans accounted for three-fifths of the guest artists on Clark's series. Nevertheless, the "teenybopper" reputation of the show diminished its status with not only viewers but also critics. Worse, observers considered the best days of *American Bandstand* long past, in contrast to Cornelius' hip show. *The New York Times* declared, "'Soul Train' is to the old 'American Bandstand' what champagne is to seltzer water." *The Los Angeles Times* said derisively, "Dick Clark and American Bandstand just keep on be-boppin.'"[18]

Soul Train had other new competitors targeting African American audiences besides Dick Clark. The show *Black Omnibus* billed itself as an "exciting black experience." The series showcased new talent and performances by veteran entertainers, not unlike *Soul Train*. It was also syndicated, as Cornelius' series was; *Soul Train*, at last, was not the only syndicated television series targeting an African American audience. *Black Omnibus* even had its own deep-voiced host in baritone actor James Earl Jones. Like *Soul Unlimited*, however, *Black Omnibus* had a short broadcast life. Even the celebrity of Jones and the talent his show could attract proved no match for Cornelius and his dancers.[19]

Soul Train suffered not from competing shows but from uncooperative markets. Some cities committed to broadcasting the program but either scheduled it around midnight on a weekend day or did not air episodes for weeks at a time. In Chicago, where teenagers could at least watch the local weekday version on channel 26, WBBM Channel 2 usually aired the show on Saturdays at 1:00 P.M. As a CBS affiliate, however, the station often preempted *Soul Train* to televise the sports events offered live by the network. Sometimes the scheduled *Soul Train* episode would air the following Saturday morning at 12:30 A.M. The syndicated show occasionally would not air at all in Chicago. In October and November 1973, when the program was peaking in popularity, WBBM frequently substituted college football for the dance show.

When Cornelius experienced these droughts in committed markets, he could rely on his friend Jesse Jackson to successfully address the problem. "Jesse Jackson was the power that kept *Soul Train* on the air," remembered George O'Hare. "When he picks up the phone and calls someone, he gets a return call." When Jackson received the news about one particular prolonged absence of the show from WBBM's Saturday afternoons, he "went to bat" for Cornelius. He called the station and asked why *Soul Train* had stopped airing, and a station representative explained that the station stopped broadcasting shows that lacked sponsorship. Jackson then informed him of *Soul Train*'s financial backers, to which the representative replied, "Somebody didn't *tell* me it was sponsored." Channel 2 then resumed airing the program.[20]

WBBM eventually caved in to consumer demand and pressure from Jackson and provided a more stable time slot for the syndicated *Soul Train*. On December 8, 1973, the station moved the show's Saturday afternoon airing from its usual slot of 1:00 P.M. to 4:00 P.M. As a result loyal viewers no longer suffered preemption of the series for sports events. The new time slot for the show was previously the home of another syndicated show — the weekly nature documentary *Animal World*. The California-based *Soul Train* thrived in Chicago at 4:00 P.M., and WBBM kept the program there for the next four years.

Meanwhile, the media provided another problem for Cornelius. In late 1973 journalists began to change their reporting of *Soul Train*'s racial exclusivity. The *Los Angeles Times* was among the first periodicals to call attention to critics arguing that the absence of other groups of people "provokes indignant references to segregation and racism." Unsurprisingly, Cornelius disagreed with the accusations, but he did not refute them by mentioning that white people were welcome to audition for *Soul Train*. After all, by this time the show had gained significant press coverage for its landmark televising of young African American culture, and an admission of openness to white people stood to complicate that coverage. Cornelius instead astutely diverted the discussion from his show to the state of television programming. He argued, "These people are forgetting that there are still scores and scores of all-white shows on television."[21]

Moreover, the critics were placated in November 1973 by the appearance of an act consisting *mostly* of white people. In earlier episodes musical guests had used white musicians as part of their backup, but now whites were the main performers. The ten-piece jazz ensemble Tower of Power performed two songs in an episode airing that month — one of which was a five-minute, live rendition of their R&B hit "What Is Hip." The majority of the white members played in the horn section. The two African American members played the organ and sang lead.

Soul Train, however, managed to give Tower of Power as Afro-centric an image on television as possible. Close-ups of the African American lead singer Lenny Williams comprised the majority of the televised performance, and he stood in front of the band on the stage as he sang. Despite this imagery, he was not the actual leader of the group; rather, Emilio Castillo, a member of the all-white horn section, had founded the ensemble in 1968. In addition, episode director B.J. Jackson included several shots of the all-black Soul Train Gang surrounding and outnumbering the mostly white group on the set. By filming African Americans extensively during a performance by white artists, *Soul Train* maximized the potential appeal of the group to the urban black audiences the show targeted.

Still, Jackson gave credit to the white members of Tower of Power where it was due. Whenever the horn section played a particularly rhythmic riff, the camera went to the white men playing those notes. In addition, a white trumpeter playing several solos within "What Is Hip" received a considerable amount of camera time, though still a fraction of Williams' camera time. *Soul Train*, as a result, was one of the first television programs to visually define "soul" music as something that white people could play as well as African Americans could. The enthusiastic response of the Gang to the songs demonstrated acceptance by African Americans of white brassy "soul."

The attention of the *Los Angeles Times* to *Soul Train*'s racial policies reflected changes in network television programming since the premiere of the series two years earlier. *The Flip Wilson Show* was no longer the only network variety series hosted by an African American. During the 1972–73 season, comedian Bill Cosby hosted his own program, and the following year Sammy Davis, Jr. starred in *NBC Follies*. All three programs, however, featured white as well as black guests and cast members. The increase in integrated shows featuring African American leads made the all-black *Soul Train* more conspicuous to critics.

None of these developments in network television had any relevance to Cornelius. He told the *Los Angeles Times* of his frustration in pitching ideas about African American series to networks. His sales pitches fell on deaf ears, because executives did not think that his ideas appealed to the "general market." Thumbing his nose at the networks, he remarked of *Soul Train*'s success, "I owe the industry itself nothing."[22]

As a single producer with independence from network interference, Cornelius further distinguished himself from people like Dan Rowan and Dick Martin of *Rowan & Martin's Laugh-In*. The two hosts lamented that the press ignored them and instead reported the workings of NBC or their show's producers. After all, the names Rowan and Martin were in the title of the program. In contrast, reporters only talked to Cornelius about the business affairs of *Soul Train*. They left no confusion as to who ran that show.[23]

He certainly did not need the medium of television in order to receive exposure to his fans. He received bookings as a host for various events. On August 16, 1973, Cornelius performed as a host of Soul '73 at the Lincoln Center in New York. He appeared for one of the sixteen days of the event. Soul '73 consisted of nineteen concerts and three religious services, and it was a sequel to the "Soul at the Center" concerts of the previous summer. Seeking to "span the spectrum of black creativity," the event not only featured R&B stars but also gospel concerts and, for the children, a performance by the racially integrated juvenile rock group the Short Circus from the educational public television series *The Electric Company*. Ellis B. Haizlip, a producer of the television series *Soul!* on public television, also produced Soul '73. Cornelius' appearance at a function developed by his competitor demonstrated confidence in the success of *Soul Train*.[24]

The popularity of the series and its cast gave Cornelius and company opportunities to perform beyond the walls of the *Soul Train* soundstage. They took the series to the famed Apollo Theater in New York, performing a theatrical version of the show to a live black audience on August 19, 1973. By that time the theater had developed a reputation for making or breaking the careers of African American entertainers. Artists feared that audiences would boo them during "Amateur Hour" and that they would literally get swept off the stage. For the Soul Train Gang to survive their gig was no small accomplishment, especially considering that "soul brother No. 1" James Brown was booed there a few months earlier after having long established stardom. The Gang, however, had already won over the audience in a sense just by starring in a popular urban-marketed television series, and they had an advantage over Brown in their lack of political endorsement of President Nixon.[25]

The music Cornelius chose for the Gang at the Apollo gig came only from groups who owed their television popularity to him. Cornelius demonstrated his significance to the event by placing his name before those of all the other performers in the advertisement printed in the *New York Times*. The groups the Sylvers and The Whispers had appeared on the syndicated *Soul Train* at least twice by August 1973. The Whispers had not sung on other shows, but the Sylvers had appeared on *American Bandstand* once. The Moments had performed on *Soul Train* only once at the time but had not appeared on any other programs. Thus, all three groups largely gained television exposure through Cornelius.

The Soul Train Gang was depicted as Cornelius' creation to a greater degree than the music groups were. As usual, none of the dancers received any individual recognition in the advertisement; on the other hand, neither did any of the individuals comprising the groups. The Gang, however, received a completely different billing in the *New York Times* than on the show. The newspaper referred to the Gang as the "Don Cornelius Dancers." It was an inaccurate reference, for although he produced the show in which they appeared, he had nothing to do with the teenagers' dances. He had always used Clinton Ghent and Ronnie Paul Johnson for matters related to the choreography on the program.[26]

Starting in the fall of 1973, the dancers themselves received considerable attention from reporters. In addition to discussion about their movements, journalists described their wardrobe and hairstyles. The *Los Angeles Times* described the Soul Train Gang as "costumed, filigreed, marcelled [*sic*], enameled, plaited, and decaled from coif to clog." The clothing choices for the dancers had evolved by 1973 from the "street clothes" of the Chicago dancers from the show's first year. Much of the description in the newspaper was comical yet unglamorous; the reporter likened two female dancers to "fretful water birds stalking pavement for the first time, for their tiny dresses are like bits of plumage and their skinny legs perch shakily atop shoes with rigid, carved-out platform soles eight inches tall." Other references to the teenagers were beneficial to them. Some articles identified regulars by name, as when the *L.A. Times* mentioned Damita Jo Freeman and Jimmy "Scooby-Doo" Foster as two of the best dancers among the cast.[27]

The host did not always need the dancers when performing outside of *Soul Train*. He went without them into the world of motion pictures by filming a cameo appearance as himself in the feature-length movie *Cleopatra Jones*. Tamara Dobson played a government agent attempting to squash a drug syndicate led by a white woman. The film was one of several in the early 1970s that featured African Americans in dramatic roles as violent protagonists battling white antagonists bent on harming African Americans or Africans. Such movies comprised the "blaxploitation" genre, and film studios used not only African American actors to play the characters but also top R&B musicians to score the flicks. Joe Simon and Millie Jackson provided songs for *Cleopatra Jones*. Cornelius's role solidified his status as an African American celebrity, for the filmmakers gambled on the targeted audience's established familiarity with Cornelius in making the cameo successful. Blaxploitation movies usually cast musicians for cameos. Thus, the film's use of Cornelius for a cameo demonstrated that he had become a force in the R&B music industry.

Warner Brothers Pictures, which distributed *Cleopatra Jones*, benefited doubly from Cornelius' presence. The company released the film in July 1973, shortly before the start of the third syndicated season of *Soul Train*. He helped give the movie some "star power," as the actors were not as well-known in the media as Cornelius was that year. He used an episode of his show to promote the movie that November by having Millie Jackson as a guest star singing "Hurts So Good," which she had crooned for the film's soundtrack. In the movie the song played during the lovemaking scene of the romantic lead characters.

During the 1973–74 season, *Soul Train* promoted other movies through guest performances. Two of the films were dramas like *Cleopatra Jones*. Gladys Knight and the Pips appeared on the show to sing the song "On and On" from *Claudine*, which starred Diahann Carroll as a single mother. Although the Impressions — without Curtis Mayfield by this time — did not perform any numbers from *Three the Hard Way* for their *Soul Train* episode, they timed their guest spot to the release of the movie to theaters in the spring of 1974.

Another movie whose musicians Cornelius invited to *Soul Train* was a concert film similar to *Wattstax*. Both features were filmed in late 1972, and the Rev. Jesse Jackson contributed to both. Moreover, the other movie — *Save the Children* — consisted of footage from a music festival facilitated by Jackson's organization Operation PUSH. Artists appearing on both *Soul Train* and in *Save the Children* in the 1973–74 season included Chicagoans Jerry Butler and Curtis Mayfield, as well as Motown performers the Jackson Five, the Temptations, Marvin Gaye, and Gladys Knight and the Pips. *Save the Children*, however, came to theaters in the fall of 1973, months after the release of *Wattstax*.

Cornelius also capitalized on *Soul Train*'s four million viewers and the press's attention to the show's dances by making the show's dance contest an annual event. For the third such competition in the fall of 1973, he flew in thirty-eight participants from nineteen cities for the finals. The *Los Angeles Times* called the contest "an event of crucial importance to all *Soul Train* fans and certainly to everyone in the studio." Among the finalists in Los Angeles was Walter Payton, who ironically would later play professional football in Chicago. One of his nicknames during his career, "Soul Train," resulted from his appearance.[28]

Pervis Staples (left) with Emotions members Theresa Davis, Sheila Hutchinson and Wanda Hutchinson, and Ronnie Paul Johnson at the Chicago premiere of the movie *Wattstax*. Courtesy Theresa M. Davis.

Entertainers did not even have to be seen on stage in order to benefit from the series. For the episode airing on October 27, 1973, Cornelius finally replaced King Curtis's "Hot Potatoes" with a new theme song written just for the show. "TSOP (The Sound of Philadelphia)" by the group MFSB (Mother Father Sister Brother) made its debut as the new theme in the ninth episode of the 1973–74 season. The new song had strong horn and string sections, distinctive bongo drumming, and an upbeat tempo — all of which characterized the music of the Philadelphia International record label. Co-producers Kenny Gamble and Leon Huff developed the unique sound. The company had just started hitting its stride, achieving crossover appeal with popular African American groups the O'Jays, the Stylistics, and Harold Melvin and the Blue Notes; all of these artists had recently topped not only the soul charts but the pop charts as well. In fact the call "People all over the world" from "TSOP" had origins in Gamble-Huff's chart-topping song "Love Train" for the O'Jays.

The song choice was rather ironic, considering the locations of the series and the Philadelphia International label. Los Angeles was the home not only of *Soul Train* but also of Motown Records, which had just relocated from

Don Cornelius Productions

SOUL TRAIN

FINAL DANCE CONTEST
KTTV STUDIOS
Sunset and Van Ness
MARCH 19, 1972

ADMIT: *Ronnie Bauchman*

Present this card at gate

Pam Brown

10:00am

Don Cornelius Prod.
1857 Virginia Road
L.A. 90019

LOS ANGELES CAL
PM
13 MAR
1972

United States 8¢
EINSTEIN

Mr. Ronnie Bauchman
1920½ W. 22nd Street
L.A. 90018

Pam Brown

Ticket for a dance contest on the syndicated *Soul Train*. Courtesy Ron Bauchman.

Detroit the previous year. In bypassing Motown for Philadelphia International for a theme, however, Cornelius tacitly demonstrated that the latter label, not the former, was now "The Sound of Young America." In addition, *Soul Train*'s musical alignment with Philadelphia reestablished the city's preeminence in televised music. The show's competitor *American Bandstand* had severed its ties with Philadelphia's record labels and bands when relocating to the West Coast one decade earlier.

Along with the new theme came significant cosmetic changes to the program. Lighted train tracks now stood behind the "Soul Train" sign, which also showed more elaborate lighting. The train lights behind Don Cornelius' lectern now flashed. The railroad signs disappeared. The animated cartoon no longer presented a rickety locomotive in the countryside but rather a sleek black train blowing an ornate, psychedelic puff of smoke across a city. It was a perfect visual symbol for the change in theme song, for the lush string and horn arrangements of "TSOP" were more fanciful than the guitars and keyboard playing on "Hot Potatoes" and "Familiar Footsteps," which "TSOP" also replaced for the commercial "bumpers."

The new look of the stage also reflected Cornelius' confidence in *Soul Train*. For the 1973–74 season, he eliminated the gimmickry of the previous year. In addition to the decreased reliance on cameos, he phased out the "Create-A-Dance" segment. The new episodes tended to consist of dance floor sequences, performances by guests, the Scramble, and the Line. The show consequently became more stylized and formulaic, but it also had more of a

Set of the syndicated *Soul Train* in the 1971–72 season. Courtesy Ron Bauchman.

95

focus on both Cornelius and the Soul Train Gang. Meanwhile, Dick Clark borrowed the "Create-A-Dance" idea for his new dance series *Action '73*, which replaced his *Soul Unlimited* as a substitute for his *American Bandstand*; but he dubbed his program's dance segment the "Dance of the Month."

By replacing "Hot Potatoes" with "TSOP," Cornelius severed an important tie to the show's Chicago roots. In addition, celebrities were showcased less than before. Guest artists had to compete not only with the dancers but also with the flashing lights of the giant "Soul Train" name behind them for the viewer's attention. Cornelius no longer replaced the giant series name with the name of an established artist during guest performances. Now Aretha Franklin and James Brown had to share the stage with the huge "Soul Train" sign just like newcomers such as Blue Magic and Sister Sledge.

On April 20, 1974, "TSOP" reached the top of the "Billboard 100" chart — a feat rarely accomplished by television show themes, especially for programs in syndication. The song was, in fact, the first from a syndicated television series to enter and top the chart. "TSOP" became the show's definitive theme. It also significantly influenced popular music for years. KC and the Sunshine Band borrowed a horn riff of "TSOP" for "(Shake, Shake, Shake) Shake Your Booty," which itself became a chart-topper in 1976. Two years later the disco group Love and Kisses took the same riff for its song "Thank God It's Friday" — the theme to the feature film of the same name, which, ironically, Motown produced.

After "TSOP," songs with a "train" theme became a genre within the genre of soul music. BT Express scored a hit with the song "Express," which received airplay on *Soul Train*; the largely instrumental song included the sound effects of train whistles and the chanting of the word "chug." In 1974 Motown's Jr. Walker and the All Stars, whose biggest hit was "Shotgun" from nearly one decade earlier, recorded the novelty tune "Dancin' Like They Do On Soul Train." The group, however, did not perform the song on the series, nor did the tribute become the program's new theme. Without television promotion and significant play on radio, Walker's blatant attempt at cashing in on the *Soul Train* name faltered.

By playing "Philly Soul" songs, *Soul Train* popularized heavily orchestrated songs with sexually charged lyrics. The tunes had slow beats and, like funk music, extended instrumental sections. Because Cornelius only played slow songs for guest appearances, many "Philly Soul" songs could only appear on the show if the singers showed up to perform them. As a balladeer of popular romance songs, Barry White was in frequent demand on the show. On the other hand, he had to appear often in order for the program to have opportunities to play his songs when his label released them. When he was absent from *Soul Train*, so was his music. The female vocal group Love Unlimited, which featured his wife Glodean, occasionally performed similar songs on the program.

White, however, had competition in the "sexual ballad" genre from outside Philadelphia. In early 1974, *Soul Train* devoted one episode to Marvin Gaye, whose lusty album *Let's Get It On* also featured sexual instruction wailed over heavy orchestration. For his episode he sang only songs from that album, which was unusual. Previous guests had promoted older songs as well as current ones. Moreover, such a guest usually sang hits that spanned the length of his or her career, instead of performing only hits from the latest album. The exclusive focus on *Let's Get It On* showed that Cornelius saw further potential in the sales of that album, which had been out for half a year by the airing of the episode. *Soul Train* visually complemented the sexual appeal of Gaye's album by having him sing on the main floor surrounded by mostly female members of the Soul Train Gang — an unusual arrangement, for the guests usually sang on the center riser and towered above the dancers.[29]

The "Let's Get It On" episode also demonstrated *Soul Train*'s new apolitical stance. Just three years earlier Gaye had gone in a strong political direction with his album *What's Going On*, which decried racism, pollution, and the Vietnam War. The success of the album led to countless "message songs" about urban African Americans and their problems. The lengthy tracks serving as background music for the complaints were a template for other artists, especially Curtis Mayfield, with the albums *Superfly* and *Back to the World*. Either Cornelius or Motown, however, made a conscious decision not to revisit Gaye's anguish over Vietnam. After all, in 1974 U.S. forces had been out of the war for one year. In addition, the decision was cost-effective. Motown released several songs from the *Let's Get It On* album as singles, and Gaye's singing of only the album's songs allowed the record label to save considerable money by promoting multiple singles from the same album on the same episode.

Meanwhile, female artists also increased the sexual content of their performances. Their feminism had less to do with rights than with telling lovers to meet physical requests or, in some cases, demands. The new direction helped women land guest spots when *Soul Train* offered fewer to them; by 1974, the series often went without female guests — soloists or female members of groups — for two to three weeks at a time. Sylvia Robinson pioneered the new sound for women by delivering breathy coos and moans in her song "Pillow Talk." Lyn Collins switched from political to sexual content by bellowing, chant-like, "Rock Me Again and Again and Again and Again and Again and Again." Through the group Rufus's stylized funk instrumentation, lead singer Chaka Khan demanded, "Tell Me Something Good," and reassured, "You Got the Love." As these women adapted to new trends, earlier vocalists like Laura Lee and the group the Honey Cone suddenly disappeared from the show after multiple appearances during the first two syndicated seasons.

After the theme to *Soul Train* was dubbed "TSOP," the show capitalized upon its new image as a champion of R&B music from the "City of Brotherly Love." Philadelphia-based musicians did not have to belong to Philadelphia International in order to receive exposure on *Soul Train*. In one episode of the 1974–75 season, all three of the musical guests — Blue Magic, Sister Sledge, and Major Harris — hailed from the "City of Brotherly Love." None of them were signed to the label.

Other locations and labels received significant attention from Cornelius at this time. They had not developed regional music styles that captivated listeners as Philadelphia had done in 1973. They did, however, have artists with lengthy, successful careers. Motown artists frequently appeared on *Soul Train*. In two episodes the Jackson Five were the only guests. Chicago-based Curtis Mayfield, another popular artist on the show, managed his own label: Curtom Records.

The prominence of "Philly Soul" on *Soul Train*, however, symbolized Cornelius' growing detachment from Chicago-based R&B. Thanks to the success of the show, the host now had the clout to book top R&B acts from across the country on a regular basis, and he proceeded to do so. The increased nationwide bookings meant less opportunity for singers from Chicago to appear on the series. As a result, most of the Windy City performers of the first two syndicated seasons — Brighter Side of Darkness, the Five Stairsteps, General Crook, Laura Lee, and Peaches — did not return to the show after 1973.

When Cornelius had faith in an artist's career, he used his resources to promote that musician. In an unprecedented move for the show, he allowed one of the biggest national recording stars to bring his own musical guests. Like the Jackson Five, James Brown also received permission from Cornelius to monopolize the episodes in which he sang. He used his appearances to promote his protégés. Lyn Collins, who recorded a version of his hit song "Think" in 1972, accompanied him on the show twice. Brown had so much clout in the R&B industry that his stars had an episode to themselves without him in 1973. Collins appeared in an episode that also featured Brown's backing band — Fred Wesley and the JBs — but no Brown. Later that year Maceo Parker, Brown's saxophone player, appeared with his group the Macs for a performance of his employer's song "Soul Power," but the "Godfather of Soul" himself was once again absent.

Don Cornelius provided the venue for the defining moment of another performer's career. This artist, however, was decidedly non-musical. By early 1974 African American comedian Richard Pryor had become a popular stand-up act, appearing frequently on *The Flip Wilson Show* and even landing a role in Paramount Pictures' feature film *Lady Sings the Blues*. Around this time Pryor performed at Don Cornelius' Soul Train Club. His act was recorded and released that May as the album *That Nigger's Crazy*. The album was a success, immediately selling over one million copies.

Pryor's monologue dealt with previously taboo subject matter in comedy routines. As a result, he introduced pressing concerns among African Americans to comedy fans in a groundbreaking manner. Similarly, Cornelius broke new ground in television as *Soul Train* presented African American musical expression through the medium in an Afro-centric context. In addition, some of the "message songs" on the program highlighted the same issues covered in Pryor's jokes. In this regard Cornelius and Pryor were a perfect match.

By providing venues for both Richard Pryor and Curtis Mayfield, Cornelius unwittingly played a major and controversial role in popularizing the imagery of African Americans addressing themselves with the racial slur "nigger." On the album recorded at Cornelius' comedy club, Pryor used the word to identify African American characters in his monologue. *New York Times* reporter James McPherson gave context to the utterances of the word: "When Pryor says 'nigger,' he is usually about to define a human type in all his complexity. It is to his credit that he is able to start with an abstraction and make it into a recognizable human being. If he does his work well enough, it will be difficult for even the most offended listener, white or black, not to say, 'I've seen this man before.'" Meanwhile, the "master storyteller" Mayfield gave the slur a similar function in two "message songs" he pantomimed on *Soul Train*. He performed "Pusherman" from the soundtrack to the motion picture *Super Fly* in a January 1973 episode, and the next season lip-synched "Future Shock" in two different episodes. The former song described an

African American seller of illegal drugs as a "nigger in the alley," and the latter song had the phrase "preying on niggers," partly as a means to rhyme with "figures."[30]

Pryor's album and Mayfield's appearances were among the first productions in American popular culture of African Americans saying the word. Before then media generally identified whites as the speakers when the word was uttered. Newspapers from the 1890s to the 1910s commonly referred to African Americans as "niggers," some while using the exaggerated dialect of blackface performers to quote from African Americans. By the 1960s, however, white audiences were more likely to hear the racial slur either from newscasts about civil rights demonstrations or from racist fictional characters in theatrical feature films, such as rural police chief "Bill Gillespie" of the movie *In the Heat of the Night* (1967). As a result, African Americans complained that the insult's exposure by African American entertainers to mainstream audiences would, in McPherson's words, "[move] the word from the pool halls and barber shops back into public usage."[31]

Cornelius' televising of Mayfield singing "nigger" was especially remarkable, because television series of the 1970s generally avoided the word as much as possible. Even among the topical and controversial programs produced by Norman Lear, reverence trumped "shock value." On the situation comedy *All in the Family* (1971–79), racist protagonist "Archie Bunker" called African Americans "spades" and "coloreds." When confronted about his language, however, his wife reasoned, "It's better than when he called them *coons*." In the mid–1970s, *Good Times* also used other words, such as in one of its less celebrated catchphrases, "*Negro*, please!"

On June 5, 1974, Don Cornelius and the Soul Train Dancers performed as part of Sly and the Family Stone's concert in Madison Square Garden, where Sly Stone married Kathy Silva on stage. Over 20,000 people attended, and most knew in advance of the couple's plans to wed in concert. Cornelius served as the master of ceremonies, telling the spectators, "There is a religious nature to the ceremony you are about to witness." In contrast to the family-friendly *Soul Train*, this gig attended by Cornelius and company had what *Time* magazine called "an atmosphere heavy with cannabis." Another difference between this concert and *Soul Train* was that most of the audience at the wedding was white.[32]

Cornelius also appealed to more conservative elements. The National Association for the Advancement of Colored People (NAACP) invited him to serve as the master of ceremonies for the Image Awards of 1974. The invitation was a testament to the breadth of his appeal, for he had now won the respect of the elders of the civil rights movement as well as hip R&B musicians and counterculture journalists. Moreover, Cornelius had broadened his political scope, for within the movement he had only associated himself professionally with the Rev. Jesse Jackson, who was considerably more liberal than the NAACP.[33]

In its early years, *Soul Train*'s guests appealed to a wide variety of age groups. Adult viewers in their thirties or older often saw artists whose careers had begun when they were teenagers. Fans in their late teenage years or early adulthood could watch plenty of new, hip acts. Meanwhile, pre-pubescent and adolescent devotees of the show were occasionally treated to singers their own age, such as Foster Sylvers, the Five Stairsteps, and the Jackson Five.

By 1974 the Soul Train Line had become an important part of urban African American early adolescent socialization. That year the academic journal *Sociology and Sociological Research* published a report about the dance party's role as a "rite of passage" for some urban African American youth. Such parties tended to have a communal aspect. The youngsters usually formed a "Soul Train Line" during the party, at which point an attendee danced between two rows of pre-pubescent peers. These spectators then decided whether to approve the performance and allow the attendee into the peer group.[34]

The dancing on *Soul Train* even won the respect of Broadway. In the early 1970s, a wave of musicals with African American casts entertained audiences, especially *Raisin* and *The Wiz*. As a result the emergence of African American dance on television via *Soul Train* dovetailed with the new popularity of theatrical African American dance. In late 1974 one critic who saw a preview of *The Wiz* cheered, "Little Dorothy is dancing down the Yellow Brick Road like it led to *Soul Train!*" In addition, Broadway stars like Ralph Carter of *Raisin* and Stephanie Mills of *The Wiz* later started R&B careers and pantomimed their songs on *Soul Train*.[35]

Meanwhile, the record label Adam VIII capitalized on the popularity of *Soul Train* and the music on the show. In 1973 and 1974, the label, which sold albums through television marketing or "telemarketing," packaged compilations of R&B music with the title of Cornelius' show. *Soul Train* benefited, too, because the commercials for the albums gave the series more television exposure. In addition, the advertisements essentially introduced the series to unfamiliar television viewers by tying the name of the show to the music offered on the albums. The album *Soul Train — Hall of Fame* (1973) contained popular crossover hit songs from the 1950s to the early 1970s. *Soul Train — Hits That Made It Happen* (1973) consisted mostly of songs that the program had broadcasted; many of the selected artists had performed the songs on the show in 1972 and 1973. The label's final *Soul Train* album, subtitled *Super Tracks* (1974), was similar in concept to *Hits That Made It Happen*, except that the songs came from the episodes from between 1973 and 1974.

Of the three albums, *Hall of Fame* reflected *Soul Train* the least. Rather, the album cashed in on the contemporary nostalgia craze in the United States. Throughout the 1970s Hollywood set films like *American Graffiti* (1973) and television programs such as *Happy Days* (1974–84) in the time periods of the 1950s and early 1960s. Some musicians who had peaked in popularity in the 1950s — Chuck Berry, Ricky Nelson, and Elvis Presley — enjoyed new hits in the 1970s by recreating their old styles of music. "Soul" musicians, however, had hardly warmed to nostalgia. One notable exception, the vocal group the Pointer Sisters, combined Andrews Sisters–style harmonies and the fashion of the 1940s with funk instrumentation for the 1973 hit "Yes We Can Can," which they sang on *Soul Train*.

Hall of Fame did not represent the heritage of *Soul Train*. All of the songs collected in the album were national crossover hits. As a result, the Chicago-based performers and the local hit songs that helped make *Soul Train* a hit series on WCIU were absent. In addition, no Chicago-based artists with nationwide hits like the Impressions or Major Lance were on the album. Adam VIII completely overlooked the Windy City–based dance crazes that adolescents throughout the country performed. Barbara Lewis, who had recorded songs as a teenager in Chicago, later relocated to Detroit and recorded the *Hall of Fame* song "Hello Stranger" (1963); she appeared on *Soul Train* in the 1970s but never performed that song there.

Some of the artists had not appeared on *Soul Train* by the album's release in 1973. Therefore, the program did not contribute to their careers, despite their inclusion in the show's vinyl hall of fame. Otis Redding never had the opportunity to perform on *Soul Train*, having died in an airplane crash four years before the syndicated debut. Fellow "inductee" Frankie Lymon succumbed to a drug overdose in 1968. Sly and the Family Stone eventually appeared in 1974, but Mickey Baker of the duo Mickey and Sylvia never did. The year of the album's release, Sylvia sang her crossover hit "Pillow Talk" on the show.

In addition, *Hall of Fame* did not attract the same audience as *Soul Train* did. The album's crossover content helped maximize potential appeal to white customers as well as African Americans. In contrast, *Soul Train* targeted urban markets. Many episodes featured guests whose songs never made the popular music charts despite their popularity in urban radio. The occasional booking of R&B artists with mainstream hits gave the show a better chance of attracting viewers, but *Soul Train* did not need them in order to be popular.

On October 11, 1974, the *New York Times* finally confirmed what Cornelius had been declaring for almost two years. *Soul Train* was one of the two series most watched by African Americans; Redd Foxx's situation comedy *Sanford and Son*— the second-place show in overall network television ratings in the 1974–75 season — was the other. By this time other shows with all-black casts included *Black Journal, Black Perspective on the News, Soul!, That's My Mama,* and *Good Times,* which ranked seventh in the Nielsen ratings overall. *Soul Train*'s feat is especially remarkable, because the other series mentioned aired either on public television or network television, in contrast to the syndicated *Soul Train*.[36]

Missing from the roster of African American television that season was one of *Soul Train*'s most formidable contemporaries in televising black music. In early 1974 NBC aired the last new episode of *The Flip Wilson Show,* and repeat episodes spanning the entire four-year run lasted until June. The show had lost viewers to the nostalgic, Great Depression–set drama *The Waltons* for two years; in the 1973–74 season, *The Waltons* was the second highest-rated network series (behind only *All in the Family*). In contrast, *The Flip Wilson Show* was not even among the top thirty; it ranked thirty-ninth, for example, in the last week of October 1973. To the very end, however, Wilson continued to provide big-name African American singers for audiences before Cornelius did. Both the Pointer Sisters and Gladys Knight and the Pips sang on *The Flip Wilson Show* in the fall of 1973. The former group did not board *Soul Train* until two months after Wilson's series ended, and the latter performed their chart-topping crossover hit "Midnight Train to Georgia" to Wilson's audience seven months before belting it out to the Soul Train Gang.

Knight's lapse was uncharacteristic of her relationship to *Soul Train*. She and the Pips had been very supportive of the show. They had appeared on the very first syndicated episode to introduce two songs. In late 1972 Cornelius had allowed her not only to debut two more tunes but also to pantomime her five-year-old hit "I Heard It Through the Grapevine," which the dancers enjoyed despite its stylistic incongruence with the current funk and early disco songs they frequently heard by then. Nevertheless, her decision to go to *The Flip Wilson Show* first in 1973 for "Midnight Train to Georgia" showed that his show was still powerful competition for Cornelius even as it faced cancellation.

Another development contributing to the demise of Wilson's program was the popularity of series with all-black casts. Both *The Flip Wilson Show* and the situation comedy *Room 222* used integrated casts until midway through the 1973–74 season. The shows, especially *Room 222*, had become relics of the pre–*Soul Train* era, when networks offered imagery and rhetoric promoting interracial cooperation in the wake of urban riots and the assassinations of the Rev. Dr. Martin Luther King, Jr. and Senator Robert F. Kennedy of New York. The continuing de facto segregation of cities and the anger of white parents towards the busing of students across racial lines to black public schools slowly changed *Room 222* from a relevant ideal to racial escapism. By the time both *Room 222* and *The Flip Wilson Show* left the air, *Good Times* had already premiered.

By this time *Soul Train* had become famous for both the moves of the dancers and the racial exclusivity of its guest roster. *Soul Train* was synonymous with "black music television" in the fall of 1974. Such an association acknowledged not only the success of the series but also the lack of similar programming either on the networks or in syndication after three national seasons of *Soul Train*. When the second-season premiere of *Don Kirshner's Rock Concert* featured only African American artists and "plugs" for their labels, critic John J. O'Connor called the episode "a tribute to Don Cornelius, producer of the 'Soul Train' TV series."[37]

For some people the all-black casting of *Soul Train* had a political context. In February 1975, Warren Foulkes wrote in *Black World* magazine that the dancing on the series was unique because African Americans were dancing among themselves. He considered the moves part of a secretive socialization among African Americans, noting that outside of the series, they might suppress their feelings of oppression. Calling for the release of African Americans from frustration and pressure stemming from their oppression at the hands of white people, he stated that in the meantime, the dance moves allowed the dancers to release pent-up feelings in a controlled manner. He likened the movements on *Soul Train* to a barometer by which an observer could gauge the discomfort level of African Americans as a community.[38]

The politics, however, went beyond the Soul Train Gang, according to Foulkes. Imagery of social dissatisfaction in the African American community also lay in the set design. He noted that trains, as a mode of transportation, signify having a means of escape from a location. The railroad tracks that adorned the dance floor, meanwhile, suggest a destination.[39]

To Foulkes, *Soul Train* even had a religious dynamic. The program was an African American ideal. He likened Cornelius to a mystic and each episode of the program as a ceremony. The host's status as a mystic showed in his ability not only to talk to the young dancers in their lingo but also to chat with celebrity guests with ease. In addition, Foulkes curiously referred to the vastly different practices of Catholicism and Islam for the same program. He compared Cornelius' hosting to a papal visit and referred to an opportunity to dance on the show as "a trip to Mecca."[40]

By the time *Black World* published Foulkes's article, "Mecca" was settling into a sort of rut. The media blitz had cooled. Major newspapers no longer discussed the show as a novelty. Although *Soul Train* still featured "TSOP" as the theme song until the fall of 1975, the song had long vacated the charts when the year started. When Cornelius began making changes to keep the series fresh that year, he changed the character of the show — so dramatically that the changes rendered Foulkes's Afro-centric article nearly obsolete.

5

"You Can Bet Your Last Money"

Beyond Soul Train *and Soul Music*

In 1974 the Rev. John and Rose Watley moved with their three children to Los Angeles. It was the latest of several moves for the itinerant preacher and his family. The middle child, fifteen-year-old daughter Jody, was a talented dancer who adored the syndicated *Soul Train*. Attending the Rev. James Cleveland's Cornerstone Institutional Baptist Church the Sunday after the move to Los Angeles, she received an invitation from *Soul Train* regular and fellow worshipper Glen Stafford. He asked her to temporarily serve as his partner, and she responded by hollering, "Yes, yes!" She later remembered, "The funny thing is he didn't even ask me if I could dance. He just liked the way I looked."[1]

As a substitute she did not make a lasting impression on the *Soul Train* staff. When Stafford's regular partner returned to the show, Watley struggled to gain admittance into the studio for tapings. "I had to find people who would bring me on the show, because I wasn't a regular," she noted. "I would hide under a blanket in the back seat of someone's car until we were past the guards at the studio gate. Sometimes I would be able to stay in the studio all day. Other times they would tell me to leave." Despite the setbacks she doggedly pursued spots on the program. "I was determined to be a regular," she remarked.[2]

Eventually she paired with Jeffrey Daniel, and they became one of the show's most popular couples of the mid–1970s, if not of the entire run of the series. "Jody became more than just a regular," host Don Cornelius reminisced. "She and her partner, Jeffrey Daniel, set the standard for the '70s and '80s *Soul Train* dancer. They were very creative, their dancing abilities were

106

undoubted and they always seemed to know what to wear." Unsurprisingly, they made frequent trips down the Soul Train Line during their tenure.[3]

The couple also became a symbol for the evolution of *Soul Train* from 1975 to 1979. They appeared on the series as it began to change its look as well as its sound. Cornelius rewarded the loyalty and creativity of the couple by using them for the growth of the *Soul Train* franchise. As the careers of Watley and Daniel ascended, so did *Soul Train*.

In 1975, Cornelius began taking serious gambles with *Soul Train*. To be sure, the show itself had always been a gamble. The host had taken a major chance by producing a weekly, all-black program for syndication. That gamble paid off, and *Soul Train* became a mainstream hit partly because of the novelty of the racial exclusivity of the series. By the mid–1970s, however, Cornelius had to do more than televising African Americans dancing to African American music in order for his show to survive. He dispensed with many of the show's traditions over the next few years, but many other changes the series experienced were beyond his control. By 1979 all of the changes made *Soul Train* significantly different from the show that had caught the nation's attention eight years earlier.

Other people not affiliated with Don Cornelius Productions attempted to capitalize on the popularity of *Soul Train* through a lackluster stage show bearing the *Soul Train* name. In New York City, a stage show entitled "The Easter Soul Train of Stars" took place in March 1975. The event was a three-hour concert featuring six artists. Of all the performers — William De Vaughan, Ebb Tide, Joe Quarterman, Jenny's Children, Shirley and Company, and Betty Wright — only Wright received accolades from the press. The concert suffered poor management, with too much time elapsing between acts. Even worse, the event had racist overtones; a disc jockey and a person in a gorilla suit appeared on stage to entertain whenever the music stopped.[4]

Meanwhile, the real *Soul Train* entered a transition period from "soul" music to other genres. "Soul" music, which had given the series its individuality on television, lost its appeal with audiences in the mid–1970s. Part of the problem lay in new music styles eclipsing soul music in popularity. Social messages sung over drums, guitars, and a keyboard gave way to calls for one-night stands set to lush orchestration and mechanical beats. The word "love" became a euphemism for sex and was attached to various items in three chart-topping songs in 1976 — Ohio Players' "Love Rollercoaster," Diana Ross's "Love Hangover," and the Miracles' "Love Machine."

Disco music — the genre of the aforementioned "love" songs — had crossover appeal, which provided benefits and problems for *Soul Train*. Listeners beyond the urban African American audience targeted by *Soul Train* enjoyed disco. As a result, the series attracted disco fans as well as urban blacks. Disco, however, was a technical genre instead of improvisational. A singer did not have to sound "soulful" to have a disco hit; in fact, many popular disco songs had few to no lyrics. Thus, songs that played on *Soul Train* also appeared on network variety shows of the day. The debut of *The Brady Bunch Variety Hour* on ABC in late 1976 featured a disco medley including Van McCoy's "The Hustle" and Donna Summer's "Love to Love You Baby."[5]

In addition, Cornelius had to compete with those variety programs when booking guests. Before the disco boom, his guests tended to have television gigs on *American Bandstand* or *The Midnight Special* as well as *Soul Train*. Now he competed with different shows that catered to various audiences on any day of the week. Weekday morning talk shows such as *Dinah* (1974–80) and *The Mike Douglas Show* now booked African American musical acts.

The soul singers who had appeared on *Soul Train* in the show's early years switched genres for their guest spots of the mid–1970s. If soul fans were disappointed, at least the artists maintained their popularity with young African American listeners by adapting to their trends. James Brown lost musicians to George Clinton's funk group Parliament and started making disco music with the Ohio Players. No longer did he sing of black pride or politics. The O'Jays recorded the disco song "I Love Music," an uncharacteristically upbeat song when compared to earlier hits "Backstabbers" and "For the Love of Money." With *Superfly* now as recent history, Curtis Mayfield began releasing disco songs and ballads as singles after years of musically lamenting the drug trade, poverty and the high price of meat.

Soul Train, however, survived the musical transition better than some of the labels whose songs the program had promoted. Some of the larger labels either bought independent African American labels or wooed away their artists with more lucrative contracts. Other soul labels simply collapsed. Holland-Dozier-Holland's Hot Wax label folded. Stax went bankrupt. Many of Motown's great singers — the Four Tops, Martha Reeves and the Vandellas, Gladys Knight and the Pips, and the Jackson Five — had left the company by the mid–'70s. Some artists stayed in Detroit when Berry Gordy took the label to Los Angeles, while others defected because of declining record sales, unpaid royalties, and lack of creative control over songs. The label continued to develop popular solo and group acts, but only the Commodores among new performers had the same degree of success as the classic singers.

In addition, the label dropped its R&B subsidiary Soul Records in 1978, as disco peaked.[6]

The disco craze inspired the Adam VIII label's promotion of urban audience-oriented music. After years of promoting R&B album compilations by using the *Soul Train* name, the label changed tactics in 1975. The first of several disco compilations—*Disco Party*—was released that year. As with the *Soul Train* albums, *Disco Party* contained many songs that *Soul Train* had promoted in recent episodes. Some of the hits, however, were not disco songs but rather rock numbers like "Lady" by Styx and "You Ain't Seen Nothin' Yet" by Bachman-Turner-Overdrive. Including those rock songs in a *Soul Train* album would have made as little sense, and as the *Soul Train* media blitz subsided, the show's publicity needed to reflect its content as much as possible.

As the African American recording industry underwent a transition, Don Cornelius decided to get into the business. He founded Soul Train Records with *Soul Train*'s talent coordinator Dick Griffey in late 1975. Cornelius hired arrangers to flesh out his musical ideas for his groups. He usually knew how he wanted a song to sound, and arrangers would simply try to accommodate Cornelius' wishes. When trying to convey his musical desires to his staff, he occasionally *sang* the parts he wanted. This creative arrangement influenced the *Soul Train* program as well as the label. After dropping "TSOP" as the theme song to *Soul Train* at the end of the 1974–75 season, Cornelius composed each of the theme songs subsequently used over the next twelve seasons, and he chose his own musical protégés to perform the songs.[7]

Griffey, meanwhile, knew how to create, groom and package acts. He had first entered the music business in 1966 — the same year that Cornelius took his broadcasting course. At the time Griffey was a promoter for clubs and concerts in the Los Angeles area. Through his experiences he learned how musical entertainers had to look, move and sound in order to entertain audiences. He decided which artists would sing the lyrics for Cornelius' musical ideas.[8]

Each business complemented the other. Soul Train Records provided promotion of the *Soul Train* name in music stores and print advertisements for the label's soloists and groups in trade magazines. The program, meanwhile, served as a means to televise the acts to nationwide audiences. Now that soul and disco were crossover pop styles, artists on other labels had begun to bypass *Soul Train* for network shows when debuting their songs. By having his own performers, however, Cornelius guaranteed that his series would introduce his label's songs to R&B consumers.

One of the first groups Cornelius signed to the label consisted of a few members of the Soul Train Gang. The label dubbed the group the Soul Train Gang, and the host subsequently renamed the show's teenage cast the Soul Train Dancers. He tried hard to promote the Gang. He successfully recruited Stevie Wonder as an arranger on the group's first album. Their theme songs to *Soul Train* opened and closed the program from 1975 to 1978. The group appeared twice on the show in 1976.

The formation of the group represented the peak in popularity of both the Soul Train Gang and the Soul Train Dancers. Despite the promotion of the two albums the group made and the television appearances, the Gang did not generate any hit singles. As for the Dancers, Cornelius had done all he could for them by 1975. After having taken them on tour with him and having formed a group from some of them, he did no more promotion of cast members. His last major gesture was literally to give them greater voice in the show; starting in the 1975–76 season, he concluded every episode by wishing "love, peace, and"—but let the dancers shout, "Soul!"

Cornelius and Griffey also invited The Whispers to record on the Soul Train label. The group had appeared on *Soul Train* since the show's first syndicated season, when they sang for a different label. Even after the group left Soul Train Records, Cornelius found uses for them on the show. The Whispers not only kept appearing as guests over the next two decades but also sang the theme song to the series—"Up on Soul Train"—in the early 1980s.

Label mates Shalamar also enjoyed success thanks in part to *Soul Train*. The group initially consisted of session singers. In 1977 their album *Uptown Festival* became a crossover top ten hit, and the title single achieved mainstream success by placing in the top thirty. Cornelius promoted them by having them appear on his show to sing two songs from the album. In yet another decisive break from the "Philly sound" the host had formerly embraced for his show, the song "Uptown Festival" was a medley of Motown tunes.

Uptown Festival was an astute exploitation of two of the most successful trends of the 1970s — disco and nostalgia. By using old Motown hits, the label drew from successful crossover R&B songs to maximize the number of potential buyers. The album was on par with other nostalgic popular music of the decade such as the soundtrack to the movie *Grease* (1978). Very few R&B artists of the 1970s, however, covered old songs, and even fewer released such songs as singles for radio play. *Uptown Festival* and Donna Summer's disco cover of Richard Harris's 1967 song "MacArthur Park" were notable exceptions.

When Cornelius and Griffey decided to reorganize Shalamar as a permanent band the next year, they demonstrated great talent for creating successful groups. Mining talent from *Soul Train*, they invited regular dancers Jeffrey Daniel and Jody Watley to replace the band's departed backup singers. The pair was *the* most popular couple on the program at the time, according to the *New York Times*. The record executives, therefore, capitalized not only on the couple's ability but also their familiarity to television viewers. Shalamar later recruited a backup singer named Jermaine Stewart, who had spent his formative years in Chicago and had danced on WCIU's *Soul Train* in the early 1970s.[9]

Cornelius had more confidence in the new lineup than Griffey did. "Since Jody and Jeffrey were the most recognizable dancers on the show then, I said, 'Let's use them,'" the host recalled. Griffey initially refused, noting, "Jody Watley can't sing." Cornelius countered ironically by minimizing the importance of musical talent: "It doesn't matter, only the look matters." He then, however, argued that some singing talent might have possibly existed in her. "She had told me her mother had been a gospel singer. I had some cocka-mamie idea there must be some kind of singing in her genes," he theorized.[10]

Still, Watley herself needed convincing that "only the look matters." "I had never thought of singing professionally," she confessed. "I was a dancer so I was a little nervous. But I knew it was a good opportunity, thought about it overnight and said yes the following day." Just as "the look" had helped her land a spot on *Soul Train* years earlier, it now gave her a recording career. Daniel also agreed to join, and Shalamar was reborn.[11]

The revamped group had middling success with its initial releases. *Disco Gardens*, the first album by the "new" Shalamar, performed much worse on the charts than *Uptown Festival* and barely made *Billboard*'s "Top-200 Chart." Then Howard Hewett replaced Gerald Brown as the lead singer in 1979. Shalamar immediately scored a crossover top ten hit with the disco song "The Second Time Around." Griffey had developed a successful sound for the group, which the *New York Times* favorably called "a smooth compromise between bubblegum rhythm-and-blues and gospel-based soul."[12]

In March 1978 Cornelius and Griffey parted company professionally and dissolved Soul Train Records. Cornelius devoted his full attention to *Soul Train*, but Griffey reorganized the Soul Train Records as the S.O.L.A.R. (Sound of Los Angeles Records) label. Cornelius did not, however, completely abandon the artists he had helped to develop. Shalamar and The Whispers continued to sing on *Soul Train* for years. As the former group began to splinter, solo acts Watley, Stewart, and Howard Hewett appeared for a few episodes each.

Soul Train gave Shalamar exposure that not every artist for Soul Train Records or S.O.L.A.R. received. Artists with proven or potential hit songs still took priority over others. Shalamar boarded the "train" several times. Only The Whispers appeared more times than Shalamar — a distinction that owed more to its number of visits dating back before the label's formation than its number of S.O.L.A.R. hits. Less successful groups the Deele, Midnight Star and Lakeside and soloist Carrie Lucas sang less frequently on the program. Meanwhile, in the years that the group Klymaxx was signed to S.O.L.A.R., they never appeared on the show; they later made hit songs "The Men All Pause" and "I Miss You" after signing to another label.

Cornelius remained loyal to people who helped develop music for Soul Train Records. He hired Bruce W. Miller, an arranger for a song on "Uptown Festival," for the sessions of *Soul Train*'s three theme songs used between the 1977–78 and 1979–80 seasons. Miller also arranged an album for The Whispers and worked on music for O'Bryan — a singer Cornelius mentored. The *Soul Train* producer continued to employ Miller for various projects into the 1980s.[13]

Cornelius made news in the trade periodicals during the mid-'70s largely through his management of Soul Train Records. In September 1975 *Billboard* was the first to report the formation of the label via RCA Records. *Variety* provided another article on the label's start four months later. The development was newsworthy, for it marked the first step in the growth of Cornelius' music business empire beyond television. Rarely did television stars create record labels, especially for other performers instead of themselves.

On the other hand, trends in the music industry continued to cause problems for Cornelius. Disco's rise in popularity on television meant that *Soul Train* no longer provided unique dances. When the music on *Soul Train* had a primarily urban audience, the program was the only place to see the latest dances. Now, *Soul Train*'s dancers received invitations to network shows. For example, in the months between the first and second performances of the dance group the Lockers on *Soul Train* (February 1975 to October 1976), the performers appeared on *Dinah!, Saturday Night Live,* and — ironically enough — *American Bandstand*. In addition, *American Bandstand* and *Soul Train* dancers began doing the same moves — this time without Dick Clark having to lure dancers away from Cornelius' show.

Some dancers did go on both *American Bandstand* and *Soul Train*.

Neither show paid dancers, but the shows provided national exposure, opportunities to dance on stage, and talented musical guests for dancers to meet. *Soul Train*, as a result, became a victim of its own success. The R&B music and African American dancing that the series promoted became so popular that Cornelius now had to regularly compete with other shows for the musicians and dancers he helped make into stars.

As a result, *Soul Train* became just another dance show in the mid–1970s, albeit a show that still provided a wider variety of African American music than other programs did. In the late 1970s and early 1980s, the program not only hosted disco dancers but also movers whose steps later became known as "breakdancing." The latter especially showed their routines during the Soul Train Line. Still, the "disco" label followed the series. One article lumped *Soul Train* together with *American Bandstand* and the new weekly disco dance competition show *Dance Fever* in the same sentence, merely because the group Gary's Gang performed on all three shows. The article made no attempt to distinguish any of the shows from one another. Another report also neglected to associate *Soul Train* with soul music. *The New York Times*, in writing about local adolescents producing their own dance program, observed, "Teen-agers elsewhere are watching such televised disco shows as *Soul Train*."[14]

The *Soul Train* episodes that deliberately spotlighted disco dancers did not help distinguish the series. In 1979 Cornelius allowed one of the couples to perform a dance routine for around three minutes. It was an enormous opportunity for exposure, for the length of camera time on them alone was over thirty times the usual length that a couple received if fortunate enough to be chosen to dance down the Soul Train Line. The couple gave an extraordinary performance to the song "Keep On Dancing" by Gary's Gang, with male partner Randy Thomas frequently lifting female partner Cheryl Song; he walked in circles as she elegantly posed in the air. The routine was a marked change from the "popping" and "locking" that had characterized the early syndication years. On the other hand, as a disco routine, it resembled dance performances on competing shows. Still, for their efforts, both dancers each received a twenty-fifth anniversary Johnson Products package and a $100 savings bond — a significant improvement over the weekly rations of Kentucky Fried Chicken.

American Bandstand and *Soul Train* had similar aesthetic as well as musical qualities beyond disco-oriented trends. Both programs featured new sets that resembled nightclubs in the fall of 1978. They emphasized neon lighting. Towers for dancing also appeared on both shows. Throughout the late

Johnson Products Co., Inc. | 8522 South Lafayette Avenue | Chicago, Illinois 60620 | ac 312·483 4100

January 7, 1972

Mr. Ronnie Bauchman
1920½ W. 22nd Street
Los Angeles, California   90018

Hi Soul Train Gang Member:

Congratulations! You are the lucky winner of
a years supply of Afro Sheen hair care products.

    Afro Sheen Conditioner & Hair Dress
      Afro Sheen Hair Spray for Sheen
      Afro Sheen Comb Easy Conditioner

We here at Johnson Products, Inc. pride ourselves
in having the finest of hair care products. We
hope you will continue to be a satisfied customer
for many years to come.

                Sincerely,

                Sonny Harper

                Sonny Harper

Manufacturers of ULTRA SHEEN® and AFRO SHEEN® Hair Care Cosmetics

**Letter from Johnson Products to *Soul Train* dancer Ron Bauchman. Courtesy
Ron Bauchman.**

1970s and 1980s, Clark acknowledged the popularity of R&B with white audiences by playing Billy Preston's song "Space Race" during the halfway point of each episode before a commercial break. In addition, *American Bandstand* not only promoted an increasing number of African American artists but also beefed up its roster of African American dancers. Some of the dancers coming from *Soul Train* increased their prominence on Clark's program by appearing in *American Bandstand*'s annual dance contests. On the other hand, some *Soul Train* dancers appropriated gimmickry from *American Bandstand*'s cast by wearing t-shirts with written messages — a far cry from the fancy, flashy "*Superfly* look."

Both shows also switched to darker lighting, which contributed to the similarities of their sets to nightclubs. The dark dance floors not only fit the advent of disco but also demonstrated that both series now prominently featured adults instead of teenagers. In the early 1970s, the programs featured yellow or yellow-orange backgrounds. For *American Bandstand* the bright colors reflected the happy, inoffensive pop music offered by Clark. On *Soul Train* the cheerful hues complemented the enthusiasm and extroversion of the dancers. Then in 1976 *Soul Train* switched to dark blue lighting, swirling strobe lights, and a hanging "disco ball" emblazoning the show's title. The following year *American Bandstand* followed suit except for its own "disco ball."

Still, both shows retained their individuality, however reduced. Cornelius continued to collectively introduce his dancers, while Clark did not. *Soul Train* changed its theme song at least three times between 1978 and 1988, and Cornelius continued to speak in current African American urban vernacular and advertise his series as "the hippest." *American Bandstand*, in contrast, awkwardly blended nostalgia with contemporary music. The combination dovetailed with Clark's increasing tributes to his own program's longevity while keeping the music fresh; in addition to new episodes, he produced a twentieth anniversary broadcast in 1973 and a twenty-fifth anniversary special four years later. Although playing popular songs throughout each episode, starting in 1977 Clark opened and closed each airing with Barry Manilow's "Bandstand Boogie," which added lyrics to the series' theme song of 1957 to 1969. Both the old and new version of the theme recalled the "Big Band" sounds of the 1940s. Also, the host left the modern slang and "hipness" to the artists and dancers, most of whom were white, although he slightly lengthened his hair and sideburns in the 1970s.

The Soul Train Line remained *Soul Train*'s unique centerpiece. Dancers looked forward to participating in it. Christa Lee, who joined the show in 1975, said, "The Soul Train Line was what everyone lived for on *Soul Train*. We all wanted to come down that line and get our 15 seconds." Being chosen for the Line, however, did not guarantee time on camera. "I remember getting really pissed sometimes, when I was coming on and the song was over," she complained, "or they would decide to put a more popular dancer in *my place* on line. I would be depressed all day!" In contrast, *American Bandstand* never created its own version, leaving its cast members without any opportunity to shine with exclusive camera time.[15]

In addition, *Soul Train* offered a wider variety of African American music than *American Bandstand* did. Besides old-fashioned "soul" singers and disco artists, funk musicians like the Bar-Kays accepted Cornelius' invitation to ride the "train." Funk music of the late 1970s usually consisted of a slow or medium tempo, a pronounced bass line, a synthesizer and minimal orchestration. Funk vocalists often punctuated their songs with guttural shouts not unlike those of James Brown. In contrast, most of Clark's black guests were disco singers. Funk and soul did not sell as well as disco did outside of urban radio markets.

Other aspects of disco made it a better fit for *American Bandstand* than funk. Many white musicians recorded disco songs. The genre was very accessible to any one of any racial or ethnic group who possessed a drum machine and a studio orchestra of decent quality. As a result several white performers proceeded to pantomime disco songs on *American Bandstand*. Funk, despite its less complex instrumentation, was not a genre embraced by many white pop performers. Very few of those who did produced successful hits, but Cornelius respected the efforts of the white funk group Wild Cherry by allowing the group to play on his show. Clark's couples engaged in close dancing, which underwent a phenomenal comeback in the 1970s at the same time that disco boomed. Unlike disco, funk music's often thick, plodding beats did not inspire romantic dancing in pairs.

Although *Soul Train* gained a reputation as a "disco show," several of the genre's most successful acts did not appear on the show. Their collective absence was ironic, considering the program's significant role in popularizing disco through television. Moreover, Cornelius played the missing acts' recordings on his show and the Soul Train Dancers enjoyed the songs. The most commercially successful disco act, the Bee Gees, did not perform on the show, but the dancers moved down the Line to the group's hit "You Should Be Dancing." The group Silver Connection, whose songs became top-ten mainstream hits, also did not appear, although Cornelius played one of the songs ("Get Up and Boogie") for his cast members. Meanwhile, the Village People did not board the "train" until 1980—well past their peak and years after the releases of the hits "YMCA" and "Macho Man."

When the weekly exposure of R&B to television audiences via *Soul Train* proved successful in the afternoons, networks decided to provide African American musical entertainment in prime time viewing hours. Two groups that had previously appeared on Cornelius' program got their own weekly variety series. In the summer of 1975, *The Gladys Knight & the Pips Show* aired on NBC, and for the next two summers, CBS broadcast *The Jacksons*. They were the first African American singers with their own series since the demise of *The Barbara McNair Show* in 1971. More importantly, black R&B musicians were starting to gain new outlets for exposure of their songs on television without having to rely on Cornelius.

R&B appeared in other prime time series besides network variety shows and *Soul Train*. Some artists got weekly exposure for their theme song work. Quincy Jones had the most work in this area, writing themes not only for Bill Cosby's programs but also for the situation comedy *Sanford and Son*. From 1972 to 1978, CBS aired the situation comedy *Maude*, whose theme song came from performer Donny Hathaway; and from 1975 to 1978, the weekly cop-drama *Baretta* featured Sammy Davis, Jr.'s performance of the show's theme "Keep Your Eye on the Sparrow." In addition, R&B artists occasionally tested their acting skills on network television. In 1973 the group the Three Degrees made a guest appearance as themselves on NBC's situation comedy *Sanford and Son*.

No non-variety series benefited more from *Soul Train*'s popularization of R&B more than CBS's situation comedy *Good Times*. From February 1974 to August 1979, the series sporadically featured recordings of contemporary disco groups like Average White Band, Brass Construction, Odyssey, and the Jacksons—all of whom had appeared on *Soul Train* during the same period. *Good Times* used the Jacksons' "Shake Your Body Down to the Ground" as background music in a July 1979 episode, which had aired five months after the group had first pantomimed the song for Cornelius. Janet Jackson, who had performed with her brothers on stage earlier in the decade, was a regular member of the *Good Times* cast at the time of the episode featuring "Shake Your Body Down to the Ground." She did not, however, sing on the recording. In the episode, she played an abused child whom a divorcee adopted after having successfully separated the child from her violent mother. In the episode containing the Jacksons' song, the mother attempted to win back her daughter by trying to fraudulently characterize the divorcee as an unfit parent.

Of all the aforementioned series, only *Baretta* was not a comedy, which meant that *Soul Train* remained virtually alone in presenting R&B music in a non-comedic context in the mid–1970s. The new variety series hosted by artists were an extension of the comedy sketches of *The Flip Wilson Show* that featured African American musicians. As in *The Flip Wilson Show, Gladys Knight and the Pips* and *The Jacksons* placed R&B stars in humorous skits. The artists, however, were the stars instead of the guests. Meanwhile, Cornelius continued to engage in dialogue with musicians only during interviews and usually did not laugh while conversing with them.

Despite the new competition, *Soul Train* remained the premiere R&B series. R&B artists still boarded the "train" in order to establish themselves as stars of that genre. In February 1975, singer Gino Vannelli made show history as the first white guest artist on *Soul Train*. In the 1970s Vannelli often wore tight pants and an unbuttoned shirt while singing romantic ballads onstage. As a result observers tended to compare him to fellow bare-chested, white crooners Engelbert Humperdinck and Tom Jones. He did not mind the comparisons, but he made it a point to mention, "I'm not in [the music business] for the personality business. Music is first." Indeed, he had written, arranged, produced and played instruments on almost all his recordings at the time.[16]

Cornelius asked Vannelli to come on *Soul Train* and perform his hit songs. "'People Gotta Move' was higher on the R&B charts than pop charts. I believe that was what prompted Don to personally invite me on the show," Vannelli recalled. "He simply liked the music, the sound." Still, the singer was "both flattered and in wonderment about being the first white artist on the show." He had initially thought that Cornelius had made a mistake. He was, however, intimidated less by the host than by his invitation. "Though Don always wore a tall starched collar, and snappy suits fitted like knight's armor, I found him to be relaxed, open, gracious and completely color blind."[17]

Vannelli considered his looks as an advantage when trying to win support from the Soul Train Dancers. He had already become popular on the radio through his voice and his brother Joe Vannelli's funky arrangement of the song. Although white, the singer was not blond and pale. He surmised that Cornelius, in booking him as the first white guest, was "perhaps shrewdly recognizing my ethnic looks ('off-whiteness' as he put it)." He added, "My long shock of locks, in particular, could help tear down any possible walls in viewers' minds."[18]

Overall, Vannelli's episode of *Soul Train* was a success. Awkward moments were minimal. The singer remembered, "Dancers were a bit giggly and smiley. Some posed honest questions about music and place of birth." No one affiliated with the show expressed any negative feelings about him, although they also appreciated the novelty of Vannelli's presence. "The crew [were] curious and wide-eyed by the change of pace, but respectful and accommodating, as 'tv' crews go," he complimented.[19]

Vannelli credited his appearance on *Soul Train* with enhancing his singing career. At the time of his guest spot, he embarked on a tour with Stevie Wonder. It was a most opportune series of gigs for Vannelli, because in 1975 Wonder was enjoying the success of his chart-topping album *Fulfillingness' First Finale* and top-selling songs "You Haven't Done Nothing" and "Boogie on Reggae Woman." Vannelli remarked, "In that same period [as the *Soul Train* spot], Stevie Wonder taking me on tour with him, helped build a career in ways a Montreal boy could have never imagined."[20]

His appearance on *Soul Train* enabled him to break from his contemporaries like Humperdinck and Jones. At first critics compared not only Vannelli's image but also his music to that of the other crooners. By the end of the '70s, however, journalists began calling his songs "more adventurous" than those by other balladeers. To illustrate the daringness of his work, one article noted, "Vannelli ... is one of a few white singers who have been invited to perform on the rhythm and blues [read black]-oriented television program *Soul Train*." He returned to the show in 1979 to sing another high-charting song, "Stop."[21]

The success of Vannelli's initial episode resulted partly from the hard work that went into the performance. His brother Joe Vannelli, who arranged Gino's music and played keyboard for him, was "thrilled and honored" to have received the invitation and recalled that he and the band rehearsed with Gino "in earnest" on the sound stage of A&M Records for the *Soul Train* gig. In addition, he was so focused on the performance that he "tuned out" the Soul Train Gang dancing all around the band. "I was more concerned about trying not to fumble," he remembered.[22]

Other white artists appearing in 1975 benefited from urban radio's recent embrace of futuristically dressed performers. In the previous year, the group Labelle had pioneered the blending of American rhythm-and-blues music with British "glam rock" or "glitter rock," which featured androgynous musicians wearing costumes that resembled those of science-fiction characters. When promoting their chart-topping song "Lady Marmalade" on television in 1974 and 1975, Labelle wore clothing that looked like spacesuits adorned with feathers. On the other hand, white "glam" artists Elton John and David Bowie had slightly toned down their images when they appeared on *Soul Train* to perform their urban radio hits. John sang "Philadelphia Freedom" and "Bennie and the Jets" a few weeks after Vannelli's episode, and Bowie crooned "Fame" and "Golden Years" in late 1975.

John's episode was important in that it showed a rare patriotic side to R&B. In recent years much of "soul" music had been "protest music." In fact, in 1975 Curtis Mayfield released a gloomy album with the ironic title *There's No Place Like America Today*. In contrast, John's song "Philadelphia Freedom" contained lyrics that promoted "wav[ing] the flag" and professed love for the United States. In advance of the nation's bicentennial celebration and in the wake of the recently concluded Vietnam War, the song had a healing, celebratory tone about the country. Moreover, *Soul Train*'s images of young African Americans enjoying John's patriotic "soul" music suggested that the positive message resonated with urban audiences. The dancers — and, thus, the show itself — now accepted "soul" as celebrations of American pride as well as black pride.

The disassociation of "soul" from an exclusively African American context dovetailed perfectly with the desegregation of *Soul Train*'s guest roster. The series not only showed others besides blacks making R&B but also promoted songs to which more people could relate. People who were not African Americans had a fundamental disconnection to James Brown's "Say It Loud (I'm Black and I'm Proud)." Rural and suburban dwellers had no experience in dealing with dire urban conditions described in Marvin Gaye's "Inner City Blues (Make Me Wanna Holler)." On the other hand, anyone living in the United States could feel the patriotism expressed in "Philadelphia Freedom." As a result, John's episode of *Soul Train* made "soul" more accessible to viewers.

Before 1975, David Bowie was less likely than Elton John to venture into R&B. John had already integrated aspects of contemporary R&B into his music. Part of the prominent bass line of his "Philadelphia Freedom" had come from his earlier song "Step Into Christmas." Bowie, however, had most recently produced "hard rock" songs like "Rebel Rebel" and cover versions of British rock songs of the mid–1960s, and neither genre had attracted a significant African American following. In addition, until 1973, his work had featured his white backup band "The Spiders from Mars," in contrast to the African American musicians backing him in a Philadelphia studio in 1975. His former androgynous, futuristic alter ego "Ziggy Stardust"—a role he played in his concert performances from 1972 to 1973—also did little visually to endear him to teenage African Americans.

Bowie's venture into R&B also caught the music industry by surprise. Music journalist Robert Christgau noted that Bowie had become inaccurately characterized as having "gone disco." The author initially rationalized the reference by mentioning Bowie's African American back-up singers, his album produced at Sigma Sound in Philadelphia (thus cashing in on the "Philly Sound" R&B trend), and his appearance on *Soul Train*. Then, Christgau countered by bluntly theorizing that for these commentators on Bowie's changes, "'disco' is once again being used as code for 'nigger.'" The writer used Bowie's appearance on Cornelius' show to prove the argument that Bowie's songs did not inspire disco dancing: "The kids on *Soul Train* may be impressed by Bowie, as they are by Elton John, but like Elton he inspires no fancy stepping—no stepping at all, in fact."[23]

Even if the Soul Train Dancers did not move to Bowie's music, they still recognized his music as legitimate R&B. He nearly squandered the goodwill his song had earned him by acting out of sorts on the show. Most of the questions the dancers asked of him before his performance of "Golden Years" related to his acting career. Then the last question came from a gentleman: "When did you start getting into soul music? You know, when did you start wanting to do soul music?" He then complimented, "I mean, you're doing it." The singer then gave the man an incoherent response about street corners, attending clubs, and listening to James Brown in the 1960s. Bowie also laughed nervously through the interview. A stone-faced Cornelius then mercifully ended the question-and-answer session and introduced Bowie, and the ghost-faced guest began to perform his song.[24]

Soul Train invited Bowie to appear as his career was in transition—a constant state for him in the 1970s. When interviewed by Cameron Crowe of *Playboy* magazine, Bowie was more candid about his musical direction (or lack thereof) than with Cornelius. The artist claimed to have no pretensions regarding his music. He admitted that he had not produced an authentic R&B sound. Rather, he called his R&B "thoroughly plastic" and dubbed his first Philadelphia-based album "the definitive plastic soul record." He underscored his music's phoniness by declaring, "'Fame' was a put-on that worked." Just as he had discarded his "glam" alter ego "Ziggy Stardust," he did not seem committed to continuing a career as a "plastic soul" artist. "I'll do anything until I fail. And when I succeed, I quit, too."[25]

The group Average White Band was the most understated of all the white performers who broke ground on the show in 1975. The members did not use any visual gimmickry for their appearance on *Soul Train* in November, unlike the "glam" John and Bowie. Nor did the band emphasize sexual appeal, as Vannelli had done. On the other hand, their casual looks did not hinder their appeal to Cornelius. A very popular group that year, producing a crossover chart-topping hit with "Pick Up the Pieces," the Average White Band played three songs in its episode, whereas the other white guests only pantomimed to two.

The integration of *Soul Train*'s guest roster barely made headlines. Integrated series had become commonplace by 1975. The appearances of major white stars like Bing Crosby on *The Flip Wilson Show* had helped broaden the host's appeal beyond African American audiences back in 1970. The drama series *Room 222* had presented an integrated faculty and racially diverse classrooms at a time when mandatory busing was a controversial issue for school systems nationwide. In addition, one month before Vannelli's guest spot on *Soul Train*, CBS had introduced the situation comedy *The Jeffersons* (1975–85), which featured the first interracial married couple as regular characters on a television series. Vannelli believed that he had made his *Soul Train* debut during "a good time for black/white relations." Concerning the media, he noted, "The arts were doing their part to break down time-honored barriers. Dr. King's death had not been that long ago."[26]

The introduction of white artists to *Soul Train* also had significance, because for the first time, African Americans decided to integrate an all-black show. Previously white producers and hosts had used African American entertainers to break down color barriers. Now, however, Vannelli, John, and Bowie had to prove their worthiness to appear before Cornelius and the Soul Train Dancers and have their music accepted as "soul." Their success required a redefinition of *Soul Train* as a show. Whereas having an all-black show once defined "soul," the definition now expanded to white musicians whom black dancers liked.

Cornelius best demonstrated this new turn of events when introducing the Average White Band in 1975. He started by mentioning the members' birthplaces of Scotland and England. He then, however, noted that they sounded as if reared on "cornbread and black-eyed peas." Thus, with stereotypical references to "soul food," he attempted to legitimate the band's presence on the show to African American audiences. He concluded by acknowledging the uniqueness of a white soul group from Europe by noting that they had to be "seen to be believed." The band did not disappoint, and the Soul Train Dancers warmly applauded the group.

Whenever artists gave especially exciting performances, the dancers did more than clap for them. The Supremes returned to *Soul Train* in 1975, pantomiming "This Is Why I Believe in You"—a song with an extended ending that sounded like "running music" in African American churches. As the group members fervently clapped and stomped to the accelerated tempo, the Soul Train Dancers whooped and hollered as if having a spiritual experience. When David Bowie went on the show, he started "Fame" with a waddle-like shuffle that unimpressed the adolescents. As the song progressed, his movements became more forceful, and the dancers rewarded him with loud cheers during his dance.

As in the early 1970s, the guests and dancers of the late 1970s continued to have good relations with each other. During a break in taping an episode, a performer told a couple that they looked good together. On occasion, the socialization extended beyond the *Soul Train* stage. Moreover, the motives were sometimes more romantic, as opposed to the Jackson Five learning dance moves from Damita Jo Freeman. Christa Lee remembered having attended a taping of a performance by the sibling group the Sylvers in late 1975. "I went out on a date with Leon Sylvers after we met on the show," she recalled.[27]

Meanwhile, Cornelius continued to alter his public persona. He flirted with network television after years of declaring that he owed networks nothing for his success. In May 1975 he served as the host of an episode of NBC's late-night music variety show *The Midnight Special*. It marked his first time promoting music on television in manners beyond his control. Instead of serving as host/producer, he was merely the host; Burt Sugarman produced.

The Midnight Special was very far removed from the African American aesthetics that Cornelius had developed on *Soul Train*. The title of the show came from an old blues song about a train that carried women on their way to visit their incarcerated men at Parchman State Penitentiary in Mississippi—a prison farm. Ironically, Parchman at the time was undergoing fundamental changes that made the song obsolete within a few years; in 1972, a federal judge had ruled that the prison's conditions were unconstitutional, and he oversaw the prison's transformation from a fenceless farm to a series of fenced concrete cellblocks. Nevertheless, the song's theme of sexual release while in prison contrasted starkly with the idea of a train as a means of liberation, which

Warren Foulkes had argued regarding *Soul Train*'s symbolism. Also, the main voices for *The Midnight Special*— Johnny Rivers's cover of the title song and the announcing talents of Wolfman Jack — were white, unlike *Soul Train*'s Cornelius, announcer Sid McCoy, and the group MFSB.

Cornelius' episode of *The Midnight Special* also has significance in its guest roster. Most but not all of the acts were African American. He was able to promote The Whispers, who had signed on to Soul Train Records. Flautist Herbie Mann, however, was white. Cornelius' embrace of multiethnic guest lists on a show other than his own further indicated his willingness to expand beyond his reputation as a host who sought only African Americans to entertain African Americans.

Meanwhile, *Soul Train* continued to generate a sizable amount of appeal among African American celebrities. Actors still made cameo appearances, but the cameos were less frequent as the 1970s. Even more rare were visits aboard the "train" by government figures. One of the last political guests of the series was Lieutenant Governor Mervyn Dymally of California, who boarded for the final episode of the 1977–78 season. A successful state-level Democrat, he had served in California's government since 1962 and had won the position of lieutenant governor in the 1974 election. His *Soul Train* appearance in May 1978 happened in the midst of his reelection campaign. The incumbent, however, lost to Republican challenger Mike Curb. Dymally received only 43 percent of the vote, as opposed to his opponent's 52 percent.[28]

Dymally's appearance illustrated one of the first political stances taken by *Soul Train* since the end of the Vietnam War. By allowing him on the show, Cornelius demonstrated support for him. No episode from that election year featured Curb. Dymally's loss, on the other hand, proved that the challenger did not need to appeal to African American television viewers to win political office in California. After having successfully promoted "TSOP," Richard Pryor, and Shalamar, the *Soul Train* magic now started to falter.

Cornelius attracted other top talent in Hollywood besides actors. Animator Sam Pal worked on an opening sequence for *Soul Train* in the late 1970s. Although the sequence underwent revisions into the 1990s, Pal's animation of the locomotive remained in the opening. He was one of very few connections made by Cornelius to figures of "classic Hollywood" (people involved in moviemaking before the introduction of the modern ratings system in 1968). In the 1960s the film studio Metro-Goldwyn-Mayer had credited Pal as the "coordinator" of the short animated cartoon *Cannery Rodent*, which stars Tom (Cat) and Jerry (Mouse). As a result of his participation,

Soul Train had better animation in its opening and commercial bumpers than in previous years.

Director J.D. Lobue, who replaced B.J. Jackson as *Soul Train*'s regular director, gave the show his own visual imprint. He improved the cinematography of the program, especially by integrating camera tricks into the episodes. His opening sequences featured a three-way split screen of the dance floor. Also, during the "Soul Train Line" segments, the show no longer roughly jumped from one line to the other. Instead, Lobue provided a "wipe" of the new camera shot to "clear away" the old. As a result, smoother transitions from line to line appeared.

Many of the dancers of the first syndicated season were gone by the end of the decade. As the original high school students graduated from their schools, they left *Soul Train* too. By the end of the fourth syndicated season, Pat Davis, Jimmy "Scooby-Doo" Foster, and Damita Jo Freeman had stopped appearing regularly. Freeman became a well-respected choreographer for major entertainers upon departing the "train." She also acted, having a role in the motion picture *Private Benjamin* in 1980, and a recurring part in the television series adaptation of the film between 1981 and 1983. One scene from the movie features a "Soul Train Line" of sorts as Goldie Hawn dances among female co-stars to Sister Sledge's disco song "We Are Family." Freeman earned the respect of Dick Clark, on whose *American Bandstand* series she appeared while a *Soul Train* dancer. He took pride in bragging about her post–*Bandstand* career, claiming her as one of "the kids" of his show. In 1999 she reunited with him, working as the choreographer for his amateur talent series *Your Big Break*.[29]

As the dancers who helped *Soul Train* become a hit left the show, Cornelius had the task of replacing them with new dancers who could help keep the program's ratings and publicity high. This challenge was not easy to meet. The series had already lost some of its individuality when many of its guests and dancers gained enough mainstream appeal to perform regularly on other shows like *American Bandstand*. New dancers to become mainstays in their own right (eventually) included Jeffrey Daniel, Sharon Hill, Tyrone Swan, Jody Watley, and Asian American cast member Cheryl Song. When Christa Lee joined the Soul Train Dancers in the fall of 1975, Tyrone Proctor — a dancer from the program's early years — still appeared on the show.[30]

Soul Train began replacing some of the departed teenagers with adult professional dancers. Part of the reason for the change lay in disco's popularity. In the early 1970s, much of the music of *Soul Train* did not appear on other shows. As a result, the adolescents had more creative freedom to dance however they wanted on the show. In contrast, disco dancing had a professional image, which the slick routines of the theatrical feature film *Saturday Night Fever* (1977) solidified. Because other television series featured professional dancers moving to disco hits, *Soul Train*— one of television's first promoters of disco — could not afford to present amateurish dancing and compete effectively for viewers.

Having connections with cast members enabled new people to join the show. Often a guest of a Soul Train Dancer later became a part of the cast. Sometimes, however, complete newcomers experienced strokes of good fortune. Christa Lee, a new student at Pepperdine University in the fall of 1975, went to the *Soul Train* studio soon after having moved from New Jersey for school, and she saw regular cast member Jeffrey Daniel waiting in line for the doors to open. "I recognized him as a regular and asked him how I could get on the show," she remembered, "and he said I had to go through Chuck, I think he was the producer." As the studio doors opened, Daniels's partner Jody Watley had not yet arrived, so he turned to Lee and asked, "Can you dance?" She responded, "Of course!" He then invited her. "Well, come on. You can be my partner."[31]

Once inside the studio, Lee continued to experience good fortune. Dancing with a prominent cast member allowed her to be on the center riser with him — a privilege usually reserved for longtime cast members. Lee, in turn, was later able to have her twin sister join the cast, too. The producer was impressed by the novelty of twin dancers on *Soul Train*.[32]

Despite being new cast members instead of the original ones, the Soul Train Dancers of the middle and late 1970s became famous for dancing on the program, just like their predecessors. Christa Lee was only on the program for the first few months in the fifth syndicated season. "My twin sister and I stopped dancing," she recalled, "because my mother paid for us to go to school and not to party and get bad grades, so after [one] semester we were summoned back to [New Jersey] to continue at out local community college — BOOOOOOO!" Still, even her brief tenure earned her some fame, for people in New York and New Jersey asked her for her autograph.[33]

The recognition that the Lee sisters received as ex-Soul Train Dancers also resulted in some very exclusive perks. "We got [into] Studio 54 and became regulars there because of our popularity on the show," Christa Lee noted. Studio 54 was a New York discotheque whose patrons were wealthy, famous, or both. Wealth and fame, however, did not guarantee an entrance into the facility. Thus, the nightclub's welcoming of the Lees was no small accomplishment.[34]

On the set, however, Cornelius was the star of the show, and he began to distance himself from the dancers from the mid–1970s onward. He rarely ventured beyond his lectern, except to greet guests and Scramble participants. Moreover, the rare occasions in which he did interact with the adolescents were sometimes awkward. His cool demeanor towards them occasionally became cold. "I remember asking him a question and he did not even look at me when he answered," Lee sadly recalled. "I felt like a little peasant girl."[35]

Shortages on the set hardly helped to bridge the gap between the host and his cast. Although the show remained a success at the time, Cornelius occasionally did not have enough resources for the Soul Train Dancers. A two-piece meal from Kentucky Fried Chicken remained the standard food rations on the set. Lee, however, remembered having to quickly enter the line for the food, because "sometimes they did not have enough to go around." Thus, some dancers appeared on the show and did not receive compensation in any form, whether money or a meal.[36]

In the late 1970s, references to *Soul Train* crept into mainstream music. Three songs by two artists immortalized the show in different contexts. Johnnie Taylor's "Disco Lady," a number-one pop hit in 1976, recommended that a woman dancing to his satisfaction should appear on the program. In "I Want You," from that same year, Marvin Gaye complimented the moves of a woman he had previously seen on the show. The next year's chart-topper "Got to Give It Up, Part 1" featured him calling out to Cornelius, who had unexpectedly dropped in on his recording of the song. It was the second number-one song since "TSOP" to pay tribute to the show.

At the same time, references to drugs — especially marijuana — on the program were bolder than in previous years. In several episodes performers on the show discussed narcotics and recreational drug use in a lighthearted manner. As a result, the balance that earlier entertainers like Curtis Mayfield had tried to strike between glorification and condemnation of drugs was eliminated. Such content in family programming was daring. For example, as the situation comedy *The Brady Bunch* ended its five-year run in 1974, drugs were never mentioned by name or shown on the program. In contrast, on *Soul Train* that same year, comedian Franklyn Ajaye joked about a Spanish teacher translating her students' first names into her language. The dancers snickered when he said that she called Mary Jane "Marijuana."

Then in November 1978, Rick James boarded the "train" to sing a number that paid homage to marijuana: "Mary Jane." It was one of the first times that the music on *Soul Train* glorified recreational drug use. Moreover, he made his television debut with that episode. Thus, *Soul Train* became the first series to feature an African American entertainer who fashioned a "stoner" characterization for his act. Such figures had populated white rock music since the emergence of the music of San Francisco's counterculture in 1967. But back then, "soul" singers either crooned about love, created new dance crazes, or sang political numbers. By eleven years later, drugs had inspired R&B songs, too.

Also in November 1978, *Soul Train* aired another drug-related milestone. On the weekend following Rick James's episode, the comedy duo Cheech (Marin) and (Tommy) Chong made an appearance. Their performance was significant for several reasons. *Soul Train* rarely featured comedians who were not African American. Also, no entertainer whose act or characterization centered exclusively on drug abuse had previously appeared on the show. When the "Cheech and Chong" episode aired, the team's hit movie *Up in Smoke* had already been in theaters for over one month. The film focused on two people trying to join a rock band while maintaining their stash of marijuana. As a result, *Soul Train* was in the unique position of capitalizing on the popularity of a movie about "stoners." Indeed, the *Los Angeles Times* called Cheech and Chong "freaked-out, doped-up whackos" and proclaimed that *Up in Smoke* was "the first rock 'n' roll dope movie."[37]

On the *Soul Train* set, the "drug culture" was nothing new in 1978. For years dancers were exposed to performers whose behavior suggested use, if not abuse, of narcotics. When Christa Lee was on the show in 1975, she did not notice drug use among the Soul Train Dancers, who were nonplussed by the behavior of some artists. However, because Cornelius only booked acts that had appeal with urban audiences, the Soul Train Dancers of 1978 would have been familiar with the drug culture-related material of Cheech and Chong. Cheech and Chong put on an act and received calculated laughs.[38]

Soul Train's exploitation of Cheech and Chong — characters epitomizing "sex, drugs, and rock 'n' roll" — demonstrated new standards in family entertainment and served as a latter-day symbol of the same counterculture from which Cornelius' weekly call for "love, peace, and soul" had derived. The program's drug references were part of a trend in television entertainment that predated the show by a few years. In the late 1960s, variety shows *The Smothers Brothers Comedy Hour* and *Rowan & Martin's Laugh-In* pioneered jokes about narcotics, and network censors unfamiliar with the vernacular of the drug culture unwittingly allowed the jokes. By 1973 both series were off the air, and variety programs aimed specifically at young audiences were few and far between. However, two years later, the show *Saturday Night Live* premiered, and its repertory company not only told drug jokes but also demonstrated the injecting of heroin or the snorting of cocaine in broad, exaggerated manners. By 1978 even the Middle American television personality Johnny Carson was quipping about Quaaludes and marijuana in monologues as host of *The Tonight Show. Soul Train* caught Cheech and Chong as new social permissiveness about drug-related discourse allowed the duo to emerge "out of the smoke-filled closet," according to the *Los Angeles Times.*[39]

The 1978–79 season was a major year of movie promotion for *Soul Train.* Cornelius promoted two more feature films — which, despite being musicals, were completely different from one another. Frankie Valli, a white singer recently separated from his group the Four Seasons, scored a hit with the theme to the film *Grease* and performed it on the show. The movie, although capitalizing on disco's popularity with the theme, did not star any African American characters as leads. In contrast, another episode of *Soul Train* featured a performance by Diana Ross and Michael Jackson from *The Wiz*— the all-black Broadway musical adapted into a movie by Motown. By helping Hollywood soundtracks become hits and working with movie studios in securing film clips, Cornelius gained power in the film industry.

That season of movie promotion, however, was uncharacteristic of *Soul Train* in the late 1970s. After 1974 *Soul Train* had fewer movies to promote through its musical guests. Before the 1978–79 season, *Soul Train* had not promoted movie music since Aretha Franklin sang "Sparkle" from the film of the same name in November 1976. The popularity of blaxploitation movies had sunk. Hollywood made fewer films featuring violent African American detectives or "soul" concerts, and some of those pictures did not receive exposure on *Soul Train.* Motown acts did not appear on the show to perform songs from movies produced by the label; Diana Ross sang nothing from *Mahogany* on the program, and none of the artists from the disco film *Thank God It's Friday* appeared. Meanwhile, few movies with all-white or integrated casts had songs by African Americans in soundtracks.

Nevertheless, booking Cheech and Chong and Frankie Valli were major accomplishments, and Cornelius capitalized on his growing power in Hollywood and on *Soul Train*'s crossover appeal by surrounding himself with rock-and-roll stars instead of movie-soundtrack soul singers. In October 1979 the *New York Times* announced that he would appear in the theatrical feature film *Roadie*, which focuses on a young white man's experiences as an electrician for a rock music tour. Instead of making a cameo appearance, as in *Cleopatra Jones*, Cornelius played a character named "Mohammed Johnson." His co-stars included rock musicians Blondie, Alice Cooper and Meat Loaf, as well as veteran comedian Art Carney of the classic television series *The Honeymooners* (1955–71). Ironically, Cornelius also starred in the movie with Gailard Sartain of *Hee Haw*—a television series Cornelius had derisively mentioned as an example of mismatched syndicated programming in urban markets.[40]

Still, *Soul Train* catered primarily to urban markets, and as late as 1979, Cornelius felt compelled to explain some of his programming choices. When Gino Vannelli returned that year, Cornelius proudly crowed that the singer with the top-ten hit "Stop" had made his television debut on *Soul Train* back in 1975. The host, however, failed to mention that Vannelli had desegregated the show with that episode. In addition, when interviewing Vannelli after the first performance of his return episode, Cornelius specifically noted that the singer had multiracial appeal at his concerts and asked for his opinion on the reasons for his diverse following. Vannelli responded by listing African American jazz and rock-and-roll artists who had influenced his music.

Not every song from a white artist received such scrutiny from Cornelius. In the same episode as Vannelli's return, veteran hard rocker Rod Stewart's hit "Da Ya Think I'm Sexy" played during the "Soul Train Scramble" segment. Cornelius did not explain why he chose to broadcast that song. To be sure, Stewart's song was a disco tune that sounded like countless others from both black and white artists. In contrast, Vannelli's "Stop" was a ballad and, therefore, not part of a genre affiliated primarily with African Americans.

The "glitter soul" that Labelle had promoted in the mid–1970s had transformed into "galactic soul" by the late 1970s. An increasing number of acts wore costumes reminiscent of spacesuits from science-fiction movies. The electric synthesizer became a more frequent prop on stage. Even the opening cartoon sequence boasted a "space" theme. No longer chugging through a city, the animated locomotive now circled planet Earth among the stars in space. The imagery on the stage and in the cartoon reflected the growing presence of space in American entertainment, most notably in the television series *Space: 1999* and the motion picture *Star Wars*.

Cable television provided a boost to *Soul Train* as the 1970s ended. WGN Channel 9 in Chicago became a regional cable station. In the fall of 1977,

Soul Train started airing on WGN after having had WBBM Channel 2 as its syndicated Chicago home for the previous six years. The distribution system on syndication made WGN's cable broadcasts of *Soul Train* important. Different cities across the country continued to broadcast different episodes each week. In contrast, WGN transmitted the same episode to the various markets across the South and Midwest that carried the channel. Thus, at least in the central time zone, the show had some broadcast consistency.

Despite all the changes on *Soul Train* from 1975 to 1979, the show still inspired people. African American symphony orchestra conductor James Frazier, Jr. taught urban schoolchildren the similarities that symphonies had with R&B music like the *Soul Train* theme. Other exploiters of the series were not as altruistic. Some people still tried to make money off the familiarity of the *Soul Train* name. In 1979 the stage show "French Feelings" at New York's Drake Hotel consisted of the music of the "soul band" named Soul Train Bleu.[41]

Soul Train also continued to provide riveting television. The 1979–80 season opener — a tribute to Minnie Riperton — differed from other episodes featuring only one performer, for Riperton had died of cancer on July 12, 1979. One of the most touching and poignant episodes of the series, the tribute featured an interview with singer Stevie Wonder, who worked on an album of hers. When fellow guest Wintley Phipps sang two tributes to Riperton, the Soul Train Dancers did not dance. The "Soul Train" sign's light was turned off for his first song, and the director superimposed photographs of Riperton over Phipps's other performance. The show had no "Soul Train Line" segment, but one of the show's couples performed a routine in Riperton's memory. At one point Cornelius himself seemed to forget that she had passed away; introducing a song from her last album, he said, "This is one she *calls*, 'I'm a Woman.'"

In addition, the Riperton tribute led to some unprecedented cooperation between Cornelius and his competition. Mike Douglas allowed *Soul Train* to rebroadcast two of her performances from his daytime talk show. Over the past few years, Cornelius and Douglas had competed for top-name R&B guests; the Supremes and the Jackson Five were among the artists appearing on both shows. For the tribute, however, Cornelius acknowledged the source of the clips when introducing them, and he played them without cutting away to the dancers on his own program.

As *Soul Train* departed the 1970s for the 1980s, the series was at a crossroads. It no longer had a consistent identity after having lost its collective foundation of both the all-black format and "soul" music. Cornelius began the new decade with the challenge of integrating romantic ballads, funk, and disco into each episode in a balanced manner. Even more difficult obstacles awaited him as the 1980s progressed, some of which threatened the survival of not only the show but also the producer himself.

6

"Still the Hippest Trip"

Soul Train *Loses Preeminence and Grows Older*

In 1980 *Soul Train* began its second decade on a very high note. The series continued to feature R&B acts with successful crossover singles despite the disco backlash of the previous year. The show still attracted Hollywood stars for cameos; actresses Kim Fields of the NBC situation comedy *The Facts of Life* (1979–88) and Jayne Kennedy of the same network's "human interest" show *Speak Up, America* (1980) made appearances in the 1980–81 season. The program also boasted a new theme song by The Whispers, which Cornelius used for three years — the longest tenure for a theme since King Curtis' "Hot Potatoes."

The same year, Cornelius himself enjoyed success in the entertainment industry outside of *Soul Train*. In June, United Artists released the movie *Roadie* to theaters. Reviewers were kind to the film. *Variety* stated that Cornelius "slickly embodied" his character, concert promoter Mohammed Johnson. The *Los Angeles Times* identified actors by name instead of the characters they played; it referred to the tour the title-character joined as "Don Cornelius' Rock 'n' Roll Circus." The critics accepted his portrayal of a character involved in "white" rock music — quite an accomplishment, because to television audiences he still embodied "soul," not "rock."[1]

Cornelius understood the limitations of his character's appeal and, therefore, did not exploit the movie on his television series. *Roadie*, after all, was a different kind of movie than *Cleopatra Jones*, which was a film marketed to African American audiences. In that movie Cornelius played himself, and he promoted the film by allowing an R&B singer to perform a song from it on *Soul Train*. In contrast, his program did not feature Meat Loaf, Alice Cooper, Blondie or any other musical act from the "rock 'n' roll movie" as guest stars. Pop music had effectively become re-segregated. Whereas only five years earlier, three white acts boarded the "train," only Teena Marie crossed the musical color line onto *Soul Train* in the 1980–81 season.

Cornelius did promote movies as the decade began — just not his own. Moreover, he booked acts that had worked in major motion picture releases, not just those targeted to urban demographics. In 1980, Irene Cara sang the theme to her movie *Fame*. The film presented an ethnically diverse group of students pursuing stardom while training at the New York High School of the Performing Arts. *Soul Train*'s promotion of the movie was ironic, considering that high school students once performed on the television show and sought fame from television exposure.

Another large-budget movie *Soul Train* promoted did not fare as well as *Fame*. In 1980 the Village People performed the theme to their movie *Can't Stop the Music*. The members starred as themselves — stereotypical male icons — and fictitiously depicted their rise to fame; the other leading characters were white. Few people saw the film. It was released one year after Chicago's "Disco Sucks" rally, and the movie did not have major stars or well-respected actors supporting the group. The studio had merely counted on disco music and the Village People to draw the audiences.

Can't Stop the Music was a poor fit for *Soul Train* despite the disco music they shared in common. *Soul Train* presented African Americans dancing to their own music in a venue created and maintained by an African American. On the other hand, *Can't Stop the Music* only focused on the importance of white people in the formation of one of disco's most successful acts. Moreover, the movie was a throwback to films made before the 1960s, in which African American musicians played music while isolated from white people listening or dancing to the music. In addition to the racial segregation, the older movies and *Can't Stop the Music* also made African Americans sexless by neglecting to give them romantic interests.

As disco waned, Cornelius started the decade by promoting rap music — a genre in its commercial infancy. In the 1980–81 season, both Kurtis Blow and the Sugarhill Gang performed raps in their own episodes. The latter act had more mainstream success with "Rapper's Delight," which became a top-forty hit. Despite the genre's growing popularity, its lack of commercial potential at the start of the 1980s meant few invitations for rappers to appear on *Soul Train*. Before 1985, no more than three rap groups went on the show per season.

One person benefiting significantly from *Soul Train* in 1980 was Dick Griffey. His S.O.L.A.R. record label experienced such a phenomenal year of hits that the *New York Times* dubbed it "the Motown of the 80's." The label was churning out hit after hit, as Motown had done in the 1960s, and Griffey borrowed such practices from Motown boss Berry Gordy as promoting artists as "family oriented" and packaging acts for national tours. The acts still promoted their material, written primarily by Leon Sylvers of R&B family group the Sylvers, on Cornelius' show. As of March 1980, The Whispers had a top-ten album, an R&B chart-topping number, and a mainstream hit song. Shalamar also saw its song "The Second Time Around" top the R&B charts and cross over to pop. That same month five of the label's eight acts — The Whispers, Shalamar, Lakeside, Dynasty, and Vaughn West — took their collective tour "The Solar Galaxy of Stars" to New York.[2]

Cornelius astutely capitalized on Griffey's success by frequently booking the label's acts as guests throughout the 1980s. The label did not maintain its high level of success as the decade progressed. *Soul Train*, however, gave some of the artists the opportunity for a hit song by performing on the show. In April 1981 an episode featuring only guests from the S.O.L.A.R. label aired. The biggest crossover hits came from the label's oldest groups. Shalamar scored with "Dead Giveaway" in 1983 and "Dancing in the Sheets" the following year, by which time ex–*Soul Train* dancers Jeffrey Daniel and Jody Watley had left the group. The Whispers triumphed later in the decade with "Rock Steady."

Many of the acts on *Soul Train* in the 1980s were fragments of former groups that had performed on the show in the previous decade. Cornelius did not exhibit partiality towards certain members of defunct groups. Both the group Shalamar and soloist Jody Watley appeared on the program late in the decade. Meanwhile, Cornelius tapped Jeffrey Daniel to host *620 Soul Train*—a British adaptation of the series that featured British R&B acts as well as clips of old *Soul Train* episodes from the United States.

In the early 1980s people not affiliated with *Soul Train* continued to capitalize upon its success. In New York the Yvon-Maye Travel Agency offered a disco train to people ringing in the year 1980. The train provided music and dancing for passengers while traveling from New York to Montreal. The agency had earlier created the Disco Soul Train. Then in 1982 owners of about twenty bars and restaurants in African American neighborhoods in Detroit developed a bar-hopping bus tour called the Soul Train Party. The organizers wanted to cash in on the sixty million dollars in estimated revenue expected from the Super Bowl, which took place in the city's Pontiac Silverdome. Just as one decade earlier Cornelius had complained about the lack of African American syndicated shows like *Soul Train*, the bar owners created the party after the Michigan Host Committee failed to involve African American establishments in its Super Bowl bar tour.[3]

The exclusion by cable network Music Television (MTV) of African American artists helped *Soul Train* remain the only show to consistently showcase African American music on television. In the first few years after MTV's debut in August 1981, the network largely aired New Wave music videos, especially British imports. Dick Clark's *American Bandstand* gravitated to the genre and largely discarded the disco artists who had sustained the show in the late 1970s. No African Americans made their debuts on that show in 1980 or 1981, and only about one-fourth of the guests during those two years were African American. "One of the things that music videos did was obviate the need for a white pop star to go and do a dance show," Don Cornelius noted. African American artists kept *Soul Train* on the air, for "black artists not only didn't have other media to turn to, they were not given decent video budgets, and for a long time ... they could not get air play."[4]

Thanks to the new cable network Black Entertainment Television, however, *Soul Train* was no longer the only game in town for exclusively catering musical television to African Americans. In 1981 the two-year-old network launched the weekday series *Video Soul*, which consisted of R&B music videos introduced by another deep-voiced African American personality — Donnie Simpson. Now, instead of waiting until Saturday to watch people dance to the most popular songs on urban radio, viewers could see the latest dances and hear the latest songs throughout the week. Also hurting *Soul Train* in terms of immediacy was that the syndicated status of the show still meant that some cities were one week behind in televising episodes seen in larger markets seven days earlier. Cornelius rectified the situation in 1985 by arranging for Tribune Entertainment to syndicate via satellite, which allowed every market carrying *Soul Train* to air the same episode.

The few African Americans whose videos played on either channel were able to either start or revitalize their careers without having to rely on *Soul Train* for television exposure. This development demonstrated that the series had begun losing its preeminence as a force in televising African American culture in the early 1980s. Michael Jackson, a frequent guest in the 1970s, stopped appearing on the show when MTV began playing videos of his songs from the *Thriller* album in 1982. Both Tina Turner and Aretha Franklin experienced successful comebacks in the mid–1980s after developing pop sounds and spiky, New Wave hairdos for their respective heavily played MTV videos.

Meanwhile, Eddie Murphy, already a television and movie star, bypassed Cornelius to MTV to launch a singing career, scoring a crossover hit with the Rick James production "Party All the Time."

Even worse for *Soul Train* was that the show lost its television monopoly of introducing the latest African American dances to viewers. Michael Jackson, who unveiled his version of the "Robot" on *Soul Train* in 1973, introduced the definitive dance of his career — the "Moonwalk" — on another program in 1983. The special telecast *Motown 25: Yesterday, Today and Forever* featured his professional reunion with his brothers, in which they sang a medley of their Motown hits. Then he started his solo performance of his hit "Billie Jean," and during the song's break he did the "Moonwalk." It was a combination of moves he had seen on television by James Brown, Sammy Davis, Fred Astaire, and — ironically — the *Soul Train* dancers.[5]

After NBC premiered *The Cosby Show* in September 1984, *Soul Train* no longer was the only place where television viewers could see African American performance on a program produced by African Americans. The show, a situation comedy produced by and starring comedian Bill Cosby, topped the Nielsen ratings from 1985 to 1990. Despite its different genre, *The Cosby Show* had some commonalities with *Soul Train*. Cosby's show was outwardly apolitical, just as Cornelius' show had become by the start of the 1980s. Both programs promoted African American music and dance, but *The Cosby Show* did so less frequently. Cosby and Cornelius are a year apart in age, but their choices in songs to publicize were strikingly different; the former featured jazz music and invited middle-aged and senior jazz artists as guests, but the latter stuck to the more contemporary R&B, rap, and occasional New Wave.

In addition, as in the 1970s, Cosby and Cornelius televised R&B in different contexts. The former continued to couch the music in humor. The fictional Huxtable family comically pantomimed old songs by Ray Charles and James Brown, and Stevie Wonder made funny noises on his synthesizer for the characters. Meanwhile, Cornelius still presented African American music in a straightforward manner. The only other television series to give R&B a non-comedic image was *Fame* (1983–87), based on the motion picture. The overwhelming ratings and press coverage of *The Cosby Show* in the 1980s demonstrated that most television viewers preferred Cosby's approach to Cornelius.[6]

All of these developments, however, paled in comparison to Cornelius' illness, which almost ended the series in its entirety. Near the middle of the 1982–83 season, he suffered from a brain tumor. In January 1983, however, he had successful brain surgery and a remarkable recovery. He was miraculously able to produce thirty-one episodes for the season. He developed a new theme song — "Soul Train's A-Comin'" — and rising solo star O'Bryan sang it. With the new theme came a slight revision of the opening sequence in order to correspond with the song's tempo, which was much slower than The Whispers' theme song for the series.

Some aspects of *Soul Train* had not drastically changed. Cornelius continued to tape four episodes during two consecutive days of every month. The tapings took place on Saturdays and Sundays. The production company offered the same lunch during every taping day. The meal of the day remained Kentucky Fried Chicken, and Shasta was the accompanying beverage. Vera Dunwoody, who appeared on the show from 1987 to 1992, said, "We used to joke that Don must be part owner in a franchise!" Dancers were free to deviate if they wanted a change from the usual offerings. Dunwoody either went to a nearby eatery during the break or brought her own lunch.[6]

Among the dancers a hierarchy remained. As in the 1970s, the new decade of *Soul Train* featured dancers placed on stage according to skill. For the Soul Train Dancers, the center riser on the set was still the most coveted spot. Dancers on the center riser had guaranteed time on camera and in significant amounts per episode. Most of the cast had to spend time on the floor or in corners of the stage before moving upward. In addition, the center riser was where guests performed, and occasionally Cornelius permitted dancers to share the platform with the singers. One dancer, for example, appeared on the center riser with soloist Dennis Edwards, former lead singer of the Temptations, during one of his performances.

Other opportunities for extended camera time still included the Soul Train Scramble and the Line. The scramble remained the same as did the haircare prizes, but by the 1980s the director no longer superimposed a clock over the playing of the game. For some dancers the Line remained an opportunity to shine in the spotlight, as it had for countless others over the past decade. Others, however, looked at the Line in the context of the music. Lackluster moves tended to reflect the feelings of the dancers toward the choices of songs for the Line. New stars and mainstays among the Soul Train Dancers throughout the decade included Vera Dunwoody, Rosie Perez, and Cheryl Song.

The change from couples to single individuals dancing down the Line marked a major break from *Soul Train* tradition. Over the years not every couple had danced down the Line as a cohesive unit. In the show's early seasons, Damita Jo Freeman sometimes danced the "Robot," while her partner made his own moves, and Jimmy Foster's "locking" occasionally clashed with a female partner's understated shuffling. During the disco craze, close dancing was common on the Line, but in the 1980s breakdancing helped revive individual dancing. Now, the show delineated the two lines according to gender. As a result, the days of such routines as one man sliding on his stomach through a woman's open legs came to an end. On the other hand, benefiting from the freedom from partners, many individual dancers like Rosie Perez created memorable movements for the Line.

Another major change lay in the shift of the advertisements away from pan–African culture. No longer did the show exploit politically radical hairstyles like the Afro. Dancers wore their "naturals" much shorter than in the 1970s. Also, in the 1980s commercials for Johnson Products' items like Classy Curl promoted processed hairstyles. Such products allowed curls to extend beyond the shoulders. Dancers soon followed suit, foregoing the "Afro puffs" of Damita Jo Freeman for the "Jheri Curls" of Rick James.

A positive change for *Soul Train* was its greater exposure of female artists in the 1980s. Whereas no female singer appeared more than five times throughout the 1970s, three women did in the next decade. Both Stephanie Mills and Deniece Williams had already gained momentum in their careers from their appearances just before the 1970s ended. Mills landed the most *Soul Train* gigs of all the women in the 1980s — seven; Williams had six. Meanwhile, Stacy Lattisaw, who performed six times on the show between 1981 and 1990, literally grew up in front of the camera. Her debut episode aired in the month she turned fifteen years old. She was a continuation of *Soul Train*'s tradition of supporting R&B child stars like the Jackson Five and the Sylvers.

Throughout the 1980s, *Soul Train* promoted more R&B teenage acts than in the previous decade. Music producers updated the combination of "bubblegum pop" and "soul" that had served groups like the Five Stairsteps and the Jackson Five well. The new sound worked, for like the Jacksons, the new teenage artists had crossover appeal and managed to have videos aired on MTV as well as perform on *Soul Train*. The group New Edition came closest to repeating the Jackson brothers' R&B and pop chart success. Other adolescent groups of the 1980s on *Soul Train* included the sibling acts Five Star and the Jets.

Cornelius developed his own "teenage sensation" at this time — a young male singer named O'Bryan. Although the host no longer had a record label of his own, he produced O'Bryan's music for Capitol Records. Cornelius displayed a tremendous amount of faith in O'Bryan's career by allowing him to perform on *Soul Train* seven times during the 1980s; only three other acts appeared as much that decade, and no one appeared more. Moreover, Cornelius tapping O'Bryan to sing the new *Soul Train* theme was a high honor, for since 1975 only artists either developed by Cornelius or signed to his now-defunct label sang themes for the show.[7]

Another artist the host took under his wing with less success in the 1980s was California native Rosie Gaines. He discovered her singing at a club and later boasted that her voice embodied "all the great female singers of our time." On the other hand, she received much less exposure on *Soul Train* than O'Bryan — only two episodes in the entire decade. Cornelius, however, co-produced her debut album on Epic Records with her. The album *Caring* fared poorly, but the album's song "Skool-ology (Ain't No Strain)" placed at number seventy-three on *Billboard*'s "black singles" chart and was popular on the West Coast. She performed it and another single from *Caring* on the show in October 1985.[8]

Debut appearances, regardless of gender, were even more rare on *Soul Train* in the early 1980s than in any previous time in the show's history. Two or three weeks often passed between episodes featuring new guest stars, and episodes with only new guests were nearly nonexistent. To an extent, the program's increased reliance on proven talent reflected the sustained success the artists achieved in their music careers. Such reliance, however, made the show less willing to introduce new sounds to viewers — a development which clashed with the show's slogan as "the hippest trip in America." Still, with *American Bandstand* having even less use for new R&B talent at the time, *Soul Train* was effectively the only opportunity for new artists to have any nationwide television exposure.

When the Chicago-based company Tribune Entertainment took over the syndication of *Soul Train* in 1985, the show took more risks with its guest roster. More episodes featured new artists, and an increasing number of episodes had only new guests. Such experimentation had rarely taken place since the early years of syndication. The first two episodes of the 1985–86 season consisted of debuts; Go-West and Rosie Gaines appeared in the season premiere, and Sheila E. and Five Star boarded the "train" the following week.

Soul Train and Tribune developed a mutually beneficial relationship. The show now had better distribution throughout the nation. The distributor, meanwhile, had an established, hip, successful series that attracted teenage and young adult audiences. At the time Tribune's only other offering for syndication was *At the Movies* (1982–90), in which Chicago movie critics Gene Siskel and Roger Ebert reviewed films. They provided thoughtful critiques, witty banter, and a catchy "thumb's up/down" ratings system. Such content, however, did not lead to high ratings with young viewers.

By the mid–1980s, Cornelius had begun producing some of *Soul Train*'s most musically eclectic episodes. American pop music was still largely segregated, with few African American acts appearing on MTV and *American Bandstand*. Meanwhile, *Soul Train*'s guest roster became more integrated, for urban radio listeners had more diverse taste than in previous years. The series now offered a mixed bag of genres: ballads, synthesizer-laden disco, rap, and even New Wave. In 1985 the show featured New Wave group Spandau Ballet and Motown stalwarts the Four Tops in one episode. Later that year, rap group UTFO appeared in the same telecast as white novelty singer Rick Dees, whose songs that day were "Eat My Shorts" and "Get Nekked."

Cornelius occasionally added gospel music to the mix at this time. Moreover, the popularity of gospel on urban radio brought religious figures back to *Soul Train* in a different manner than in the show's early years one decade before. When the series was on WCIU, politically active African American clergymen such as Father George Clements and the Rev. Jesse Jackson were occasional guests. For the national program, however, Cornelius curtailed political rhetoric from the mid–1970s onward. The ministers appearing on the syndicated show in the 1980s did not board the "train" to preach but rather to sing or direct their choirs. When Andrae Crouch performed, he was at the peak of his mainstream television exposure. During the early 1980s he sang not only on *Soul Train* but also the variety series *Saturday Night Live* (1975–present) and the situation comedy *Laverne & Shirley* (1976–83). The Rev. James Cleveland gave his final national television performance in 1987 on *Soul Train*, accompanied by the Cleveland Singers.

Meanwhile, Cornelius made fewer musical contributions to his series. In 1984, arranger Bruce W. Miller stopped working with him after having collaborated on a horn session for a song by O'Bryan. Miller had developed music for the *Soul Train* producer for the past eight years and had arranged theme songs for the series. About his departure from the *Soul Train* staff, he simply said, "I felt it was time for me to move on." He was not easily replaced. Although the show featured at least four different themes during Miller's tenure, Cornelius did not change the theme again until three years after Miller had left. In addition, the new theme for the 1987–88 season was an updated version of the venerable "TSOP," which Cornelius did not write. It remained the theme for six seasons, which, added to the two years of the original "TSOP," gave the tune the longest tenure for a theme of the series.[9]

Soul Train, despite its musical disjointedness, was still consistent in presenting unique African American dances. The show experienced a mini-revival in the mid–1980s because of the short-lived mainstream dance craze of breakdancing. The show did not generate new buzz in the press by exploiting the trend through its dancers. Still, the program at least returned to its roots by showing dance moves that other television series did not.

Soul Train not only introduced breakdancing but also helped inspire it. The trend began in the early 1970s in the South Bronx. Poor African Americans and Puerto Ricans there challenged each other through dance in the streets and at house parties. They appropriated moves they had seen in martial arts feature films and from the *Soul Train* dancers on television. The competitors used the breaks in songs (where instrumentation replaces singing) to try to outdo each other's moves.[10]

Soul Train welcomed more rappers in the wake of breakdancing's crossover success. In 1983 a breakdance scene highlighted the movie *Flashdance*, and the following year two movies about breakdancing — *Breakin'* and *Beat Street* — were released to theaters. Breakdancer Adolfo "Shabba-Doo" Quinones starred in *Breakin'* and became one of *Soul Train*'s first Hollywood star alumni since Damita Jo Freeman, although Quinones appeared on *Soul Train* with Freeman and left before she did. Meanwhile, in the 1984–85 season, rap groups the Fat Boys and Whodini made appearances. The next season, *Soul Train* promoted the rap musical movie *Krush Groove* by booking two acts from the film for different episodes. Although neither act — Sheila E. and New Edition — performed rap, the exploitation of the film through their appearances on *Soul Train* rivaled any exposure of the movie elsewhere in television, except perhaps for on BET.

Soul Train's dance renaissance also led to some academic writers taking notice of the durable hold that *Soul Train*'s dancers had on young viewers. Adolescents continued to look to the show in order to follow trends in music and fashion. Teenagers still used the Soul Train Line for parties. An article in the Spring 1983 issue of the scholarly periodical *Dance Research Journal* noted that in urban black West Philadelphia, young children and teenagers considered *Soul Train* their favorite program. For them it was an "affirmation of Afro-American identity in the performing arts and the popular media." They perceived the dancers on television as people who had "made it" in show business. And as far as the dances were concerned, "if it looks good on *Soul Train*, it's cool by these kids' standards," according to the article.[11]

The breakdancing craze allowed *Soul Train*'s serious images of African American dance to divert some attention from the show's comical counterparts. Thanks to the breakdancing movies of the 1980s, non-comedic contexts of urban dance won mainstream appeal. Even on *American Bandstand*, the dancers attempted the complicated moves. In addition, the relatively new series *Solid Gold* (1980–88) consisted of a dance troupe's choreography to popular recordings.

Cornelius also cashed in on the dance craze beyond the walls of the studio. *Soul Train* was hip enough to attract corporations seeking programs to sponsor in exchange for airtime of innovative musical commercials. In 1984 the shoe company Pony Sport announced that it had produced a half-minute advertisement that featured children breakdancing in a "ghetto" setting. The agency promoting the commercial called it "a *West Side Story* for the 80's." Pony arranged for the advertisement to air on the major U.S. television networks, the cable channels ESPN and MTV, and the dance shows *Solid Gold*, *Dance Fever*, and *Soul Train*. As a result, Cornelius was in the odd position of selling airtime to a commercial whose dance moves had roots in the dances of his program.[12]

The success of *Soul Train* allowed Cornelius to purchase a significant part of Hollywood history. In late 1985 he bought the former Mack Sennett Studio for over $1 million, with the intention of renovating it for *Soul Train* and renaming the building DCP Television and Film Centre. Sennett, a filmmaker, had made silent-film stars out of the Keystone Kops and Roscoe "Fatty" Arbuckle at the studio over half a century earlier, and before Sennett's tenure Charlie Chaplin had worked on movies there. Sennett sold the facility in 1932, and ownership transferred several times until Cornelius' purchase. The new owner planned for the building to have control booths, a videotape production area, a sound stage, and a lounge and dressing room for guest stars, as well as offices and storage space.[13]

For Cornelius the building showed potential although it was large and vacant inside, covered with graffiti outside, and surrounded by weeds. He toured the building with Anthony Sabatino, the executive in charge of production of *Soul Train*, before buying it. Sabatino said that his boss initially looked unimpressed. "Oh my God, he thinks I'm crazy," the employee thought to himself.[14]

Then Cornelius grew more animated about the facility and told Sabatino,

"It would be a great fixer-upper." He proceeded to buy it and made front-page news in the *Los Angeles Times* for doing so. African Americans rarely bought old Hollywood studios, regardless of their condition. More notable was the host's intention to use the facilities to produce entertainment for young urban African Americans — a far cry from the 1910s, when had Sennett made films starring a broad African American slave caricature named Rastus.[15]

Over eighteen months after the purchase, however, the host made the front page of the *Los Angeles Times* for news — bad news — about the building. He sold it to Public Storage, Inc. for an undisclosed amount in June 1987. Cornelius had predicted that he could renovate the studio in half a year, but after one year and a half, it was still vacant, swallowed by weeds and graffiti. The host had failed to line up the financing to work on the "fixer-upper."[16]

The sale of the building to Public Storage infuriated at least one Californian for poor stewardship of famous movie landmarks in Los Angeles. A letter to the editor lamented that Public Storage had considered razing the building and constructing a new one in place of the old one. To him, such action threatened to dishonor pioneering filmmakers of the studio such as D.W. Griffith, Walt Disney, and Chaplin. "Have we so forgotten our roots? Are we so blindly avaricious that we can only think of more storage bins and mini-malls? No wonder the quality of life in Los Angeles continues to diminish," the writer criticized. "This city's motto should be 'Anything for a Buck.'"[17]

Despite the setback, *Soul Train* continued to receive positive press coverage as new African American dances emerged. When the group Experience Unlimited successfully launched "Da Butt" in 1988 through Spike Lee's movie *School Daze*, the newspaper *USA Today* called on Cornelius as an authority in dance promotion to comment. "Artists and record companies look for the opportunity to start a dance craze with a record. That usually doesn't happen," he explained. "If there aren't specific steps that give you the feeling you're doing something unusual, there doesn't seem to be any incentive to do the dance. Da Butt had the strongest promotional tool — film." The reporters were wise in seeking Cornelius' feedback, for after nearly two decades of promoting music through television, he certainly knew about the power of film in starting trends.[18]

The choice of interviewing Cornelius about "Da Butt" also had considerable irony. Just as Motown launched the "Moonwalk" on its own program, Experience Unlimited did not seek out *Soul Train* as the forum to introduce

"Da Butt." Thus, Cornelius was in the odd position of commenting on an African American dance his show did not start; that would have been unthinkable seven or eight years earlier. Moreover, not since the one-reel live-action musical films of the 1940s had African Americans gone to the movies in order to see new, trend-setting dances. Thus, the medium of television was losing influence to the movie industry in launching black dance crazes.

In terms of dance promotion, *Soul Train* itself received mixed reviews in 1988. A critic for the *Chicago Sun-Times* called the series "easily the most sophisticated dance show on television." Despite the largely segregated state of pop music that year, the article noted, "Undyingly a black show since its creation, it has attained crossover popularity." The journalist further recommended, "If you really want to learn how to dance, this is the place to go." *USA Today* agreed but cast doubt on the program's hip quality: "*Soul Train* is a good place to catch L.A. dance styles, although some complain that the show's taping is sometimes months behind."[19]

In the late 1980s, the television industry started to look at *Soul Train* as a relic of the 1970s instead of "the hippest trip in America," which the show still claimed in its opening sequence week after week. The first blow came from the most unlikely of fellow Saturday morning shows—a cartoon. In 1987 an episode of *Mighty Mouse: The New Adventures* (1987–89), which aired on CBS, parodied *Soul Train* as *Soul Caboose*. The stars wore outlandish 1970s garb and danced to disco.

A few years later, a humorous takeoff of the show's Soul Train Line emerged in a white rock music video. The plot of the video "Been Caught Stealing" by the band Jane's Addiction centered on people shoplifting at a grocery store. In one scene the kleptomaniacs formed two columns, and each person danced down the aisle between them. The characters were diverse, consisting of a young blonde woman, a middle-aged cross-dresser and a senior citizen, among others. They all danced poorly, and none of them dressed like any of the current Soul Train Dancers.

The *Mighty Mouse* episode and "Been Caught Stealing" were benign, however, in contrast to the FOX network's comedy variety series *In Living Color*, which premiered in early 1990. The program poked fun at African American culture in its diverse forms, thus making *Soul Train* an easy target. The jokes on the comedy show often consisted of crude references to physical ailments and disabilities, and Cornelius' show was not spared this treatment. The June 24, 1990, episode depicted *Soul Train* as "Old Train." The sketch replicated *Soul Train*'s set. Gray-haired, wrinkled dancers shuffled around in walkers. The point made by *In Living Color*'s Keenen Ivory Wayans and company was that *Soul Train* and its host were not only durable but also had elderly demographics. Although *Soul Train* had modernized its set and theme song in the late 1980s and regularly played the latest R&B music videos, the program could not hide its age, the ages of the cast or the timeworn familiarity of its formula. Wayans had experience from which to draw for his parody of the series, for the comedian had appeared as a guest on *Soul Train* in the previous year.

Wayans' spoof differed from the others in that it made more fun of the stars of *Soul Train* than of the "camp" value of the Line and the disco-era fashions of the show's early years. The sketch was typical for *In Living Color*, which blended exaggerated characterizations with a small amount of slapstick. The comedian's portrayal of Cornelius was especially devastating. He gave the host grayer hair and slower speech than the *Soul Train* host actually had. In addition, Wayans-as-Cornelius forgot his lines and mangled words. The comedic climax of the sketch was the phony Cornelius' collapse and revitalization with a defibrillator as "Old Train" was still taping. On the other hand, the sketch validated Cornelius' stardom, for *In Living Color* did not make fun of unknown figures.

In Living Color, ironically, was a descendant of sorts from *Soul Train*. Long before FOX's show, Cornelius had provided hip African American comedians a forum through his series. Richard Pryor's album *That Nigger's Crazy*, which came from a performance at Cornelius' nightclub, addressed social and political topics that *In Living Color* later covered. And long before the "Fly Girls" dance troupe strutted across *In Living Color* to hip-hop beats, *Soul Train* had introduced African American dance to television audiences.

Meanwhile, MTV began to compete seriously with *Soul Train* in televising African American music and dance. In 1988 the network launched the series *Yo! MTV Raps*. It initially ran only on Saturdays but soon expanded to weekdays as well. One year later MTV premiered a new dance show — *Club MTV*. It was similar to *Soul Train* but featured a nightclub setting.

All of these changes signaled the end of Cornelius' most durable competition. In October 1987 *American Bandstand* aired on ABC for the final time. That same fall Dick Clark took the show to syndication but was no competition for *Soul Train*, especially because both series catered to different audiences by this time. With the New Wave craze having passed, the programs no longer aired the same kind of music. Clark's program now featured mostly "adult contemporary" white musical guests like Laura Brannigan, in contrast to Cornelius' urban radio performers. *American Bandstand* aired for a single season in syndication and then for five months in 1989 on the USA cable network before ending for good.[20]

The segregation of the music industry, which had ensured the success of *American Bandstand* for so long, now worked to Cornelius' advantage. Because television hosts did not seek African American musical guests as often as they did white artists, Cornelius did not have to deal with insufferable musicians arguing about money. He kept the budget low on his show by paying his R&B guests a standard wage or "scale"—something Clark could not do with the more popular white artists. As a result, while *Soul Train* still attracted premiere R&B acts, MTV's higher budget for rock and pop acts forced *American Bandstand* into the "adult contemporary" category, which received considerably less exposure on the youth-oriented MTV.[21]

When the music video industry welcomed more R&B acts, *Soul Train* dancers significantly benefited. Having previously appeared on television, they did not need to be told to dance when the red light beamed on the camera, and they knew which moves worked well with specific camera angles. As a result, in the 1980s casting directors for videos started coming to the *Soul Train* set and, with Cornelius' permission, scouted for volunteers for video work. Vera Dunwoody, who did both the show and some video performances, noted, "Most of the [video] work was not done for pay but rather for portfolios for the dancers."[22]

Soul Train dancers enjoyed other perks besides a fuller curriculum vita. They experienced busier social lives. Dunwoody explained, "We were sought out for various clubs around LA. We were given VIP passes to Club Paradise, Club 24, Carlos & Charlies, etc. and often free drinks just to show up." Dancing on *Soul Train* remained a symbol of status in the late 1980s, and nightclubs gave the program's cast members preferential treatment to have people of stature as customers. The club managers encouraged the television dancers to wear the latest styles of clothing and to demonstrate their new moves to their fellow patrons.[23]

Makeshift photography sessions at the clubs benefited the dancers and the photographers. People offered to take Polaroid pictures of the Soul Train Dancers for five dollars per photograph. The dancers used the pictures to prove that they attended a hip establishment; the club's name usually appeared in the background. The Polaroids were especially important, because Cornelius did not allow his cast members to take pictures of themselves on the set of *Soul Train*.[24]

By the 1990s the press joined the television industry in assessing the long history of *Soul Train*. Most newspapers glossed over the phenomenon that the show had become from 1972 to 1974. Whereas reporters had taken pains to describe how different the show was from *American Bandstand* two decades earlier, the new articles identified Cornelius as "the black Dick Clark." Cornelius himself told the press, "We've always realized that we were doing *American Bandstand*." Moreover, he emphasized the derivative aspect of *Soul Train* instead of its uniqueness: "It was really the same show. A dance show is a dance show is a dance show." Now that Clark's show had ceased production, Cornelius had nothing to lose by comparing his own program to Clark's.[25]

At times the press joined the comedy shows in making fun of *Soul Train* as an artifact of the '70s. An article that discussed the nostalgia craze for popular culture of that decade described Cornelius' appearance at great length, just as newspapers had done back then. The host, however, was now retroactively hip instead of currently hip. In contrast to the 1980s, when businessmen appropriated "the slicked-back and suspendered [*sic*] Gordon Gekko" of the movie *Wall Street*, they "are now wearing sideburns, wide lapels and spinnaker-size ties that recall the sartorial style of Don Cornelius on *Soul Train*."[26]

Reporters tended, however, to revere the venerable host for having brought young urban African American culture to television when no one else had done so. They likened him to a pioneer, often mentioning his insight in tapping into an untouched demographic in television. Journalists also noted that the ratings still ensured the series' extension for years to come. And when Cornelius claimed in 1989 that the show was stronger than ever, no one questioned him. Still, the same *USA Today* article that referred to Cornelius as an authority on filmed dance referred neither to him nor his show but rather to another disco program in the headline, "Dance Fever Kicks Up Again."[27]

Soul Train's status in the media as "stuck in the '70s" had little to do with the show itself. While it had the same format of dance segments, guest segments, the Soul Train Scramble and the Soul Train Line, its set and theme song changed periodically to reflect changing tastes among young African Americans. The fashion of the dancers changed with the times. Cornelius also modified his look, having discarded the huge Afro and wide ties for more conservative apparel. Still, observers looked at the show from a context of disco, because the show had not maintained its intense crossover appeal since the disco craze ended.

Cornelius did not help matters by playing clips from earlier episodes on *Soul Train* throughout the 1980s. Starting with the 1979–80 season, several of his episodes paid hour-long tributes to artists having lengthy careers and enough "classic" performances over the years to fill sixty minutes. Then, in the new decade, non-tribute episodes often featured a single clip from the early years of the program; Cornelius dubbed this part of the show the "*Soul Train* History Book." On the one hand, the honors and retrospectives allowed artists to receive appreciation for their work after the disco crash exiled them from pop radio. On the other hand, the salutes to the entertainers gave *Soul Train* a focus on the past, which ran counter to the show's self-anointed distinction as "the hippest trip in America." While the tribute episodes usually focused on R&B artists with crossover victories, the "History Book" segments were more eclectic; one "History Book" installment reprised the Honey Cone's singing of "Want Ads" on the first syndicated episode, but another consisted of white pop singer Frankie Valli's performance of his chart-topping hit "Grease."

Nevertheless, year after year *Soul Train* remained on the air. As a show catering to an urban, African American audience with new episodes, the series was a rarity among syndicated offerings during the 1980s. The only other syndicated programs with African American leading characters or hosts in production before the latter part of the decade were the drama *Fame*, starring Debbie Allen, and the Chicago-based talk show *The Oprah Winfrey Show* (1986–present). Syndicated reruns of African American situation comedies like *That's My Mama* and *What's Happening!!* usually consisted of at most two or three seasons' worth of episodes, which meant that the rerun cycle would start again after three months of weekday airings. On the other hand, *Room 222*, despite enjoying a five-year run in the early 1970s, was too topical to have relevance among young television viewers of the 1980s. Only the durable situation comedies with standard plots such as *Sanford and Son*, *Good Times*, and *The Jeffersons* enjoyed long syndicated runs as reruns.

Then, starting in January 1989, *The Arsenio Hall Show* gave *Soul Train* significant competition in syndication. Hall's talk show provided many of the same forms of entertainment as did *Soul Train*: stand-up comedy, R&B music, and an African American host fluent in hip slang. Hall had important advantages over Cornelius. *The Arsenio Hall Show* aired on weeknights on several CBS-TV affiliates, thus giving Hall considerably more exposure than *Soul Train*. Also, Hall had the financial backing of the major movie company Paramount Pictures, which syndicated the show. As a result, Hall could afford guests that Cornelius could not. All that Hall lacked that Cornelius had was a troupe of dancers.

In January 1991, Hall competed even more intensely with *Soul Train* via his own dance show — *The Party Machine with Nia Peeples*. Like Hall's own series, *The Party Machine* boasted top-level R&B talent, thanks to Paramount's budget. The host was a young actress, who at thirty years of age was almost a quarter-century younger than *Soul Train*'s host. *The Party Machine*, however, only lasted for eight months. As a weeknight, late-night dance show, it struggled to find an audience. Hall soldiered on with his talk show, as did *Soul Train*.

Just as Hall used his clout from his show to launch another, Cornelius also started a new television series that used *Soul Train* as a foundation. On March 23, 1987, the Soul Train Music Awards made its debut. In concept, the awards had roots in *Soul Train*'s hour-long tribute episodes. In addition, the Soul Train Music Awards were Afro-centric in concept, like the pre-integration years of *Soul Train*. African Americans produced and hosted the ceremony, and the categories for awards represented African American music forms. Artists won in rhythm and blues, gospel, rap, and jazz. Cornelius promised of the ceremony, "It's not going to look like the Grammys, and it's not going to walk like the American Music Awards. It'll walk like we walk."[28]

The Soul Train Music Awards had other sources of inspiration, however, that were not African American. Like the People's Choice Awards, the Soul Train Music Awards were populist in terms of award selection. Radio programmers, music retailers, and musicians whose songs appeared on the black charts in 1986 determined who won the first annual awards. Dick Clark had set a precedent by starting the American Music Awards in 1974. Cornelius' awards gave African American artists more categories than either the American Music Awards or the Grammy Awards.[29]

The Soul Train Music Awards attracted a diverse group of personalities despite the focus on urban music. The entertainers who went on stage at various points collectively symbolized the history of *Soul Train* as of 1987. Representing Chicago, George E. Johnson of Johnson Products made an appearance. Recalling the early years of *Soul Train*, politicians such as the Rev. Benjamin Hooks and Hollywood stars like Marsha Warfield of the television series *Night Court* (1984–92) presented awards. Reflecting the show's racial integration, white musicians Kenny G., David Sanborn, and Billy Vera announced winners, as did white actress Emma Samms from the soap opera *Dynasty* (1981–89).

Cornelius' concern about racial problems in the music industry significantly motivated his development of the event. He noted the segregation of the music industry and stated that the racial separation predated his creation of the awards. "Blacks have been too important to be just a part of mainstream awards shows," he declared. "They needed their own party." Ironically, at that year's Grammy awards, two African American entertainers won awards in categories besides the usual R&B and jazz. Jody Watley, newly divorced from Shalamar, won the New Artist prize, and Whitney Houston received the Pop Female Vocalist honor.[30]

Another motivation for the Soul Train Music Awards had to do simply with keeping the *Soul Train* franchise visible to the public. By the late 1980s, the dance show had lost some ground to MTV and BET in attracting viewers with new dances and R&B songs. Cornelius theorized that one way to revitalize *Soul Train* was to create another telecast that prominently displayed the name of the dance program. "I think the show will help introduce people to, or remind them of, the weekly show," he predicted before admitting, "A lot of people are not aware that we are still on the air."[31]

The awards were an instant success for Cornelius. The host received press coverage for the ceremony to a degree he had not experienced since the mid–1970s. In fact, the Soul Train Music Awards overshadowed *Soul Train* as critics offered positive reviews of the ceremony. Few critics bothered to compare the awards telecast with the weekly series. One observer praised the festivities: "This was an understated, tasteful program from start to finish, and if it lacked the kind of strobe-lit, artificial hysteria of the Grammys and American Music Awards, it put the spotlight back where it belongs, on the singers and their songs." Thus, the Soul Train Music Awards provided an alternative not merely as an African American awards show but also as a television ceremony of classy quality.[32]

Famous *Soul Train* alumni also began to receive more press attention than the show that had started their careers. As the Soul Train Music Awards won rave reviews, journalists increasingly referred to *Soul Train* because of its connection to new pop music stars. Jermaine Stewart, a dancer on the WCIU show who later worked with Shalamar, scored a hit with the song "We Don't Have to Take Our Clothes Off." Meanwhile, Jody Watley, another ex-dancer and alumnus of Shalamar, experienced solo success with the songs "Looking for a New Love," "Don't You Want Me," and "Some Kind of Lover." In several articles and interviews, reporters mentioned the artists' earlier appearances on *Soul Train*. Ironically, the program had not received that much coverage for influencing pop music since Shalamar's peak in the early 1980s.

Watley's final years in Shalamar had been unhappy. Her position in the group had not evolved after seven years, for S.O.L.A.R. still relegated her to singing backup and dancing at the time of her departure from the band in 1983. She sang lead on only two songs, neither of which the label released as a single. The label also refused her requests to write songs. Overlooking her talents demonstrated that label founder Dick Griffey took ex-partner Cornelius' comment that "only the look matters" to heart.[33]

Frustrated, Watley hired a lawyer to negotiate a settlement that freed her from the group. Lead singer Howard Hewett sympathized with her plight. "I always felt that Jody was a unique talent with a special voice that deserved to be exploited more," he recalled. Ironically, the last album in which she appeared as a member of Shalamar was titled *The Look*.[34]

A sojourn away from the West Coast enabled her to start her solo career. She temporarily left the music business, starting a family and living in London immediately after having quit Shalamar. Within a year, however, she had begun writing songs for receptive artists. Before relocating to Los Angeles to start her solo career in earnest, she left her biggest mark in Britain's music industry by singing in Band Aid's humanitarian hit number "Do They Know It's Christmas?"[35]

More success stories besides Stewart's and Watley's followed but not exclusively in the music industry. By the 1990s former *Soul Train* dancers had also carved out careers in Hollywood. Some of their early jobs still had to do with dancing or R&B music or both. Vivica Fox starred in NBC's 1992–93 situation comedy *Out All Night*, in which Patti LaBelle played the owner of an R&B nightclub. Each episode featured a performance by a guest musician or group, not unlike *Soul Train*. Meanwhile, Rosie Perez evolved from *Soul Train* dancer to *In Living Color* choreographer — ironically on staff during production of the "Old Train" sketch — to movie actress in the comedy films *White Men Can't Jump* and *It Could Happen to You*. Her coworker on *In Living Color* — director Terri McCoy (announcer Sid McCoy's daughter) — had also worked with her on *Soul Train* but as an assistant director instead of a dancer.

For most of the Soul Train Dancers, the show did not serve as a stepping stone to stardom. Dancers had a difficult time starting successful careers in entertainment after *Soul Train*. Some of them were not star-struck at the appearances of guest stars, because the dancers themselves sought stardom, too. For some members of the show's cast, their status as "Soul Train Dancer" proved a hindrance to finding work outside of televised music. They became, in effect, typecast. In order to have more opportunities for dramatic work, they had to choose to leave behind *Soul Train* and music videos. Even then, many of the show's stars never found fame after years of trying.

By this time *Soul Train*'s reputation as a star-making series had fundamentally changed the character of the show. The program had come a long way from its first few seasons of Afro-ed adolescents in casual clothes. When Vera Dunwoody appeared on the show in the late 1980s and early 1990s, most of the Soul Train Dancers were professionals and over twenty-five years old. She herself first danced on an episode at age thirty. Moreover, the mandatory wardrobe became more gender-specific and sexualized, in contrast to the program's early years of both women and men wearing pants, sneakers, T-shirts and other general apparel. During this period of the show, the staff mandated that women wear high heels, skirts or dresses, and nylons. In a possible strike at the ascendancy of hip-hop culture, baggy clothes of any kind were banned. The staff also prohibited denim clothes, which many dancers had worn before the late 1980s.[36]

The high heels made for painful taping sessions for the female dancers. By this time, each day of filming lasted between twelve and fourteen hours. When Dunwoody first started dancing on the show, she noticed that fellow dancer Cheryl Song walked around in slippers during breaks between songs. As Dunwoody's long day in heels continued, she realized the ingenuity of Song's choice of apparel. Mercifully, in the 1980s, *Soul Train* started showing music videos in episodes, which meant shorter taping days for the dancers.[37]

In addition to the pain caused by the mandatory high heels, *Soul Train* had a dance coordinator who inflicted pain on the Soul Train Dancers as a means of discipline. She was in charge of making certain that the dancers followed Cornelius' orders and that they behaved appropriately for filming sessions. She sometimes resorted to violence to keep the dancers in line. If dancers were caught chewing gum on the set, she would hit them.[38]

Another of the coordinators also contributed to the increasingly sexualized appearances of the female dancers — or, in some cases, tried to do so. The coordinator suggested that they wear shorter skirts and lower blouses. Dancer Vera Dunwoody resisted the changes, however, because she was not seeking attention for herself in that manner. In addition, she did not need to use the show as a launching pad for an entertainment career. She had already found work as a college professor for six years when she first boarded the "train."[39]

The increased sexual content of *Soul Train* demonstrated the show's diminished status. When the series was in its prime, it could rely on the novelty of African American dance crazes and music on television to attract viewers. By the end of the 1980s, however, the novelty had worn thin, and Cornelius had already used old clips, new cartoons, and revamped sets to keep his audience. The clothing of the women had nothing to do with the quality of the music or dances; the wardrobe change addressed style instead of substance.

Eric Casem, one of the program's coordinators, admitted as much when he acknowledged that he did not seek great dancers for the show but rather stylish ones. "I'm looking for showmanship, appearance, dance ability and charisma," he noted after revealing, "I can't expect everyone to be an A-plus dancer." He considered any complaints about sexual content a matter of opinion. "I think if they were violating any principles here for family viewing, we would know about it," he said before rationalizing, "but glamour being part of the format is part of our mystique." His work on the show reflected his boss Cornelius' comment concerning Jody Watley's singing: "Only the look matters."[40]

The new dress code, however, also marked the peak in the program's evolving imagery of African American sexuality. At first the show simply featured romance ballads and couples engaged in close dancing. Then, songs from Barry White and Sylvia contained more explicit lyrics and sensual vocal sounds. Soon, guests like Labelle began dressing in overtly sexual fashions, which transferred the show's sexuality from musical to visual. The only people remaining to demonstrate sexuality on the program besides the guests were the host and his cast, and the host opted for the female cast to be the next exploiters of sexuality.

The new direction of *Soul Train* partially resulted from Cornelius' delegation of some responsibilities for the series to Casem, a longtime employee of Don Cornelius Productions. In 1980 Casem had begun work on the show as a dancer, but rose in the ranks over time. Later in the 1980s, as a coordinator, he recruited dance talent in the same manner as his predecessors Clinton Ghent and Ronnie Paul Johnson. Casem went to the nightclubs in Los Angeles to scout potential Soul Train Dancers. On the first taping day of each two-day session, he went to the line of people at the gate to the studio and chose which of them would dance on the episodes to be filmed that weekend. During tapings he decided which dancers would go down the Soul Train Line.[41]

The coordinator's sexualized look for *Soul Train* reflected his previous dance experience, in contrast to that of Ghent and Johnson. The earlier coordinators were renowned in Chicago's R&B industry for their choreography, and the most successful local groups sought the dancers' services. They brought that same professionalism to recruiting *Soul Train*'s first dancers in both Chicago and Los Angeles. Casem, on the other hand, did not have as extensive a background or as renowned a reputation in R&B. As a result, he sought different qualities in dancers than his predecessors had — most notably, sex appeal.

Casem also gave *Soul Train* a new multiethnic look. The show had not been solely African American for years. Dancers belonging to other ethnic groups, however, were few and far between. Besides Cheryl Song, very few Asian American dancers appeared on the show before the 1990s. Vera Dunwoody recalled that Casem went beyond choosing individual "token" ethnic dancers; he had a specific quota. Among female dancers especially, he allowed only a certain number of Asian Americans, Latinas, and white European Americans. He explained the show's further dismissal of Afro-centricity: "If you can dance, regardless of color, you belong on *Soul Train*."[42]

Casem's boss Don Cornelius, however, was still *Soul Train*'s biggest star. Although dancers and guests were not awestruck by each other, they held the show's host in high regard. Musical performers, when chatting with dancers, often expressed disbelief that they had actually landed a *Soul Train* gig. Vanessa Williams and other guests with families often brought their children to the set, and the youngsters also looked at Cornelius with awe. Former dancers who later returned as musical guests were humbled by his gestures of respect towards them. They felt honored that he expressed pride in their success.[43]

Cornelius' stature on *Soul Train* inadvertently caused a wedge between himself and the dancers. Their "star-struck" demeanor prohibited them from approaching him and getting acquainted with him. Consequently, the host did not have much to say to them. He became more approachable to the dancers when he facilitated Christmas parties at clubs. He arranged to have a portion of a nightclub reserved exclusively for the *Soul Train* cast, and there he conversed with dancers more openly than on the set during taping days.[44]

When Cornelius made headlines now, it was for matters having to do with the entertainment industry at large instead of merely his show. The launch of the Soul Train Music Awards and the purchase of the Sennett studio gave him positive press in the 1980s. On the other hand, the *Chicago Defender*, which rarely reported negative news about him, acknowledged his labor troubles in print. The American Federation of Television and Radio

Artists picketed *Soul Train* performances in 1989, because Cornelius did not sign a contract with the group's Chicago chapter.[45]

Meanwhile, *Soul Train's* response to the Rodney King beating showed that the series had long ceased serving as a political forum for African American leaders and musicians to motivate the youth. As racial tensions in Los Angeles heated when *Soul Train's* second decade ended, the series avoided popular urban songs that addressed the conditions. Just before the 1991–92 season ended, riots erupted in Los Angeles. The police officers in the videotaped beating of Rodney King were declared not guilty in a California court. Although rap performers such as the group N.W.A. and its former member Ice Cube offered "radio-friendly" or censored versions of their lyrical venting against the Los Angeles Police Department, songs about King and the riots did not get airplay on *Soul Train* throughout the 1992–93 season. When the debut of that season aired in September 1992, the guest artists — Al B. Sure!, Tyler Collins, and Father MC — sang only romance ballads. In contrast to the appearances of Los Angeles Mayor Tom Bradley and Jesse Jackson in the early 1970s, neither person nor their contemporary counterparts were anywhere to be found on the show. But competing series *Yo! MTV Raps* and *Rap City*, both of which targeted primarily teenagers and young adults, did air the videos of riot-related songs and consequently replaced *Soul Train* as the premiere television forums for artistic, Afro-centric political expression.

Thanks to competing programming, however, *Soul Train* could afford to play "safe" music. Urban radio fragmented in the early 1990s, and different television programs focused on specific fragments of African American music. As a long-running series, *Soul Train* had a multigenerational following and, thus, had to cater to family audiences. The guest roster in 1992–93 ranged from the young adolescent rap group Kris Kross to the durable R&B group the Commodores, who had formed the year before *Soul Train's* debut in Chicago. In addition, by showcasing older artists whose careers were starting to wane, the series could still accurately claim to provide exposure to entertainers shut out of television. Still, *Soul Train* was losing its cultural relevance as well as its hip quality. Even family-oriented situation comedies *The Fresh Prince of Bel-Air* (1990–96) and *A Different World* (1987–93) featured special episodes with storylines about the riots in the fall of 1992.

Soul Train's gravitation away from controversial music fit its status as a Saturday morning show. In the early 1990s, television networks began airing animated series featuring caricatures of R&B stars for the first time since *The Jackson Five* ended in 1973. Rappers instead of singers received the treatment.

Unlike *The Jackson Five*, the new cartoon programs did not last long, nor did they inspire imitative shows. ABC broadcasted *Hammerman*, a superhero version of MC Hammer for a season. NBC's *Kid 'n' Play*, starring a pair of young rappers, lasted just as long, despite the duo's established popularity from their hit motion picture *House Party*. Both acts, ironically, had appeared on *Soul Train* in the 1980s.

At least one West Coast rapper absent from *Soul Train* in the 1980s and early 1990s decided to publicly insult the show. Ice Cube's 1990 song "The Nigga You Love to Hate" declared that the program no longer had soul and that it "looked like *Bandstand*." The criticism was decidedly less humorous than that of *In Living Color* and, at times, more caustic and misogynistic. The song referred to *Soul Train*'s female dancers as "bitches" and said they looked like prostitutes. Because "gangsta rappers" were not invited on *Soul Train* and enjoyed more exposure on MTV and BET, Ice Cube had nothing to lose by lambasting Cornelius.

"The Nigga You Love to Hate" represented another aspect of *Soul Train*'s decline. Throughout the 1970s the series had inspired complimentary references from African American singers. They sang about *Soul Train* as the preeminent place for good black dancers on television. The program had always had its critics, but rarely did artists sing negative songs about other artists or celebrities. Rap music, however, had its share of battles in song among various rappers, and the songs criticized prominent African Americans as well as powerful white people. Cornelius, for all his power in the television and music industries, was not exempt from hip-hop's scrutiny.

Nevertheless, the criticism from underground urban music did not threaten *Soul Train*'s survival at all. The series continued to chug across the country. It remained a novelty as a syndicated weekly dance show showcasing African Americans. It was far from the only black-led syndicated show. In the 1992–93 season, other such programs included *The Arsenio Hall Show*, *The Oprah Winfrey Show*, and reruns of situation comedies *The Cosby Show* and *A Different World*. Cornelius, however, still stood out from the competition by consistently providing both music and dance. In addition, he still promoted Johnson Products, whose commercials rarely aired on other shows — including the few that African Americans like Cosby and Winfrey produced. As a result his show was valuable as a rare champion of African American businesses.

Record labels were among the African American enterprises benefiting from *Soul Train*. By this time, however, they needed the show as much as the show needed them. Motown — the label that had helped give *Soul Train* its start on WCIU — fell upon hard times, and Berry Gordy sold the label in 1988. Under new management Motown struggled to rebuild its roster in the midst of departures by artists and group breakups. Cornelius continued to support the label by booking its acts whether they yielded few hits (the Good Girls) or several hits (Boyz II Men).

Meanwhile, S.O.L.A.R. folded in the 1990s, after having shown such promise as "the Motown of the 80's." Nearly all the acts from the label either faded from the music industry or found another label around this time. Almost all of them stopped appearing on *Soul Train*. The Whispers were the sole exception but performed on the show much less frequently than before. They did not "board" the train at all between November 1990 and March 1995 — an unusually long gap for the group. They were, however, the only act from the program's debut syndicated season to still appear on the show in 1995.

At this time Tribune Entertainment sorely needed *Soul Train*. With the cancellation of *At the Movies*, *Soul Train* was now Tribune's longest-distributed program. Other syndicated offerings from the company included the journalist Geraldo Rivera's weekday talk show *Geraldo* (1987–98), his weekday news show *Now It Can Be Told* (1991–92), and the variety series *The Apollo Comedy Hour* (1992–95). *Soul Train* outlived them all, but for a time Rivera generated more press coverage than Cornelius. The reports consisted mostly of violent incidents on *Geraldo*; one guest threw a chair at another in one episode. *Geraldo*'s status as a liability for Tribune made *Soul Train* more valuable to the distributor.

Soul Train's importance to Tribune demonstrated the show's progress in two decades of syndication. When the program had begun in Chicago, Cornelius struggled to find a willing distributor in Hollywood. Now, he produced the series in California but ironically placed syndication rights with a Chicago-based firm. It was one of the show's last ties with its Chicago roots, except for the host himself and his longtime announcer Sid McCoy.

While *Soul Train* remained the same in format, the passage of time meant that fewer entertainers of Cornelius' generation would "board" the train. Deaths of several R&B musicians who had helped launch the program became reminders of Cornelius' own mortality. David Ruffin, a former member of the Temptations and a frequent guest in the 1970s, succumbed to a drug overdose in 1991. Eddie Kendricks, another ex–Temptation and a guest on the debut syndicated episode, died in 1992. Both men, slightly younger than

Cornelius, were in their fifties when they died. They last performed on the show in a joint appearance in 1988.

In addition to these deaths, other signs of *Soul Train*'s longevity emerged. Performances on the program by children of some of the former guests demonstrated the show's age. Brothers Gerald and Sean Levert, sons of singer Eddie Levert of the O'Jays, made solo appearances on separate episodes over a decade after the O'Jays first "boarded" the train. A few years after Marvin Gaye's killing in 1984, daughter Nona Gaye sang in an episode. An increasing number of guests had not yet been born when the show premiered in Chicago in 1970. The group Immature, frequent guests in the 1990s, consisted entirely of members born at least ten years after the first WCIU episode aired.

As the twenty-second syndicated season ended in 1993, Cornelius approached his fifty-seventh birthday. The oldest guest performer slated for the premiere of the next season — solo singer Keith Washington — was over two decades Cornelius' junior. When *Soul Train* had begun, the host's tastes in music styles transcended generations. Now he tried to balance the music he favored with the demands of viewers not even born when the show premiered. It proved to be a losing battle for him and almost for the program itself.

7

"And, As Always, In Parting..."

Soul Train *without Don Cornelius*

On April 10, 1993, Anthony Sabatino died of AIDS complications at his home in Los Angeles. His passing was a blow to Don Cornelius Productions (DCP), because he had worked there ever since joining as the art director for the first syndicated season of *Soul Train* in 1971. Over the next two decades, he worked on other projects and won an Emmy Award for his art direction of the children's game show *Fun House*. He had advised Cornelius on the Sennett studio purchase, and he co-produced some of the most recent Soul Train Music Awards ceremonies.[1]

When the Los Angeles newspapers and entertainment press ran obituaries on Sabatino, his work on the *Music Awards* overshadowed his latest work on *Soul Train*. Neither *Variety* nor the *Los Angeles Times* noted that he had stayed with DCP for twenty-two years or that he had risen in the ranks on the program from art director to executive in charge of production. They only mentioned the dance show in relation to his career having started there in 1971. His work beyond the series apparently carried more weight in the entertainment industry than did his loyalty to an aging dance series.[2]

Judging from Sabatino's obituaries, *Soul Train* did not have a promising legacy in 1993. If a man closely affiliated with the series for two decades did not receive posthumous honor for his work on it, then the creator of the series and the producer would not stand a much better chance. Shortly after his faithful employee's passing, Don Cornelius began to shape and promote the legacy of *Soul Train*. Meanwhile, he took drastic measures to keep the show alive for as long as possible.

In the fall of 1993, Cornelius stepped down as host of *Soul Train*, installing a weekly guest-host format. "I just took myself off because I just felt that 22 years was enough and that the audience was changing and I wasn't," he told Andy Meisler. In an interview with Neil Strauss, Cornelius cited the brand-new set of the show as a factor in his retirement from hosting. "It had a very futuristic look, which cried out for something new in the host area as well."[3]

In addition, the ex-host believed that he had lost relevance to his viewers. He had become a caricature of himself. Although he kept up with the times in terms of fashion and music, his hosting style was the same. He opened and closed each episode with the same lines in 1993 as in 1971, but "love, peace, and soul" applied more to the psychedelic funk of two decades earlier than to the emerging gritty and blunt hip-hop. "I think [younger fans] had fun watching me because I was so abstract," he admitted years later. "But they really want people who are legitimately hip, fly and funny."[4]

Yet another reason for leaving was open to interpretation. He revealed to Strauss, "I had come to believe, and I still do, that the era of the well-spoken, well-dressed Dick Clark, Don Cornelius–type in a suit and tie was over and never to return." To be sure he was convinced that his viewers could no longer relate to him as a television personality. However, his reference to a suit as unappealing to young viewers contrasted with several R&B groups of the 1990s like Boyz II Men who were still performing in suits. By saying that the "well-spoken" kind of host was "over," he implied that whoever succeeded him would not be as eloquent. He implied that his viewers would not care if successive hosts could speak well.[5]

Future hosts were not the only people on *Soul Train* lacking eloquence. Cornelius rarely allowed rappers as guests on *Soul Train* before his retirement. He experienced difficulty in relating to them and conversing with them after their performances. At least one dancer believed that Cornelius did not consider rap to be music. Indeed, he considered "gangsta rap" crass commercialism. "I'm not young and you can't sell me material that proselytizes drug use, misogyny, violence or firearms," he said of the genre, "but if I was 10 or 12, you could sell me that. And when you do something for financial gain that you know isn't healthy for another person, that's selling out." In addition, the casual wardrobe of several rappers in the 1990s — baseball caps, un-tucked shirts, sagging jeans — clashed with the standards set by the show's host and dancers.[6]

On the other hand, *Soul Train* recognized the ascendancy of rap by incorporating it into the new theme song for the 1993–94 season. The theme, while a new direction musically, paid homage to the show's most popular elements.

The song started with a reference to the venerable "TSOP" before continuing with a mechanical beat, a jazzy bass line, a minimal female chorus, and a rap performance. The rap, performed by the group Naughty by Nature, featured references to "TSOP" and Cornelius' closing catchphrase, "Love, peace, and soul."

Part of the futuristic look of the series lay in major changes to its familiar aesthetics. After twenty years the locomotive was redesigned for the stage and for the animated opening sequence. Another revision replaced a visual trademark that had originated at WCIU. Cornelius changed the font of the "Soul Train" title by making the letters thicker and angular. In addition, kente designs appeared within the letters.

Like the new rap theme, the new logo represented both the heritage and the hip quality of the post–Cornelius *Soul Train*. The letters vaguely resembled those of the old logo. Meanwhile, the kente imagery was part of a pan–African trend in R&B and hip-hop in the early 1990s. In addition to performing nationalist raps, musicians began wearing dashikis, Afros, and dreadlocks. Some of the hairstyles and clothes had not appeared on the show since the episodes of the 1970s.

The nostalgic pan–Africanism of the musicians did not extend to other aspects of the show. Guest hosts and dancers tended not to wear African clothes. Rather, the fashion of American club-goers remained the order of the day. The new set looked like a typical urban American nightclub.

The pan–Africanism did not mark a return to the Afro-centric casting of the early 1970s. Rather, the show remained ethnically diverse. Brian Austin Green of the soap opera *Beverly Hills 90210* was one of very few white entertainers to serve as a guest host. In addition, Seth Coltan was a white member of the Soul Train Dancers in the 1990s. "I was so excited," he recalled of his first invitation into the studio. "Since that time, I called everybody. I love proving people wrong. I don't think people think I fit the stereotype — strictly black and strictly hip-hop." He considered the cast and crew to be tolerant: "I was surprised to find everybody was accepted."[7]

With all the changes in the show, one of the only remaining human ties to its beginnings in Chicago was announcer Sid McCoy. He continued to introduce the hosts and the guests and name the sponsors. He still referred to the show as "the hippest trip in America" but was also able to declare the program's distinction as the longest running one in first-run syndication. His voice and Cornelius' presence gave the series some consistency as the music and the celebrity hosts frequently changed.

On the other hand, the occupations of Cornelius' substitutes demonstrated how far *Soul Train* strayed from its roots. In 1970, when the retired host first produced and aired the series in Chicago, he allowed only local disc jockeys to host it. In contrast, while all the guest hosts were entertainers in the 1993–94 season, none were professional musicians. They were comedians, models, or actors. As such, they did not demonstrate skill in creatively introducing a song, nor could they authoritatively discuss the music industry. In addition, only two of them — Tisha Campbell and Mystro Clark — had prior experience on the show. The remaining "conductors" were completely ignorant of the workings of the "train" they led.

The casting of comedians was especially curious for a dance show. On the one hand, some of Cornelius' choices in guest hosts demonstrated that he held no grudges against performers who had previously criticized or poked fun at his show. Both Kim Wayans and T'Keyah Keymah of *In Living Color* were among the first guest hosts in the 1993–94 season. On the other hand, *Soul Train* had previously used comedians on a sporadic basis. The fashions and the dance steps of the Soul Train Dancers had provided sufficient amusement to viewers for decades. The reliance on comedians to self-consciously deliver laughs demonstrated how much charm the dances had lost over the years.

The cost-efficient measures for the production of *Soul Train* now worked against the program. Cornelius rarely invited top, A-list stars as guest hosts. Rather, most of his hosts were rising stars seeking fame — just like the guest singers and the Soul Train Dancers. The hosts usually already had previous television experience from spots on multiple series or a recurring role in one series; thus, their careers had more heft than those of the dancers. Still, without a host secure in his or her fame to anchor the series, each episode of *Soul Train* turned into an hour of every person on the set mugging at the camera.

The show no longer had a unifying figure to whom dancers and singers alike showed respect and admiration. The hosts did not fit into any particular type. The ages ranged from adolescence (Tia and Tamera Mowry) to the forties (Sheryl Lee Ralph). What the hosts shared in common was ignorance of the music industry. When Cornelius was the host, he demonstrated extensive knowledge of people at various labels and gave substantial information on artists' careers. For many returning performers, he could claim to have given them their initial break on his show. No one replacing him had the background in radio or the musical success to comment authoritatively on the music played on *Soul Train*. Small wonder that Cornelius continued to appear on the show after his retirement, but only as an on-camera counterpart to McCoy; Cornelius opened each episode with his usual "Welcome aboard" greeting but then immediately introduced the episode's host. He returned at the end to close the show with his signature "love, peace, and soul."

Through the use of guest hosts, Cornelius exercised some of the power that he had achieved in the entertainment industry over the previous two decades. He had formerly promoted only African American comedians and musicians on *Soul Train*, and for the latter only the music labels stood to benefit from exposure as much as the singers did. By hiring specifically non-musical talent for guest hosts, however, his promotion branched out beyond music. Whereas Sears-Roebuck and Johnson Products had supported *Soul Train* in its infancy, the show now offered its services to new African American artists and their projects.

Soul Train gave significant support to television programs with African American lead actors. The shows spotlighted usually appealed to the same young, urban demographic sought by *Soul Train*. Cornelius gave *The Fresh Prince of Bel-Air* (1990–96) the most exposure of any program. Four actors from the show—Tatyana Ali, Joseph Marcell, Karyn Parsons, and Alfonso Ribeiro—"boarded" the train. The guest hosts were often not the leading stars themselves. *Soul Train* pulled in the co-stars of *Fresh Prince of Bel-Air* but not Will Smith himself, nor did Jaleel White ("Steve Urkel") of *Family Matters* (1989–97), Brandy Norwood of *Moseha* (1996–2001), or Martin Lawrence of *Martin* (1992–97) join their co-stars as guest hosts. A rare exception was Jamie Foxx of *The Jamie Foxx Show* (1996–2001) hosting during the premiere year of his series.

Television networks benefited from the plugs given by *Soul Train*'s guest hosts for their shows—an irony, considering Cornelius's unfavorable comments towards networks during the early years of his program. Some hosts starred in *Family Matters* and *Hangin' with Mr. Cooper* (1992–96) from the ABC network, which had used Dick Clark's *Soul Unlimited* to compete with Cornelius in 1973. Many others, however, came from series on new, fledging networks like FOX, United Paramount Network (UPN), and the Warner Brothers (WB) Network. The young networks aired series with African American leads, and Cornelius supported the networks by casting their actors as hosts. FOX especially received representation with hosts from its shows *Roc* (1992–95), *Martin*, and *Living Single* (1993–98).

African American actors did not have to perform roles in all-black series in order to host *Soul Train*. Some actors in otherwise all-white casts also appeared. Many of these shows were ratings successes. Booking these stars demonstrated the great star power that *Soul Train* still had after over twenty years. Kristoff St. John and Victoria Rowell from *The Young and the Restless* (1973–present), Renee Jones from *Days of Our Lives* (1964–present), and Traci Bingham from *Baywatch* (1989–99) hosted their own episodes.

Soul Train also honored the fashion industry by hiring supermodels as guest hosts. Tyra Banks, Veronica Webb, and Roshumba Williams hosted different episodes. Their appearances had a different context than those of other performers. Singers performed songs, actors promoted their series, and comedians tested their jokes. The models, on the other hand, had no product or act to exploit; their looks were their product. Their stints as hosts perfectly complemented Cornelius' statement, "Only the look matters."

The new look that Cornelius developed changed the character of *Soul Train*. The set and the cinematography diminished the presence of the guest artists and the Soul Train Dancers. The riser for the guest performers in the 1990s was larger than ever and extended to the back wall. As a result, the guests now looked small on top of the large stage. And, the performers and dancers had to compete with colored lights swirling all over the studio to hold the viewers' attention.

After years of presenting dancing complementing the songs from guest artists, the new look of *Soul Train* de-emphasized the relationship. During guest performances the cameras concentrated solely on the singers. The riser was so large that dancers no longer were positioned all around guests but only in front of the riser. In addition, the set beyond the riser was so dimly lit that the dancers were barely visible. The discontinuation of images of the dancers moving to the song during the guest performance marked a further separation of the show from its WCIU roots. When the program was in Chicago, the stage was so small that musicians performed on the main floor *with* the dancers.

The changes in staging further symbolized Cornelius' prioritization of "the look" of *Soul Train*. When the show began, graphic tricks were minimal, and the set was sparse; the risers, for example, were movable. Most of the camera's shots featured teenagers moving to music. The dancing and singing had sufficient entertainment value by themselves; no spinning lights were needed. In contrast, in the 1990s the popularity of graphically sophisticated R&B music videos on cable networks suggested that viewers wanted their music enhanced by camera tricks. *Soul Train*'s enhancement of songs and dances with graphics kept the series on par with videos in terms of technological sophistication. The inclusion of music videos within episodes further transformed *Soul Train* from a dance show to a sixty-minute extended music video.

After Cornelius retired from hosting, *Soul Train*'s era of canonization began. The R&B music industry joined the media in acknowledging the importance of the program to the industry's development. Especially outspoken in their gratitude to Cornelius were performers born in the 1970s. Their comments affirmed reports that the series continued to influence the socialization of children well into the 1980s. Vocal star Brandy, who participated in a Soul Train Music Awards ceremony, stated that after having grown up on *Soul Train* episodes, "now to be a part of something that has touched so many lives is great." Stephanie Sinclair of the group Mokenstef— a *Soul Train* guest around this time — proclaimed, "The show had a lot to do with inspiring me and giving me a background in music. It felt good to watch the dancers in the 'Soul Train' line, the big Afros, the whole Motown era." Then, adding a dynamic of economic class to her discussion of the show's significance, she noted, "For people like myself, who don't really have the money to go to a concert, *Soul Train* is your way of seeing a show."[8]

Cornelius capitalized on the attention to *Soul Train*'s past by exploiting it. Upon retirement, he began promoting the show's history more fervently than before. Instead of a "Soul Train History Book" moment, the opening sequence for the 1993–94 season featured muted old clips superimposed above animation of the program's iconic train as the rap theme song played. Young viewers were then able to appreciate the durability of the series while simultaneously enjoying music of their generation. Like the Soul Train Scramble, the new opening educated as it entertained.

Cornelius also directly contributed to the development of some of *Soul Train*'s tributes outside of the series itself. He allowed clips from the first syndicated season of the series to appear in Spike Lee's feature film *Crooklyn*. The movie illustrates the point of view of a ten-year-old African American girl coming of age in New York in the 1970s, and Lee partially reconstructed the time period with clips of the Soul Train Line, host Don Cornelius and the animated cartoon of the rickety train chugging across the countryside. Lee gives the time period an affectionate, nostalgic image, which was not lost on movie critics. One of them agreed with the director's characterization of the start of the decade as "the frolicking days of the Seventies, when Afros were in, music was original and our urban streets, for the most part, were safe." The clips of *Soul Train* visually reinforce the comments about the Afros and music. More importantly, Lee shows reverence for the show by presenting it as a family event; the juvenile characters in the film crowd around the television set when the program begins, and their eyes remain glued to the screen.[9]

Soul Train, however, was trapped between the past that Lee and *Crooklyn* celebrated and the present that media commentators lamented. Another critic described the 1970s as "growing up watching the Partridge Family, Snaggle-puss cartoons, Afro-Sheen commercials, and Don Cornelius' Soooulll Train!" In the next paragraph, the writer complained about modern times: "Simple games like stickball, kickball, jump rope or cops and robbers are being replaced by Nintendo and Sega Genesis. And programs like the "After School Specials" or "School House Rock" have been eliminated by a new wave of bang-bang shut 'em up night-time cop shows and a host of circus-type talk shows, where the characters rotate from show to show yelling and shouting all types of obscenities." He overlooked that *Soul Train*, too, was part of this new era. Critics celebrating the original music of the 1970s, which Cornelius helped popularize, failed to mention that new episodes of the show were providing a forum to the much-maligned "sampled" music of the 1990s. Thus, observers saw what they wanted to see in *Soul Train*, and responses to *Crooklyn* revealed a preference for the show's history instead of its current offerings.[10]

Cornelius was not oblivious to Hollywood's preference for *Soul Train*'s past and immediately capitalized upon it. On November 7, 1994, months after *Crooklyn*'s release, he appeared in an episode of NBC's situation comedy *The Fresh Prince of Bel-Air* as himself. The show caricatures the early years of *Soul Train* but in a much more sympathetic manner than *In Living Color* had done. In the episode the main adult characters, Uncle Phil and Aunt Viv, recall the start of their romance in the late 1960s on *Soul Train*. Cornelius plays himself from over two decades earlier, hosting the show as the characters perform exaggerated versions of dances in garish clothes of the era. As a result, he participates in the comedy program's humorous homage to how *Soul Train* used to look and sound.

Cornelius allowed historical inaccuracy in the episode, including omissions of important people who helped him launch his program. The adult characters of *The Fresh Prince of Bel-Air* claimed to have known each other on *Soul Train* in 1969. The series, however, did not even begin as a local Chicago offering on WCIU until 1970. The episode also glossed over the dance show's Chicago roots. Noticeably absent were references to the figures of that era of *Soul Train*— Clinton Ghent, Ronnie Paul Johnson, the WVON "Good Guys," Sears-Roebuck, and Johnson Products.

There presentation of the present-day *Soul Train* on *The Fresh Prince of Bel-Air* further misrepresented Cornelius' series. He tailored his show to meet the needs of the comedy series. He rarely allowed people not affiliated with his production company to shape the promotion of his series. But a television network — NBC — owned Will Smith's show and therefore was in charge of the imaging of *Soul Train* on the comedy series, despite Cornelius' long distrust of television networks. The episode was not taped at the *Soul Train* facilities but rather at a mock studio at NBC Productions. The fake *Soul Train* stage had only the logo in common with the real stage. In the *Fresh Prince*, *Soul Train* had a bright-colored background and no towers for go-go dancing — a far cry from the nightclub setting of the actual show, but *The Fresh Prince of Bel-Air* was a family program. Cornelius was producing a special episode of *Soul Train*, according to the comedy show's storyline; but *Soul Train* had not featured any special tribute episodes for years. Cornelius himself hosted the mock show, although he had been retired from hosting for over a year.

In interviews after his retirement, he often spoke negatively of his own series. He had no reservation about declaring his preference for old episodes of *Soul Train* over current ones. He enjoyed the 1970s the most. "That's when I was introduced, face to face, to all the greater stars of the '70s — James Brown, Aretha Franklin, Al Green, even Barry White," he explained. "I was new, the show was new and these guys, many were already legendary. Marvin Gaye. It was my favorite because it was so exciting to be in." Such comments worked against his trying to modernize the series and keep it on the air. Nor did he help matters by admitting that some African American artists did not want to perform on his show.[11]

Cornelius' tactic of selling the present *Soul Train* through historical imagery worked to keep the show on the air. Media attention to his retirement as host died down within a month in the 1993–94 season, but the movie critics' nostalgic responses to *Crooklyn*'s use of old clips gave the show new publicity. In 1994 references to *Soul Train* and Don Cornelius appeared in the press to a greater extent than during the program's "phenomenon" years of 1972 to 1975. In the fall of 1994, the series entered its twenty-fourth syndicated season.

A major contributing factor to Cornelius' focus on *Soul Train*'s past was his disdain for the music promoted by the contemporary show. "I think the 1990s are the era when the music industry sold out," he declared in 1995. "We're selling material that promotes behavior that's not only unhealthy for young people, it's dangerous." For all his dismay, however, he did not actively crusade for changes in the R&B industry. "Ain't my job," he quipped. "People want me to shut up and produce TV shows." For over a decade more, he proceeded to do exactly that.[12]

The former host was honored by several organizations after his retirement. In June 1997 he became the first entertainer to be honored by the California legislature. Assemblyman Kevin Murray boasted of Cornelius, "He exposed entertainers to people all over the world." The honor marked the peak of *Soul Train*'s courting of politicians and political activists over the years.[13]

Cornelius promoted *Soul Train*'s longevity instead of the performers themselves. In order to sustain the youth appeal of the show, fewer references to the past appeared in the program. After Cornelius retired, the hour-long tributes to individual acts stopped. Each episode now had at least two acts. While less old content kept the program fresh, yet another fundamental part of the show was gone. Teaching audiences about the great R&B artists of bygone years had been a staple educational element of the show, but now only the Scramble remained to serve that purpose.

The discontinuation of the tributes meant that no more artists would have retrospective episodes when they died. Quite a few former *Soul Train* guests died in the first few years after Cornelius retired from hosting. Junior Walker died in 1995. "Master Storyteller" Curtis Mayfield, paralyzed after being struck by falling lighting equipment in 1990, passed away nine years later. Even the *Soul Train* family itself suffered losses when former dancer Jermaine Stewart succumbed to liver cancer in March 1997 and former director Mark Warren lost his cancer battle in January 1999. Nevertheless, the guest hosts and new hosts did not have the professional relationships with the artists that Cornelius had and, therefore, would not have paid as personal a tribute to each deceased performer.

With guest hosts, *Soul Train* continued to draw viewers. Nationwide the ratings were mediocre in 1995. But the series still reached its target audience, and a Tribune employee bragged, "We can charge a premium price for advertisers who want to reach that audience." Thus, Tribune Entertainment continued to renew syndication of the show.[14]

Some of the competition *Soul Train* faced came from the very shows in which the guest hosts starred. An increasing number of R&B musicians won leading roles in television programs. As a result, they did not have to release a new video on MTV or BET or appear on *Soul Train* to get exposure on television. "Gangsta" rapper Ice-T, for example, won a recurring role in *Law and Order: Special Victims Unit.* However, situation comedies were the dominant genre for the artists. In addition to Will Smith of *The Fresh Prince of Bel-Air,* rapper Queen Latifah headlined *Living Single,* Brandy Norwood starred in *Moesha,* and L.L. Cool J. headed the cast of *In the House.* Comedies also featured musicians as guest stars, such as the groups Naughty by Nature and T.L.C. on *Living Single.*

Urban-targeted television shows promoted new music, just as *Soul Train* did. Whenever Will Smith released a new song, the video for it played immediately following the broadcast of an episode of his series. Even programs without musicians as actors aired new R&B songs on a weekly basis as a means to attract young viewers. The FOX network's police drama *New York Undercover* featured hit R&B tunes in opening montages that presented the episode's crime for the fictional detectives to solve. It was a tactic borrowed from NBC's long-running, stylized police show *Miami Vice* (1984–1989), which set scenes to pop music as well as R&B.

The musical diversity represented on *Soul Train* made the series an exercise in R&B vaudeville. Odd, mismatched bookings of artists in single episodes became more frequent. African American music was more fragmented than when *Soul Train* had begun. Earlier in the show's history, an episode offered a mix of ballads and either funk songs or disco songs; but the songs usually had in common soulful singing and formally dressed performers. In the 1990s, however, guests clashed musically and visually with one another. One episode featured both the balladeer Gerald Levert and the rap group Mo Thugs Family; the former sang about a cheating girlfriend, and the latter rapped about bank robberies and murder threats. Whenever the rap group Kris Kross appeared, the members wore their clothes backwards, in contrast to the other guests on those episodes. *Soul Train* had essentially evolved into an African American musical mutation of *The Ed Sullivan Show,* which offered televised vaudeville — classical and modern musical acts, stand-up comedy, puppetry, and dramatic performances all in the same hour.

Soul Train's musical diversity distinguished the show from its competitors. BET and MTV aired their videos primarily in genre-specific packages. BET played raps in *Rap City* and slow ballads in *Midnight Love.* MTV broadcasted raps on *Yo! MTV Raps* but had no separate series for R&B. Both networks only mirrored *Soul Train*'s mixed content when airing videos according to viewer popularity. Their "Video Countdown" shows offered several musical genres.

As *Soul Train* began embracing rap music, the program promoted the diversity within the genre. By this time rap had moved beyond emcees brag-ging about their rhyming skills to sparse mechanized drumbeats. By sampling and covering older R&B songs, new rap songs ironically paid homage to the music that *Soul Train* promoted in its early years. Digable Planets "boarded" the train to perform their jazzy raps. "Gangsta" rappers Ice Cube and Snoop Doggy Dogg rapped about life on the West Coast. The group Public Enemy gave its raps a political slant.

At this time, female guests experienced a decline in numbers in com-parison to appearances in the 1980s. Although three separate female acts per-formed at least six times on the show in the 1980s, no women in the following decade appeared more than five times. On the other hand, the women with the most time on the program offered diverse music. Among the female artists appearing five times were rapper MC Lyte, gospel artist Cece Winans (per-forming with brother Bebe Winans in three of her five episodes), and R&B artists Chante Moore and Zhane.

Meanwhile, the shows that had chipped away at *Soul Train*'s exclusivity in televising urban music disappeared — a further testament to *Soul Train*'s longevity. MTV cancelled *Club MTV* and *Yo! MTV Raps*. FOX abandoned *In Living Color*. BET dropped *Video Soul* but continued to offer R&B video programming in various formats over the next few years. Nevertheless, these programs made their mark on *Soul Train*, because videos were now common-place aboard the train.

The most publicized cancellation of an African American variety pro-gram in the mid–1990s was arguably *The Arsenio Hall Show*. Before 1992, Hall had only MTV, BET, and Cornelius as formidable competition for booking R&B guests. Then, Johnny Carson retired from hosting *The Tonight Show* on NBC after years of promoting mostly adult contemporary guests, and new host Jay Leno aggressively sought the same young demographics as Hall. The following year, David Letterman of NBC's *Late Night with David Letterman* started a new talk show on CBS, and competition intensified for hip musical guests. Hall's program ended in 1994.

The end of Hall's show was ironic, because one year earlier Cornelius had crowned him as the industry's best comedian. In August 1993 the *First Annual Soul Train Comedy Awards* aired in syndication. The ceremony com-bined Cornelius' drive to honor unsung entertainers — humorists, in this case — and *Soul Train*'s tradition of providing a stage to rising African Amer-ican comedians. Hall won the "Richard Pryor Entertainer of the Year Award," which was one of the ceremony's top honors. The win came just as Hall faced the new, tough, late-night competition, but the award was not enough to save him from cancellation.

Naming the "Entertainer of the Year" prize after Pryor demonstrated Cornelius' continued focus on unsung African American performers. Awarding the Pryor statue to Hall symbolized Cornelius' respect for Hall's attempts to cater to urban audiences as the late-night audience began to fragment. Pryor's routines about African American subject matter in coarse language kept him from becoming as popular in film media as other black humorists. In the 1970s, Flip Wilson censored his own jokes and enjoyed a four-year run of his variety show. Although Pryor appeared in several movies in the 1970s and 1980s, by the 1990s comedians Bill Cosby and Eddie Murphy had eclipsed Pryor by experiencing both mainstream television and movie success. Pryor, however, influenced stand-up comedians. As Hall himself quipped at the *Comedy Awards*, "If you do standup and you ain't stole nothing from Richard, you ain't doing it right." The presence of Pryor himself at the *Comedy Awards* validated the event's significance, as far as Cornelius was concerned.[15]

The *Soul Train* producer timed honoring African American comedy at an opportune moment. On television, African American stand-up comedians performed their acts in several series in the mid–1990s. When the *Soul Train Comedy Awards* aired, *It's Showtime at the Apollo* (1986–present), *Def Comedy Jam* (1992–97), and *Uptown Comedy Club* (1992–94) offered weekly black stand-up routines. Cornelius tapped into the trend by devising awards for stand-up comedians. Over a month before the *Comedy Awards* ceremony, he held the "Soul Train Stand-Up Comedy Showdown" — a contest in which comedians George Wallace, Marsha Warfield, Paul Rodriguez, and Jamie Foxx decided on a male winner and a female winner. The champions later received their awards at the *Comedy Awards* ceremony.[16]

Outside of the "Comedy Showdown," however, the *Comedy Awards* honored mostly film and television actors. As a result, the ceremony was no different than other events held by various organizations such as the NAACP's *Image Awards*. Categories included roles in motion pictures, sketch-comedy television, and televised situation comedies. For some winners, the awards did not seem to add to their careers. Jasmine Guy, the female situation comedy winner, noted after her acceptance, "I'm looking at Broadway now and working on my second album." The most famous celebrities to win awards — Martin Lawrence and Whoopi Goldberg — did not even attend the event.[17]

The *Comedy Awards* also featured musical performances, which had nothing to do with the theme of the event. No awards were given for humorous music, and no musicians competed for any of the honors. Rather, the inclusion of singers reflected Cornelius' familiarity with music telecasts as opposed to comedy telecasts. Although *Soul Train* periodically featured stand-up acts, only one five-minute routine would take place in each sixty-minute episode; music comprised the other fifty-five minutes. Interestingly, Cornelius, who gave R&B music its first serious Afro-centric television forum in *Soul Train*, argued that music *belonged* in a comedy-based event. "There's a relationship between music and comedy, and comedy reaches many of the same people as music-oriented shows," he noted, while claiming that the songs gave the ceremony "special added versatility."[18]

African American comedians celebrated the *Comedy Awards* and praised Cornelius for creating them. Although the festivities were similar to white television producer George Schlatter's *American Comedy Awards*, Schlatter's ceremony rarely gave awards to African Americans. Sinbad, who co-hosted Cornelius' event (with Debbie Allen), declared his preference for *Soul Train*'s ceremony over the *American* one. "I want to do a show that's about us," he stated. "In a perfect world, we should be acknowledged for the content of our work in the same arena as everybody else," echoed Keenen Ivory Wayans. "But since we don't live in a perfect world," he added, "shows like these are a must." Cornelius had effectively tapped into a need felt by a significant number of African American entertainers, for Tony Cornelius of Don Cornelius Productions also observed, "Sometimes we just don't get our due."[19]

The support from the stand-up industry, however, was not sufficient to sustain the event. Cornelius discontinued the *Soul Train Comedy Awards* after its initial year. It marked the first setback of the *Soul Train* franchise since the unsuccessful purchase of the Sennett studio in the previous decade. The press was kind to him by not reporting any negative stories about the disappearance of the event the following August. In fact, no major newspaper noted the ceremony's termination at all. BET attempted to fill in the gap by launching its *Comic View Awards Jam* in early 1994, continuing Cornelius' legacy of honoring unsung African American entertainers.

Cornelius, meanwhile, refocused his energies on music-based awards. On August 6, 1995, *Soul Train Lady of Soul Awards* made its debut. Just as Cornelius had created the Soul Train Music Awards to honor African American music styles ignored at other award ceremonies, the *Lady of Soul Awards* paid tribute to African American female singers. He told reporter Charles Reeves of the *Philadelphia Tribune* that the music industry did not appropriately celebrate and honor its African American female artists, especially the rappers and dancers.[20]

The *Lady of Soul Awards* mirrored *Soul Train* in its marketing to various age groups, presenting or referring to performers of nearly every living generation. Cornelius named special awards after longtime actress/singer Lena Horne (career achievements in entertainment) and Aretha Franklin (entertainer of the year). R&B, rap and jazz artists participated in the festivities. Among the winners were actress and film director Debbie Allen and the rap group Salt 'n' Pepa.

Three months later Cornelius celebrated twenty-five years of *Soul Train* via a television special. The *Soul Train 25th Anniversary Hall of Fame* not only praised the longevity of the series but also gave the stage to singers who had given the show memorable performances. Once again, Cornelius placed the artists before himself. Michael Jackson, who had not appeared on *Soul Train* after his solo career exploded in 1979, sang for the anniversary broadcast, as did Gladys Knight, who had appeared on the syndicated debut.

The *Soul Train 25th Anniversary Hall of Fame* also featured a political peak. President Bill Clinton expressed his fondness for the series. His appearance marked one of the last times that *Soul Train* courted a powerful political figure. It was also the first time that a white politician got air time on a Cornelius show. By including Clinton's tribute for an Afro-centric program, Cornelius acknowledged the president's popularity among African Americans and exhibited his power not only in the television medium but also in American politics. After all, sitting presidents rarely made television appearances outside of speeches, press conferences, and news programs. On the other hand, Clinton had already used urban-targeted television series to his advantage when, as a presidential candidate in the summer of 1992, he played the saxophone on *The Arsenio Hall Show.*

Arsenio Hall received almost as much press coverage as Cornelius for the event. The former talk show host had not appeared on television since the demise of his series. However, Cornelius chose Hall to host the event. As a result, reporters covered the festivities not only as a major milestone for *Soul Train* but also as a career "comeback" for Hall. Claiming that he did not miss his talk show, he told journalists that he "needed rest, just to enjoy life and to do things, like take my mother to lunch."[21]

The ceremony did not honor the Chicagoans who had helped make *Soul Train* possible. The oversight marked another stylized retelling of the show's history. The only significant reference to the Windy City was in the title of the broadcast, for counting twenty-five years acknowledged that the series had started in 1970, when it aired only in Chicago. Otherwise, the ceremony was full of clips of *Soul Train* episodes from only the syndicated version, as if the WCIU version from both Cornelius and successor Clinton Ghent had never happened.

Cornelius also trumpeted *Soul Train*'s longevity by releasing boxed sets of compilations of R&B songs spanning the run of the series. Rhino Records' "*Soul Train* 20th Anniversary Hall of Fame" and MCA's "*Soul Train* 25th Anniversary Hall of Fame" capitalized on the program's respective milestones, although the former was curiously released in 1994 instead of 1990. The sets were two of several in the mid–1990s that showcased R&B. Rhino itself offered "In Yo' Face: the History of Funk" and, with *Billboard* magazine, the year-by-year "Hot Soul Hits." The anniversary collections, at least, had an advantage over the others through the marketable *Soul Train* brand name, which was synonymous with great R&B performances.

Criticism of Cornelius' empire was rare at the time but evident. In 1995 *Michigan Chronicle* reporter Steve Holsey, a frequent commentator on *Soul Train*, noted that back in the 1970s, "missing *Soul Train* was something you didn't want to do." The contemporary version of the series, however, did not inspire the same loyalty. He felt that a major reason was that "now most of the female dancers seem to be putting on a sex show." He lamented that Cornelius did not use more clips of old episodes for his anniversary special. Such longings for yesteryear were unsurprising, considering that Cornelius helped promote them through *Crooklyn* and *The Fresh Prince of Bel-Air*.[22]

That same year reporter Leah Cash of San Bernadino's *Precinct Reporter* offered a more prescient critique. She lamented what she considered a decline in the quality of the various *Soul Train* awards ceremonies. She felt that the celebrities in attendance were too casually dressed for the 1995 Soul Train Music Awards — "like they were going to the park." Because the show lacked extravagance, she felt that "[Cornelius] just made calls to mega superstars, worked out a production, solicited a network, and rented the Shrine." She further noted that the security, reporters, employees of Cornelius and celebrities in attendance complained and wanted to leave early. She said that the year's *Lady of Soul Awards* suffered the same fate. Whether the awards telecasts evolved from recognition of unheralded R&B talent to classless forums for music superstars was a matter of opinion. Cash's observation that the awards had fundamentally changed in character was affirmed by events surrounding the next two Soul Train Music Awards.[23]

By the mid-1990s, the Soul Train Music Awards had established a reputation for tremendous urban youth appeal. Contrary to Cash's claims, some celebrities still held the ceremony in high regard. Members of the group TLC were especially vocal in their admiration. Tionne "T-Boz" Watkins said, "We all think the Soul Train Music Awards is one of the hippest shows around." Bandmate Rozonda "Chili" Thomas echoed, "I like the Soul Train Music Awards so much because it's all black folks coming together for one large event. It's like one big family. We [are] really embraced by our people." Thomas's comments demonstrate that young viewers and participants considered the Afro-centricity of the ceremony as significant as Cornelius had when he started the awards. Moreover, in 1995 his feelings had not changed. "I think it is important that we continue to support the various award shows," he implored, "and I am delighted with the 10 years of support the African-American community has given us with the Soul Train Music Awards."[24]

The cheerfulness of TLC and Cornelius could not prevent the problems the Soul Train Music Awards faced the following two years. In 1996, violence at the Soul Train Music Awards tarnished Soul Train's promotion of "love, peace, and soul." The show had rarely courted controversy. The most recent crime to receive major publicity related to a dancing fugitive spotted by a viewer one decade earlier. These new incidents, however, received more press coverage than the winners of the awards did. In addition, the eruptions were related to the music industry itself instead of a lone individual. By making the show informal and "hip" for urban youth, the ceremony catered to artists who were "hip" and popular with youngsters because of skills, looks, or the violence in song lyrics.

The Soul Train Music Awards concluded its first decade with negative publicity. On March 29, 1996, violence erupted at the tenth annual Soul Train Music Awards between employees of Death Row Records and Bad Boy Records. It was part of an escalating East Coast–West Coast rap tension. Death Row, founded by Marion "Suge" Knight, was the California-based label, while Sean "Puff Daddy" Combs's Bad Boy label had headquarters in New York.

Among those exchanging words at the ceremony were Tupac Shakur of the former label and Notorious B.I.G. (Christopher Wallace) of the latter. Their quarrel had preceded the awards by nearly two years. In November 1994 Shakur was shot multiple times and robbed of jewelry worth $40,000 outside a recording studio in Manhattan. A few months later he blamed Wallace and Combs for the attack and proceeded to insult them, especially Wallace, for over a year. Other rappers joined in the dispute and took geographic sides, extending the feud.[25]

As *Soul Train* struggled to redefine itself without a host and with the music industry in flux, the violence was a further blow to the show. The incident received extensive news coverage not only as contributing to the bicoastal rap dispute but also as violence occurring at a event whose name had symbolized African American family entertainment for a quarter-century.

The violence carried over into the following year. Between the tenth and eleventh annual ceremonies, tensions escalated when Shakur was shot dead in October 1996. Many of his West Coast devotees blamed Notorious B.I.G. for the killing. At a Los Angeles party in March 1997 in celebration of the eleventh annual Soul Train Music Awards, Notorious B.I.G. was killed by gunfire. He had just presented an award at the ceremony the previous evening. The 1997 Soul Train Music Awards were, in fact, the last major event he attended.

Cornelius immediately perceived that the press reported the murder as if it had happened at an event he facilitated. His production company drafted a press release to address the error. The document clarified that Wallace did not die at an official Soul Train Music Awards event. Most of the printed reports, however, did not make any connection between Cornelius and the shooting. Rather, they noted that the party the rapper attended was in celebration of the ceremony. Neither Cornelius nor his production company was named in most of the articles about the killing. Moreover, on the day of the incident, the *New York Times* specifically included a comment from Cornelius that he had not sponsored the party where the rapper died.[26]

Despite Cornelius' best efforts to distance his empire from Wallace's death the 1997 Soul Train Music Awards remains an unwitting milestone in the East Coast–West Coast rap feud. As an event in Los Angeles, the ceremony immediately placed East Coast attendees at a geographical disadvantage with the audience. Biographies of Notorious B.I.G. continue to note that the last major event he attended was the awards ceremony. Still, Cornelius made no mention of the murder after the press release. He did not even devote a *Soul Train* episode to Wallace in tribute; on the other hand, Shakur had not received his own "memorial" episode, either.

The violence in the context of the Soul Train Music Awards underscored the irrelevance of *Soul Train* to contemporary African American young adults. While artists praised the "hip" quality of the awards ceremony, they frequently described *Soul Train* as a program of their younger years instead of a contemporary one. The show had long ceased to speak to modern sociopolitical issues among African Americans. Two decades earlier in Chicago, WCIU's combination of soul music and public affairs for its version of *Soul Train* was a source of pride among African American adolescents. After all, Crescendo Ward was spared a beating from gang members because they recognized him as a dancer on the local series. In the 1990s, however, *Soul Train* no longer transcended black-on-black crime. It had become just another dance show with no more sociopolitical significance than *Club MTV* among black urban youth.

The incidents also dramatized the differences among the African American businesses involved in them. When Don Cornelius wanted to create a musical enterprise catering to African Americans, he gave it a name that had connotations of Afro-centricity. Combs and Knight, however, named their respective labels after deviant behavior instead of racial pride. On the other hand, they did not have to call attention to being black or having "soul" to sell records; Combs especially often maximized the crossover appeal of his music by sampling white rock artists such as Led Zeppelin and the Police. *Soul Train* did not have the same crossover appeal in the 1990s but rather continued to depend on a strong urban audience for survival.

The negative publicity regarding the *Soul Train* franchise and Cornelius eventually subsided. By the summer of 1997, Cornelius made news by announcing his decision to hire a full-time host. His choice was Mystro Clark — an actor who had found work mostly in television situation comedies. In early 1993 he was one of the last guests on *Soul Train* during Cornelius' era as host; instead of singing Clark performed a stand-up act. Born in 1966 — the same year that his predecessor enrolled in the broadcasting class — he was three years younger than Cornelius when Cornelius started hosting the show. In interviews Clark had the utmost respect for his boss. The new host gushed, "I couldn't help but be awestruck over the opportunity to follow in the footsteps of someone whom I've admired as much as Don Cornelius." Both hosts had military service in common; Cornelius had been stationed in South Korea in the 1950s, and Clark served in Operation Desert Storm in 1991. They also shared a penchant for peppering their monologues and interviews with hip vernacular. When Clark talked to the Temptations in 1998, he used not only the contemporary slang phrase "original gangsta" but also the much older "dig it" — a sort of vocabulary-based bridge from Cornelius to himself.[27]

Clark's comedic background, although different from Cornelius' extensive music experience, gave *Soul Train* continuity in hosting post–Cornelius. Many of the hosts from 1993 to 1997 were situation comedy stars or comedians. Clark had starred in the syndicated sketch comedy show *The Newz* in

1994, which allowed him to show off his skills in mimicking and ad-libs to nationwide audiences. Then, in 1996 his role as talk show host "Wilson Lee" in FOX's situation comedy *The Show* allowed him to demonstrate his acting chops. With *Soul Train*, Clark used elements from both of his previous programs, using his comedy talents for the real-life role of host.

Clark was not only a younger host than Cornelius but also a more youthful one. The average age of the Soul Train Dancers helped enhance this dynamic. When Cornelius started the show in his thirties, the dancers were teenagers; but he was no more than twenty years older than the youngest dancer in 1971. Even as professional adult dancers eventually dominated the cast over twenty-five years later, Cornelius was thirty or forty years older than they were. Clark, in contrast, did not have as wide an age gap with the professional dancers. As a result, he had more of an "older brother" quality, as opposed to Cornelius' "fatherly" image on the show.

Clark has only positive recollections of his tenure as host of *Soul Train*. He enjoyed hosting because he had grown up watching the show. Referring to his experience on the program as "exciting," he likened the job to "being at an amusement park every week." In addition, many of the Soul Train Dancers became his friends. As a result, his colleagues were "like a family" to him.[28]

He also had fond memories of the musical guests. He described Rebbie Jackson, the eldest sibling of the musical Jackson family and a soloist herself, as "very nice." He noted, "She had a really sweet personality." The series also gave him experience and networking opportunities for his music career, for he had begun rapping before his hosting gig began. While still *Soul Train*'s host in 1999, he recorded rap songs in a professional studio. He released his first single "Are You Ready" a few months after he stopped hosting the program.[29]

Like the guest hosts, Clark differentiated his hosting style from that of Cornelius by openly embracing rap musicians, including those associated with the "gangsta rap" genre. Among his favorite musical artists who performed on the show during his hosting years, he noted Snoop Dogg and Ice Cube, both of whom were successful West Coast rappers. Clark also recognized the East Coast by including rapper L. L. Cool J. — one of the few rappers to appear on the program when Cornelius was host — in his list of notable guests. Of course, Cornelius as executive producer still controlled the content of the series, but Clark was now on hand to welcome rap artists on camera frequently — a major shift from the early 1990s.[30]

Most remarkable is Ice Cube's appearance at all, considering his biting critique of *Soul Train* back in 1990. Whether or not Ice Cube had a change of heart, Cornelius was gracious in offering television exposure to him. If nothing else, Ice Cube's spot on *Soul Train* precipitated major changes in his public persona. Within a few years, he successfully evolved from "gangsta" rapper to Hollywood star. He acted in leading roles in family-oriented feature films such as *Are We There Yet* and *Barbershop*. *Soul Train*, thus, marked one of his first attempts to reach the family demographic that shaped the later years of his entertainment career.

Ironically, all of the prior criticism of *Soul Train* as too sexualized had more relevance as the twenty-first century dawned. The program's content had grown more lascivious than before. The sexualizing of the series went beyond skimpier clothes for female dancers. The avant-garde cinematography in the style of *Rowan & Martin's Laugh-In* returned with a sexual twist. Cameras once again rapidly zoomed in and out, as in the days when Mark Warren had directed the show, but now camera operators zoomed in on women's bosoms—a more obvious target with revealing cleavage now standard dress—as the women danced down the Soul Train Line.

The increasingly graphic, sexual lyrics of guest stars made the diverse bookings of guests for single episodes awkward, especially as more gospel songs became mainstream hits in the wake of gospel singer Kirk Franklin's 1997 crossover chart success "Stomp." Not surprisingly, few gospel musicians performed on *Soul Train* and instead chose television exposure through BET's religious musical showcases like *Bobby Jones' Gospel*. In October 2000 an episode of *Soul Train* featured not only a video from gospel singer Yolanda Adams but also a stage performance from rapper Trina's album "Da Baddest Bitch." In June 2002 the gospel group Mary Mary sang "In The Morning" in the same episode that Cee-Lo performed "Closet Freak." The former act delivered an inspirational musical message about hope during difficult times. The latter ordered his lover, in song, to "bump and grind" on the floor.

Soul Train's profile in the media remained low despite the change in hosting, but the media attention that took place demonstrated how much reporters had changed their approaches to discussing the show since the 1970s. Clark's peak in press coverage as the show's host took place when he began the job in the fall of 1997. He did not become the media curiosity that Don Cornelius was. Moreover, when important events related to the show took place, reporters still tended to interview Cornelius but ignored Clark. On the other hand, journalists did not scrutinize Clark's hosting or gauge his views on race relations, as they did with Cornelius in the early 1970s. Rather, newspapers and magazines kept criticism extremely minimal and simply allowed Clark to do his job without much fanfare.

The most publicity Cornelius received in the late 1990s came from his business ventures beyond *Soul Train*. The two annual awards ceremonies he created generated publicity via the celebrities who attended, whether they won awards or not. In addition, Cornelius made news by adding to his *Soul Train* empire in 1998 with the first annual *Soul Train Christmas Starfest*. The *Christmas Starfest* brought together gospel singers and R&B veterans and newcomers for musical performances, and an assorted bunch of celebrities made cameo appearances. After the first year, subsequent ceremonies featured cameos of entire casts of television shows — a device that allowed Cornelius to continue to promote all-black television series, just as when *Soul Train* had weekly guest hosts. Not all of the shows featured exclusively African American casts, however; stars of *The George Lopez Show, Mad-TV, The Practice, Star Trek Enterprise,* and *The View* attended the *Starfest* over the years.

The *Soul Train Christmas Starfest* served two cross-promotion purposes. Like all the other specials, this one prominently featured the name of the dance show. As a result, the *Starfest* had the potential to remind viewers of the existence of *Soul Train*. In addition, the special was named after a compact disc compilation of seasonal songs performed by R&B artists. Because Epic Records had only released the disc in 1997, it still stood to benefit in sales from the nationwide televising of its namesake when the first annual festivities began in 1998. Barely over a year later, however, *Soul Train* began a season of unprecedented television exposure, which resulted from the appeal of one of its personalities with his viewers.

In early 2000, Shemar Moore became the *Soul Train* host. He was the first host who had no ties to the program when Cornelius hosted it. Like Clark, Moore was an actor. He had previously found work playing himself— as a guest panelist on game shows *Match Game* and *Hollywood Squares*. As a result, he already had established his amiability as a television personality. In addition, he had starred in the movies *Hav Plenty, Butter,* and *Mama Flora's Family*; and he had won guest roles on several situation comedies.

Despite his television experience, he was unsure about the hosting job. "When [Cornelius] first approached me about it, I really thought he was kidding me," Moore recalled. He considered his voice a hindrance, saying, "I don't have the smooth, Mr. Baritone Man thing."

Cornelius responded by simply patting him on the back and saying, "I like who you are and what you represent."

"With that kind of support from him, I had enough guts to give it a try," Moore decided.[31]

The new host won a Daytime Emmy Award during his tenure on *Soul Train*, but not for his work on that show. At the time he began hosting, he had a recurring role on the CBS soap opera *The Young and the Restless* as "Malcolm Winters." After six seasons, he won the Emmy for Outstanding Supporting Actor in May 2000, only a few months after having started on *Soul Train*. While on stage to receive his award, he called his mother on his cellular telephone to tell her the news. He had created another memorable moment at the Daytime Emmy ceremony of the previous year, announcing that Susan Lucci of the ABC soap opera *All My Children* (1970–present) broke her losing streak for the Leading Actress award after eighteen consecutive nominations.[32]

Moore's success in the television industry clashed with Cornelius' promotion of *Soul Train* as an "underdog" series with little power in that industry. As Cornelius had expanded his business success with *Soul Train* as the foundation and found film work tied into his hosting job, Moore continued to act in roles with no connection to his role as host. When asked in 2001 how long he would continue as host, he replied, "It's all going to depend on scheduling and flexibility. If I'm still able to chase all my acting jobs and still be on *Soul Train*, I would love to do it for years to come." For a few years, he struck a productive balance. He starred in television movies *How to Marry a Billionaire: A Christmas Tale* and *Chasing Alice*, and he landed a role in the theatrical feature *The Brothers*. He stayed on *The Young and the Restless* for two seasons after winning his Emmy. He then started a new recurring role in the science fiction drama *Birds of Prey* (2002–03).[33]

Moore's fame as a major African American presence in Hollywood hardly resulted from *Soul Train*. Most of his press coverage during his years on the show had little to do with the show. Reporters referred to him as "Daytime Emmy Winner" or "star of *The Young and the Restless*." Many articles did not even mention the dance series or Moore's job with it when discussing him. Such oversights rarely occurred when Cornelius and, to a lesser extent, Mystro Clark were the hosts.

When journalists did discuss Moore's hosting gig, they did not subject him to the same scrutiny Cornelius got. At the time *Soul Train* entered syndication in 1971, reporters complimented Cornelius on his extensive knowledge of the

R&B music industry. They often noted his experience in R&B radio. In contrast, journalists tended to be more superficial when covering Moore. Words that frequently appeared in newspaper articles about the new host included "sexy" and "hottie"—a far cry from when reporters merely mentioned Cornelius' psychedelic wardrobe, not his looks, in the 1970s.

Still, Moore's stint on *Soul Train* allowed him to have what very few television stars could claim — six days per week of television air time in new productions. Monday through Friday, he was on *The Young and the Restless*. On Saturdays he hosted *Soul Train*. His exposure, ironically, mirrored that of Dick Clark in the 1970s and 1980s. While hosting *American Bandstand* on Saturdays, Clark spent each weekday moderating *The $20,000 Pyramid* and its successive inflationary series.

The six-day spread also allowed Moore the opportunity to diversify his audience. *The Young and the Restless* aired in the late morning hours, attracting the prime demographics of college students, retirees, and stay-at-home parents. Teenagers missed the show because of school attendance. But they could spend part of their Saturday mornings watching *Soul Train*.

Although Moore did not need the exposure, he hosted several events related to *Soul Train*. He presided over Cornelius' various awards shows and the ceremony commemorating *Soul Train*'s thirtieth anniversary. As a result, he was becoming the new face not only of *Soul Train* but also of Cornelius' empire. Cornelius called upon Moore to a much greater degree than upon Mystro Clark, who only hosted the weekly series. Having an Emmy winner as a host certainly added prestige to the *Soul Train* ceremonies, and as a soap opera star, Moore's popularity among women made him a fitting choice for the *Lady of Soul Awards*. Moore even hosted a non-televised thirtieth anniversary party that Cornelius held in Las Vegas at the House of Blues in the elegant Mandalay Bay Hotel.[34]

As *Soul Train* entered its fourth decade as well as the twenty-first century, the show moved beyond pitching products to becoming a product. Rhino Records collaborated with Cornelius a second time for the production of yet another compact disc series *Soul Train: The Dance Years*. Each disc contained songs released in a particular year. Some of the recordings had appeared in earlier music compilations. In addition, several of the musicians represented in "The Dance Years" did not perform their songs on the show. Still others never appeared on the series.

The Dance Years further linked *Soul Train* to *American Bandstand* in that the creators of both shows had become content to romanticize their shows simplistically as products of their times. As early as the 1970s, Dick Clark redefined the memory of his show by having male dancers in a twenty-fifth anniversary special wear black leather jackets, which contrasted with the actual coat-and-tie rule of the show in the 1950s and 1960s. Similarly, Cornelius pitched his program as a survivor of the disco era by attaching the "Soul Train" name to a compilation of crossover disco hits. In the show's actual dance years, however, *Soul Train* featured lesser known balladeers and funk pioneers. Disco artists appeared on a variety of programs, and a few of the performers never boarded the *Soul Train*. The discs covering the mainstream R&B hits of the early 1970s were more reflective of the show's music than later retrospectives, for the R&B singers of the decade's beginning were more likely to have appeared on *Soul Train* than anywhere else on television.

The packaging of the compact discs was the aspect of the compilation series that was least like the television series. The front cover displayed *Soul Train*'s logo of the 1987–88 through 1992–93 seasons, but the discs only covered the 1970s. On the back cover and the disc itself, the show's newest logo prominently appeared. The liner notes made hardly any connections between the songs and their presentations on *Soul Train*. Nor did the notes describe any important developments in the program for each year covered in the compact disc series.

Unlike the previous boxed sets, *The Dance Years* attached the *Soul Train* name only to the 1970s. As a result, Rhino Records followed Cornelius' lead in promoting that particular decade as the peak of the series. The restriction of the compilation to the 1970–79 period, however, implied that in the years 1980 to 2000, *Soul Train* did not provide dance music or dances of comparable quality. The exclusion minimized the contributions the series still made to popular culture; the "breakdancing" craze, for example, kept the show popular with youths and the press in the 1980s.

The Clark-Cornelius similarities stretched into marketing. To help promote the collection, Cornelius took the bold step of collaborating with a television network. The music network Video Hits One (VH1) aired an infomercial that featured customer testimonials as well as *Soul Train* clips of artists singing some of the *Dance Years* songs. At the time, the network had just concluded a successful run of repeat broadcasts of *American Bandstand*'s episodes of the 1975–1985 period, and Clark capitalized on the show's renewed popularity with tie-in products. For the first time in years, press coverage of Clark's show in reruns rivaled that of the new episodes of *Soul Train*; even the magazine *Rolling Stone*, which had not written favorable articles about

Clark in the 1970s, commented on *American Bandstand*'s renaissance. Meanwhile, Shemar Moore hosted the thirty-minute *Dance Years* advertisement. Cornelius had not aired many of those old segments for nearly thirty years.

Unlike Clark, Cornelius decided not to rerun *Soul Train*. He had an advantage over Clark because new episodes of *Soul Train* still were airing when he was marketing *The Dance Years*, whereas *American Bandstand* had been off the air for six years before the VH1 rebroadcasts began in 1995. Cornelius had two tracks: he sold products related to the show by celebrating its history and by taking liberties with its past, but kept the series free of much historical content in the new millennium. *Soul Train*, after all, still billed itself "the hippest trip in America." The introduction to each episode, however, boasted that it was television's longest running syndicated program.

The television promotion of *The Dance Years* was simultaneously familiar and novel. Television commercials for *Soul Train*–sponsored compilation albums first aired in 1973, when the Adam VIII label did the compiling. Then, Cornelius had not yet built his empire of awards shows and merchandising. To return to simple television spots for a product based on the series implied that thirty years after *Soul Train*'s debut, the show still needed the exposure. But the infomercial's broadcasts on the cable network VH1 broke new ground, because Cornelius prided himself on not relying on networks for the survival of his program. Now that his advertisement aired on a network owned by media giant Viacom, he could no longer claim to owe the industry nothing.

The advertising had significantly changed by the new millennium. George Johnson's television commercials for hair products were consigned to history. L'Oreal became the new owners of Johnson Products before altogether dissolving the business. The show was not lacking in sponsorship, but now it aired commercials by Sprite and McDonald's, just like any other series marketed to adolescents and young adults. The spots for Afro Sheen Cosmetics had at least given *Soul Train* some individuality. Johnson was one of the show's last links to its Chicago days, and his financial generosity had enabled national syndication back in 1971.

Despite the growth of Cornelius' empire, he continued to portray himself as the underdog. In August 2001, he complained to reporters that MTV had unfair booking practices. The network refused to book artists on its *Video Music Awards*— MTV's most lucrative annual broadcast — if they appeared on other shows, which included Cornelius' award telecasts. Because MTV had more money and power in the entertainment industry than Cornelius, he stood to lose acts like Alicia Keys for the *Lady of Soul Awards*. The network soon relented, having already experienced recent anti-trust lawsuits from others.[35]

The Keys controversy demonstrated Cornelius' isolation from television network politics. Having syndicated his own series for thirty years and having a pool of R&B talent for the choosing for most of those years, he never had to compete strongly for artists. Non-compete clauses like the one MTV devised were very common in the industry. Eight years earlier Arsenio Hall had lambasted Jay Leno of *The Tonight Show* and the show's network, NBC, for implementing a similar clause, which drained Hall's pool of guests. MTV executives argued that they were within their legal right to draft their own clause, but Cornelius considered the arrangement a violation of anti-trust laws and said so in a letter to the U.S. Department of Justice. He also opposed it on moral grounds; the clause was not a *fair* thing to do. Challenging a law or practice on the issue of morality was a civil rights tactic.

MTV's granting of an exception of its clause to Cornelius yielded mixed results. On the one hand, his victory meant that he could continue to avoid playing by network rules. On the other hand, he now had no incentive to compete with networks and did not do so. An MTV spokeswoman said that anyone who thought non-compete clauses were an unusual industry practice was "naïve." Cornelius succeeded in conveying his underdog image, but appeared naive — hardly a good reputation for someone in television for three decades. He had won the Keys battle while losing the war of increasing television competition.[36]

The Keys incident also illustrated Cornelius' isolation within African American media companies. When he protested MTV's clause, he was alone in his outspokenness. He specifically called attention to his ceremony's Afrocentricity and the African American ethnicity of Keys in his complaint: "How can a pop channel that made a name for itself by openly banning videos by black artists during its early years now threaten African American acts with retribution if they choose to perform on a competing, black-owned media project such as *Soul Train*?" No other major African American organization openly complained that the network was racist, which weakened Cornelius' claims of racism. MTV's exemption to Cornelius did not extend to other televised African American ceremonies like *The Source Awards*, a hip-hop ceremony that was taped within days of the *Lady of Soul Awards*; but nobody from *The Source* aligned with Cornelius. As a result, Cornelius did not further pursue the matter when MTV excused only the *Lady of Soul Awards* from the non-compete clause.[37]

The inspiration for the *Source Awards* ceremony, created by *The Source* magazine, was similar to that of the Soul Train Music Awards in 1987. Hip-hop was a marginalized genre of music although gaining crossover appeal, just as soul music had been in the 1970s and 1980s. As a result, *The Source* did not suffer heavy competition for appearances by hip-hop artists at its awards festivities. Similarly, Cornelius had access to performers in 1987, because most of the artists he initially sought were not mainstream celebrities but rather marginalized R&B stars. As R&B became more popular outside of urban demographics and fostered superstars in the 1990s, he invited the stars but had to compete with others to secure the bookings. MTV's non-compete clause had little effect on the *Source Awards*, because hip-hop was a small portion of the *Video Music Awards*.

MTV's contemporary relationships with African American record labels also undermined Cornelius' criticisms of the network's historic racism. Artists from labels like Def Jam and Bad Boy received extensive airplay on MTV. The popularity of those performers, especially through the videos the network played, helped to make the labels' leaders — Russell Simmons and Sean Combs, respectively — into young millionaires in a relatively short amount of time. No contemporary artist or label executive came to Cornelius' defense to protest the network's actions. To do so would have meant criticizing their major promoter. They did not owe their careers as much to Cornelius as to MTV.

Still, Cornelius' shows remained familiar icons of popular culture. Meanwhile, a business with no ties to *Soul Train* spoofed the series for a television commercial. In the fall of 2003, the clothing franchise Old Navy advertised its sale on cargo pants with a television spot illustrating the fictional show "Cargo Train." Old Navy lent some authenticity to the commercial by arranging for *Soul Train*'s host Shemar Moore to act as the host of "Cargo Train." The advertisement marked Old Navy's second reference to *Soul Train*; an earlier commercial had the show's popular theme "TSOP" playing in the background.

The commercial was a mixed blessing for *Soul Train*. On the one hand, the spot proved that the series had become a cultural icon. Old Navy did not have to do much beyond approximating the *Soul Train* logo's font and creating a Soul Train Line to give the feeling of the show. On the other hand, many Old Navy advertisements of this period paid tribute to kitsch. "Cargo Train" showed that *Soul Train* had considerable value as kitsch. Focusing on flamboyant dances and gimmickry like the Line minimized the contributions that *Soul Train* had made to the television and music industries since 1970.

When Moore stepped down as host in 2003, he did not remain out of work for long. As with his acting jobs during his hosting tenure, his post–*Soul Train* work had no connection with the show. Moore continued to appear as a guest star in several series. He landed a leading role in the successful theatrical movie *Diary of a Mad Black Woman*. He then won a recurring role in the television drama series *Criminal Minds* (2005–present).

On October 11, 2003, yet another actor — Dorian Gregory — became the *Soul Train* host. He had appeared as a guest in many of the same shows as the guest stars of *Soul Train*. Like his immediate predecessor Shemar Moore, Gregory had demonstrated his real-life and dramatic television appeal. He won regular roles in the series *Baywatch Nights* from 1996 to 1997 and *Charmed* from 1998 to 2005. He also appeared as himself in the lightweight panel discussion program *The Other Half*— a male version of the hit ABC daytime talk show *The View*. Cornelius lured Gregory away from *The Other Half* for *Soul Train*— an ironic development, for Dick Clark was the host and producer of the panel show. Unlike Moore, Gregory did not become a breakout star during his time on *Soul Train*. Rather, he kept a low profile, not unlike Mystro Clark, and stayed with the dance show through the 2005–06 season.

Cornelius did not use Gregory as he had Moore. Gregory did not replace Moore as the face of Cornelius' empire. The new host instead was restricted to hosting duties on *Soul Train*. He never presided over the Soul Train Music Awards; that was left to singers Brian McKnight and Kenneth "Babyface" Edmonds and actor Nick Cannon. For the *Lady of Soul Awards*, Cornelius enlisted McKnight, singer Tyrese Gibson, and comedian Arsenio Hall.

Meanwhile, Cornelius received high honors from both the television and music industries. The March 2005 *TV Land Awards* ceremony lovingly paid tribute to shows that had become an important part of American television history. As part of the celebration of *Soul Train* that year, Toni Basil, a former member of the Lockers, choreographed a dance number to a soul music medley. Cornelius received TV Land's Pop Culture Award and a standing ovation from the audience. He modestly dismissed some of the claims people had made about his show, saying that he did not deserve credit for getting kids "off the streets and in the house" to watch his program. He did acknowledge that *Soul Train* influenced fashion and popular culture by promoting hip trends.[38]

That same year he received a Grammy Award for non-performing contributions to the music industry. He received two standing ovations upon accepting his statue, and tears filled his eyes as he stood at the lectern. But the award was not only a sentimental, moving event but also a humorous one.

Fellow honoree Mavis Staples quipped that she and Cornelius attended high school in Chicago together: "I think I was a virgin; Don was a senior."[39]

After the 2005–06 season ended, Tribune syndicated reruns through the fall of 2006 — a longer hiatus than usual for *Soul Train*. Then Cornelius finally offered audiences something different — reruns of episodes from the 1970s and 1980s. Starting in December 2006, Tribune began syndicating *The Best of Soul Train*. Unlike VH1's *The Best of American Bandstand*, the older repeats of *Soul Train* arrived without much advance fanfare and did not generate the same amount of industry chatter as *Bandstand*. Still, devotees of *Soul Train* expressed appreciation for *The Best of Soul Train*. Messages on the show's unofficial Yahoo Internet group tripled from November to December 2006. Subscribers praised hearing long forgotten songs and seeing dancers whom they had not seen on the show since the 1970s or 1980s. Some of the former dancers left messages about their work on the series.

The Best of Soul Train did not completely recapture the experience of watching the show in the 1970s. All of the original commercials were absent. Cornelius censored the advertisements for Johnson Products within the show, including the plugs at the beginning of the "Soul Train Scramble" segments. Within a month, the closing credits disappeared; each rerun ended right after the "love, peace, and soul" sign-off. In addition, awkward juxtapositions of past and present took place with the airings of the reruns. The new commercials for major corporations Coca-Cola Products and American Airlines revealed how far *Soul Train* had come from the days of Afro-Sheen and Kentucky Fried Chicken. Colorful, computerized title graphics for *The Best of Soul Train* were superimposed over the old footage just before commercial breaks.

Gregory sought other television work. He landed a role in the series *Show Stoppers*. He appeared as himself in the documentary *Life on the Road with Mr. and Mrs. Brown*. The press did not report Gregory's separation from *Soul Train* when the 2005–06 season ended. Journalists did not ask about his status when Cornelius started airing the old reruns. The show lost its host without any fanfare — a far cry from the departures of Cornelius and, to a lesser degree, Clark.

As for the *Soul Train* empire, its momentum had slowed since the heady 1990s. The *Lady of Soul Awards* did not take place in 2004 but returned the following year. Cornelius advertised the 2005 festivities as the tenth annual despite missing a year. The eleventh annual event did not take place in 2006. Cornelius discontinued the *Christmas Starfest* after the November 2005 broadcast.

Of all the *Soul Train*–related annual events, only the Soul Train Music Awards remained active after 2005. Cornelius gave the twentieth annual ceremony the following year a significant amount of promotion. Many A-list celebrities attended, which helped the event garner considerable publicity. Hosts Vivica A. Fox and Tyrese Gibson were Hollywood movie actors with ties to the show as a former Soul Train Dancer and a musical guest, respectively. Academy Award winner Jamie Foxx won a music award that night. Other major stars present ranged from newcomers like Chris Brown and John Legend to young but durable performers Mariah Carey and R. Kelly to R&B elder statesman Stevie Wonder. Members of the recently disbanded group Destiny's Child also appeared to receive their awards.

Meanwhile, the *Soul Train* franchise had one final project. VH1 arranged to air repeat telecasts of Cornelius' television specials of the 2005–06 season. It was his first long-term partnership with a television network. The relationship also had considerable irony, for Cornelius had quarreled with another Viacom property, MTV, over Alicia Keys only five years earlier. "VH1 has been looking to work with Don Cornelius and *Soul Train* for ages," said network executive Ben Zurier. "*Soul Train* is a premium brand in the worlds of R&B, hip-hop, and soul, and its expertise in what's hot today and what we love from the past is a perfect fit with what we do at VH1." For all the talk about the value of the *Soul Train* name, however, the flagship dance show was noticeably absent from the list of programs the network aired in rerun. Indeed, VH1 broadcast everything except *Soul Train*; the *Lady of Soul Awards*, the *Christmas Starfest*, and the *Music Awards* went on the network within one month of their original syndicated broadcasts. The exclusion demonstrated that *Soul Train* was a "premium brand" but not a premium show.[40]

The network deal and the successful 2006 Soul Train Music Awards could not stave off the decline of the *Soul Train* franchise. VH1 did not renew its arrangement with Cornelius for the 2006–07 season. With the other awards shows and the *Soul Train* program itself out of production by early 2007, the thirty-first annual Soul Train Music Awards gave Cornelius' empire its first burst of media attention in nearly one year. Most of the publicity initially resulted from the names of the celebrities announced as nominees in February. The following month journalists covered the ceremony and reported the names of the winners. Some of the reporters gave Cornelius his first unfavorable press coverage in years by lamenting the absences of the majority of the winners of competitive awards.

Moreover, the 2007 Soul Train Music Awards demonstrated that in terms of press coverage, Cornelius had now come full circle. From *Soul Train*'s premiere until 1972, the guest musicians got more press coverage than Cornelius. Now, after thirty-five years, the performers at the Soul Train Music Awards were more central than Cornelius, whether for their award speeches or their absences. The few articles mentioning him mostly centered on allegations that scheduled performer Jennifer Hudson did not want to appear at the ceremony.

The enormous success of the BET Awards later that year confirmed the decline of the Soul Train Music Awards. Stars were present to accept awards, and well-respected entertainers gave special performances. Eddie Levert sang a tribute to his recently deceased son Gerald, and Yolanda Adams, Gladys Knight and Patti LaBelle joined him during the song. Diana Ross, who had not promoted her solo hits on *Soul Train*, attended the ceremony to receive a tribute from her five children and singers Stevie Wonder and Chaka Khan. Jennifer Hudson, the *Dreamgirls* star, not only appeared at the BET Awards without controversy but also sang a song from the movie — "And I Am Telling You I'm Not Going" — with Jennifer Holliday, who had originally recorded it for the Broadway show on which the movie was based. Whether BET had more prestige than the *Soul Train* name or had more money (through owner Viacom) than Cornelius to entice major entertainers to attend, the cable network had now bested him in his own black awards genre as well as in televising African American culture.[41]

Despite Cornelius' latter-day comparisons of himself to Dick Clark, the *Soul Train* producer failed to note that the *American Bandstand* producer saw profits in his production company drop because he relied too much on specials instead of weekly or weekday series. In 1989, when Clark's dance show ended, he had only the annual *American Music Awards*, *Academy of Country Music Awards*, and *New Year's Rockin' Eve* telecasts remaining on the air. Cornelius similarly erred in building his television empire on specials. In his case, the awards ceremonies faltered before the flagship *Soul Train* series did. Yet after 2006, he, like Clark in 1989, lacked a weekly series in production, and the annual Soul Train Music Awards event did not have a promising future. As industry analyst Harold Vogel of Merrill Lynch & Co. astutely observed, "You can't make it on specials alone."[42]

For the moment, *Soul Train* is literally fading into history. Reruns continue to air, but no resumption of production is in sight. The press has not expressed interest in the show's future — a sad fate for the longest-running syndicated program in television history. When covering Cornelius, reporters are content to identify *Soul Train* as a program — not a program on hiatus. When he receives awards, no one calls him the host of *The Best of Soul Train*, although the weekly broadcasts have gone by that title for months. By airing the "classic" episodes for the duration, Cornelius is at least partially allowing the viewers to judge for themselves why the "train" chugged for as long as it did.

Epilogue

"Love, Peace, and Soul": The Legacies of Soul Train

Cornelius hardly saw himself as a television pioneer. In interviews throughout his career as the producer of *Soul Train*, he acknowledged that his program did not break new ground conceptually. "*Soul Train* was not something that hadn't been thought of by other people," he told reporter Jae-Ha Kim in 1991. "It's something that people have wanted for many, many years. But I think I was the first one who was able to make it happen, through persistency and just having the belief that it filled a viable need in the entertainment industry."[1]

The producer's choice of the past tense "filled" is telling. It implies that either *Soul Train* no longer fills the need, or the need no longer exists for *Soul Train* to fill. The show is certainly not the only one to broadcast R&B music or the latest dances. BET and MTV have expanded on *Soul Train*'s ushering in of black music television by implementing innovative filming techniques and providing filmed R&B more frequently than one hour per week. *Soul Train* continues to showcase R&B but is not the only televised venue.

The concept of having "soul" has taken on a derisive quality. When the theatrical feature film *Soul Plane* was released in 2004, reviewers were familiar with the source of the title. Whereas *Soul Train* had presented the best of R&B music for years, *Soul Plane* told the story of an inept crew of an all-black airline. Racial stereotypes abounded in the movie. Although African American businesses have been the butt of humor since the days of the dilapidated "Fresh Air Taxicab" of *Amos 'n' Andy*, African Americans were now complicit in caricaturing Afro-centricity. *Soul Train* gave "soul" a comedic context by having comedians host the show and by failing to strongly challenge the devastating parodies of it in the media.

Soul Train has a mixed legacy in the press. For his awards shows and anniversaries of the series, reporters continue to hold Cornelius in high regard. They also marvel at his power in the entertainment industry and portray him to this day as an underdog. Journalists usually ask him about the show's roots and its ability to survive in the difficult television business.

The show itself is only held in high regard for its longevity. Very few journalists have commented on the show's contributions to the entertainment industry and have instead focused on the program's significance to African Americans. Cornelius influenced this development by routinely discussing *Soul Train*'s success with African Americans and by minimizing the uniqueness of the program. Despite the fact that *Soul Train* became a synonym for Afro-centric television in the 1970s and challenged Dick Clark's supremacy in music television, Cornelius in recent years has admitted to aping *American Bandstand* and has called all dance series — including his — the same.

Soul Train was important in the R&B industry. The episodes collectively serve as a time capsule of the evolution of the music genre from 1970 to 2006. Especially valuable are the episodes featuring guest artists who have died and groups that have disbanded. *Soul Train* televised some forms of R&B when no one else would. The funk musicians of the 1970s were rarely invited to other series because of the music's lack of crossover appeal. As a result, for many of them, their only television appearances were on *Soul Train*.

Cornelius showed through *Soul Train* that Afro-centric programming could be successful. No longer did white producers and hosts alone have to showcase R&B to mainstream audiences. Now African Americans catered directly to urban viewers. His urban marketing paved the way for entire networks, such as the defunct United Paramount Network and Warner Brothers Network, to create urban programming blocks of hours in the 1990s and early 2000s.

Soul Train is known more for its success than its struggle. Journalists rarely approach anyone but Cornelius to discuss the show's history, longevity or other relevant issues. The best-known dancers such as Damita Jo Freeman receive sporadic coverage. Even Cornelius' most loyal staffers are rarely interviewed. Longtime employees such as coordinator Pam Brown and announcer Sid McCoy, both of whom worked on the program since its syndicated debut, are largely absent from the discussions about the series.

Among all the celebratory news articles about the long run of *Soul Train*, little coverage focuses on the WCIU version of the program. Outside of Chicago newspapers, the media does not mention E. Rodney Jones, Ronnie

Paul Johnson, or Clinton Ghent in its overviews of the early years of the program. More importantly, Cornelius himself has made few references to his former radio and television colleagues of the Windy City, but frequently mentions George Johnson of Johnson Products as a critical figure in the production of *Soul Train*. As a result, the retrospective articles simply discuss *Soul Train* as an instant hit after only one local year without showing how others besides Cornelius and Johnson contributed to the series and helped it survive.

But even WCIU's *Soul Train* influenced television. Just as the program introduced Afro-centricity and political activists to dancing teenagers, BET combined public affairs with urban R&B hits for the series *The Center*. BET's program also shared *Soul Train*'s WCIU schedule, for both shows were weekday after-school programs. The major difference lay in *The Center* presenting music videos instead of adolescents dancing to popular songs.

Soul Train pioneered televising dance contests judged by a panel of celebrities. When disco music became popular, the program *Dance Fever* (1978–87) revived televised dance competition. The tradition continues in several contemporary reality series such as *So You Think You Can Dance* (2005–present) and *Dancing with the Stars* (2005–present).

The show popularized some of the most controversial trends among African Americans in the twentieth century. Dancers wore clothes that drug dealers would wear, and artists used the program as a forum for saying "nigger" among other African Americans. Both developments became opened Pandora's Boxes for African Americans as a whole. The criminal lifestyle continues to be glorified in some R&B and hip-hop music, some of which the series promoted after the 1970s. Meanwhile, the issue of African Americans' use of the n-word still causes internal division, as emphasized in debates among African Americans over the practicality of the National Association for the Advancement of Colored People's ceremonial "burying" of the word at a mock funeral on July 10, 2007.

Soul Train's glorification of recreational drug use in November 1978 still resonates in African American popular culture nearly three decades later. The show introduced "stoned" personas Cheech and Chong and Rick James to urban viewers that month. More recent manifestations include rap artists Snoop Dogg, Method Man, and Redman. Comedian Dave Chappelle imitated James on *Chappelle's Show* (2003–06), exploiting and caricaturing the singer's "high" persona for a generation of viewers not yet alive in 1978. And African American descendants of Cheech and Chong's dope movie genre are the films *Half-Baked*, *How High*, and the *Friday* films.

Another legacy of *Soul Train* is that it remains Don Cornelius' show more than a show belonging to his audience. In recent years, former record labels Motown and Stax have opened museums, inviting guests to learn about their respective contributions to the music industry. At least four books about *American Bandstand* have been published since the mid–1970s, and Dick Clark keeps the name in cultural circulation via an American Bandstand restaurant chain and DVD sales of the recent television series *American Dreams* (2002–05), which fictionalized Clark's dance show during its years in Philadelphia. In contrast, Cornelius has invited audiences to remember his series only once per week through the Saturday broadcasts of *The Best of Soul Train*. Without Tribune Entertainment's continued syndication of the series, it would not have a constant contemporary cultural presence. No restaurants, no dramas.

As a result of *Soul Train*'s cultural absence, Cornelius has had to confront a growing grassroots movement commemorating the series through piracy. As reruns of *Soul Train* episodes from as early as 1971 began playing in Japan with subtitles years ago, people started recording the episodes and selling them on DVD. In a message addressing the bootlegged videos, *Soul Train*'s official Web site (run by Don Cornelius Productions) asks people not to order or purchase them. Potential customers were able to save their money anyway when clips from the pirated reruns began appearing on the free Internet site YouTube in 2006. As of this writing, scenes from the Japanese reruns, *The Best of Soul Train*, the years of *Soul Train* without Cornelius as host, and even the British adaptation *620 Soul Train* commonly appear on YouTube.

The Web site for DCP, www.soultrain.com, perpetuates Cornelius' isolation from the viewers of his shows. The site provides no means to give feedback on the programs or the site itself to anyone at DCP; neither a street address nor telephone number for the company is listed, and the company offers no e-mail addresses — not even to the webmaster. It has no message board for commentators to exchange ideas with one another. The Web site presents further evidence of a decline in DCP's franchise.

The Web site suggests that DCP is out of touch with its own franchise. He has no links to connect www.soultrain.com with any webpages that sell the various *Soul Train* compact disc collections, although Amazon.com, for example, continues to peddle them. In addition, the DCP Web site doesn't update information on telecasts. None of the show information has been updated since 2005. The webpage on the Soul Train Music Awards does not list any presenters or winners after 2005 but does include an advertisement for the 2006 awards. The 2007 ceremony was not being promoted on DCP's Web site as of August 2007.

Now that the most successful current music and dance series have become interactive, *Soul Train* and www.soultrain.com may benefit from following suit. A major part of the appeal of modern talent shows like *American Idol* (2002–present) and *So You Think You Can Dance* is that viewers participate in the voting process. MTV's long-running *Total Request Live* (1998–present) similarly allows the audience to choose which videos to air, and BET has offered several video countdown shows for its adolescent audiences. Ironically, if *Soul Train* were to take viewers' requests about which songs to play or which dancers should go down the Line, it would not be the first time; the WCIU version took suggestions from its audience concerning song playlists. And if the series is revived and thrives, it would once again beat the odds — yet another Cornelius tradition.

Appendix A

Recurring Guests on the Syndicated Soul Train

Three acts had ten or more *Soul Train* appearances: The Temptations, The Whispers, and Barry White.

Soul Train *Episodes in the 1970s (1971-72 through 1979-80 seasons)*

Two Appearances

Herb Alpert, Archie Bell and the Drells, Bohannon, Johnny Bristol, James Brown, Randy Brown, B.T. Express, Jimmy Castor, Chairmen of the Board, Gene Chandler, Chic, Otis Clay, Merry Clayton, Con Funk Shun, Crème D' Coca, Lamont Dozier, Ronnie Dyson, Brenda Lee Eager, Ecstasy, Passion & Pain, Aretha Franklin, The Gap Band, Graham Central Station, Garland Green, Michael Henderson, High Energy, Hodges, Smith, James & Crawford, Thelma Houston, Leroy Hutson, Luther Ingram, Jermaine Jackson, Jackson Sisters, Rick James, Denise La Salle, Labelle, Lakeside, Ramsey Lewis, Cheryl Lynn, Hugh Masekela, Johnny Mathis, George McCrae, Dorothy Moore, Melba Moore, Mothers Finest, New Birth, Ohio Players, The Originals, Danny Pearson, Esther Phillipps, Wilson Pickett, Bonnie Pointer, The Pointer Sisters, Richard Pryor, Martha Reeves, Ritchie Family, D.J. Rogers, Rose Royce, Side Effect, O.C. Smith, Southshore Commission, Stargard, The Stylistics, Foster Sylvers, The Temprees, Rufus Thomas, Tower of Power, The Tramps, Ike and Tina Turner, Gino Vannelli, Tata Vega, Junior Walker and the All-Stars, Johnny Guitar Watson, Lenny Williams, Charles Wright.

Three Appearances

Roy Ayers, Bobby Bland, Blue Magic, Pattie Brooks, The Brothers Johnson, G.C. Cameron, The Commodores, Creative Source, The Delphonics, The Emotions, Friends of Distinction, Leon Haywood, The Honey Cone, Willie Hutch, The Independents, The Intruders, B.B. King, Laura Lee, Love Unlimited, L.T.D., Mandrill, The Manhattans, Barbara Mason, Marilyn McCoo and Billy Davis, Jr., The Miracles, Johnny Nash, Natural Four, The Persuaders, Minnie Riperton, Sylvia Robinson, Shalamar, Bunny Sigler, Joe Simon, Sister Sledge, The Staple Singers, The Supremes, Switch, Joe Tex, Fred Wesley, Deniece Williams, Syreeta Wright.

Four Appearances

Ashford and Simpson, Bar-Kays, Brass Construction, Jerry Butler, The Chi-Lites,

The Dells, The Fifth Dimension, The Impressions, The Isley Brothers, Michael Jackson, Millie Jackson, Jackson Five/ The Jacksons, The Main Ingredient, The Moments, Billy Paul, Freda Payne, David Ruffin, Edwin Starr, The Undisputed Truth, War, Al Wilson, Betty Wright.

Five Appearances

Bloodstone, Lyn Collins, Tyrone Davis, Al Green, Kool and the Gang, Gladys Knight and the Pips, Lou Rawls, Smokey Robinson, Rufus, The Spinners, Tavares, Barry White.

Six Appearances

The Four Tops, Harold Melvin and the Blue Notes, The O'Jays, The Sylvers, Johnnie Taylor, The Temptations, Bill Withers.

Seven Appearances

The Dramatics, Curtis Mayfield, Bobby Womack.

Eight Appearances

Eddie Kendricks, Billy Preston.

Eleven Appearances

The Whispers.

Soul Train *Episodes in the 1980s (1980-81 through 1989-90 seasons)*

Two Appearances

Gregory Abbott, Colonel Abrams, Donna Allen, The Beastie Boys, George Benson, The Boys, Robert Brookins, Bobby Brown, The Busboys, Irene Cara, Carl Carlton, The Chi-Lites, Club Nouveau, Desiree Cole-man, Tyler Collins, Michael Cooper, Dazz Band, Chico Debarge, The Deele, George Duke, Dennis Edwards, Richard "Dimples" Fields, Force MDs, The Four Tops, Rosie Gaines, Johnny Gill, The Good Girls, Larry Graham, Guy, Heavy D and the Boyz, Thelma Houston, George Howard, Latoya Jackson, Al Jarreau, Miles Jaye, Michael Jeffries, Howard Johnson, Glenn Jones, Junior, Johnny Kemp, Kiara, Kool and the Gang, Krystol, Little Richard, LL Cool J, LTD, Carrie Lucas, Manhattan Transfer, Mantronix, Mary Jane Girls, Melba Moore, Meli'sa Morgan, Billy Ocean, David Peas-ton, Pebbles, Anita Pointer, Ray, Goodman and Brown, Rockie Robins, Run-DMC, Brenda Russell, Shannon, SOS Band, The Spinners, Surface, Keith Sweat, A Taste of Honey, Tavares, Tony Terry, Third World, Today, Troop, Luther Vandross, Beau Williams, Vesta Williams, Womack and Womack, Betty Wright.

Three Appearances

Anita Baker, The Bar-Kays, Cherrelle, The Commodores, Con Funk Shun, The Controllers, Sheena Easton, Five Star, Full Force, Giorgio, Nona Hendryx, Howard Hewett, Miki Howard, Freddie Jackson, Janet Jackson, Jermaine Jackson, Rebbie Jackson, Rick James, The Jets, Kashif, Lillo, Lisa Lisa and Cult Jam, Michael McDon-ald, Alexander O'Neal, Ray Parker, Jr., The Pointer Sisters, Patrice Rushen, Sister Sledge, Skyy, The System, Johnnie Taylor, The Temptations, Vanity, Jody Watley, Karyn White, Whodini, Eugene Wilde, Shanice Wilson, Angela Winbush, Bobby Womack.

Four Appearances

Regina Belle, D'Train, Debarge, Al Green, Klymaxx, Levert, Midnight Star, The O'Jays, Ready for the World, Starpoint, The Time/ Morris Day, Barry White, Yarbrough & Peo-ples.

Five Appearances

Cameo, James Ingram, Evelyn King, Patti Labelle, Cheryl Lynn, Teena Marie, Jeffrey Osbourne, Shalamar, The Whispers.

Six Appearances

Atlantic Starr, Lakeside, Stacy Lattisaw, Deniece Williams.

Seven Appearances

The Gap Band, Stephanie Mills, New Edition, O'Bryan.

Soul Train *Episodes in the 1990s (1990-91 through 1999-2000 seasons)*

Two Appearances

3T, A+, After 7, All-4-One, Another Bad Creation, Az, Az Yet, Regina Belle, Big Bub, Blaque, Mary J. Blige, Bizzy Bones, The Boys, Boyz II Men, Brand New Heavies, Horace Brown, Case, Chubb Rock, D-Nice, D'Angelo, Das Efx, Davina, Day Ta Day, Divine, DJ Quik, Nate Dogg, Marc Dorsey, George Duke, Kevon Edmonds, EPMD, Eve, Ex-Girlfriend, Father MC, Rachelle Ferrell, A Few Good Men, For Real, Eric Gable, Johnny Gill, Goodfellas, Peter Gunz, Lalah Hathaway, Heavy D, Hi-Five, Hiroshima, Dave Hollister, Miki Howard, Ice Cube, Imajin, IMX, Jade, Jeru the Damaja, Glenn Jones, Miss Jones, Shae Jones, Juvenile, Chaka Khan, Kid 'n' Play, Patti Labelle, Eddie Levert, Lisa Lisa, Lo-Key, Lords of the Underground, Monie Love, Mack 10, Teena Marie, Maxwell, Jacci McGhee, Men at Large, Men of Vizion, Yvette Michelle, Missy, Mona Lisa, J.T. Money, Keith Murray, Mya, Aaron Neville, Ol' Skool, Patra, PM Dawn, Portrait, Prince Markie Dee, Public Announcement,

Public Enemy, Busta Rhymes, Riff, Robyn, Pete Rock and C.L. Smooth, Run DMC, Sam Salter, Erick Sermon, Sisqo, Solo, Soul 4 Real, Sparkle, Take 6, Quindon Tarver, Temptations, Tony Terry, Gina Thompson, The Time/Morris Day, UMC Uncle Sam, Barry White, Karyn White, Whitehead Brothers, Christopher Williams, Angela Winbush, Stevie Wonder.

Three Appearances

69 Boyz, 112, 702, Atlantic Starr, Before Dark, Big Daddy Kane, Brandy, Chico De Barge, El De Barge, Destiny's Child, Jermaine Dupri, Faith, Warren G., Howard Hewett, Ideal, Intro, Freddie Jackson, Jagged Edge, Jodeci, R. Kelly, Kurupt, Levert, Cece Peniston, Jesse Powell, Usher Raymond, Redman, Chantay Savage, Shai, Somethin' for the People, Tracie Spencer, Keith Sweat, SWV, Tamia, J.T. Taylor, TQ, Ralph Tresvant, Tyrese, Chris Walker, The Whispers, Bebe Winans, Yo Yo.

Four Appearances

II D Extreme, Monica Arnold, Eric Benet, Blackstreet, Brownstone, Color Me Badd, Da Brat, X-Scape, Goodie Mob, H-Town, Joe, Donnell Jones, Montell Jordan, Kris Kross, Kenny Lattimore, Monifa, Naughty by Nature, Next, Outkast, Kelly Price, Rome, Keith Washington, Jody Watley, Shanice Wilson.

Five Appearances

Jon B., Tevin Campbell, Deborah Cox, Dru Hill, Gerald Levert, LL Cool J, MC Lyte, Chante Moore, Silk, Snoop Doggy Dogg, Sounds of Blackness, Al B. Sure, Tony! Toni! Tone!, Cece Winans, Zhane.

Six Appearances

Ginuwine, Aaron Hall, Immature, Brian McKnight, Mint Condition.

Soul Train *Episodes in the 2000s (2000-01 through 2005-06 seasons)*

Two Appearances

3LW, Ali, Allure, Ashanti, ATL, Regina Belle, Eric Benet, Rhian Benson, Big Tymers, Bilal, Horace Brown, Sleepy Brown, Busta Rhymes, Cam'ron, Blu Cantrell, Nick Cannon, Case, Zane Copeland Jr., Deborah Cox, Da Brat, Jermaine Dupri, Dwele, Rachelle Ferrell, Kirk Franklin, Goapele, Macy Gray, Ginuwine, Vivian Green, Deitrick Haddon, Heather Headley, IMx, Isley Brothers, Frankie J., Freddie Jackson, Jagged Edge, Jaheim, Javier, Syleena Johnson, Donnell Jones, Montell Jordan, K-Ci & Jojo, Kenny Lattimore, Li'l Kim, Li'l Wayne, Loon, Mack-10, Mario, Angie Martinez, Mary Mary, Mya, Nappy Roots, Nivea, Smokie Norful, Ray J. Norwood, Omarion, Lorenzo Owens, Pretty Ricky, Pru, R.L., Shaggy, Silkk the Shocker, Carl Thomas, Truth Hurts, Urban Mystic, Michelle Williams, Won-G, Ying Yang Twins.

Three Appearances

3LW, B2K, Bow Wow, Cee-Lo, Mr. Cheeks, Nate Dogg, Fabolous, Floetry, Tyrese Gibson, Dave Hollister, Marques Houston, India Arie, Glenn Lewis, Li'l Romeo, Brian McKnight, Chante Moore, Musiq, Ruff Endz, Tamia, Keke Wyatt.

Four Appearances

Avant, Master P, Nelly, Tank.

Appendix B

Guest Hosts, 1993–97

Guests Who Hosted the Most Episodes (two each)

Tyra Banks, Tisha Campbell, TK Carter, Tommy Ford, Vivica Fox, T'Keyah Keymah, Paula Jai Parker, Sheryl Lee Ralph, Stephanie Roberts, Kristoff St. John.

Television Series with Multiple Actors as Guest Hosts

Family Matters: Telma Hopkins, Darius McCrary, Kellie Williams, Michelle Williams.
Fresh Prince of Bel-Air: Tatyana Ali, Joseph Marcell, Karyn Parsons, Alfonso Ribeiro.
Hangin' with Mr. Cooper: Mark Curry, Holly Robinson.
Jamie Foxx Show: Christopher Duncan, Jamie Foxx.
Living Single: T.C. Carson, John Henton.
Martin: Tichina Arnold, Tisha Campbell, Tommy Ford, Carl Payne.
Moesha: Lamont Bentley, Sheryl Lee Ralph, Countess Vaughn.
Sister, Sister: Jackee Harry, Tamera Mowry, Tia Mowry.
Young and the Restless: Shemar Moore, Victoria Rowell, Kristoff St. John.

Guest Hosts Who Previously Appeared When Don Cornelius Was Host

Tisha Campbell, Mystro Clark, Vivica Fox, Aries Spears.

Appendix C

Chronology

September 27, 1936: Don Cornelius is born in Chicago, Illinois.

1966: Cornelius enrolls in a three-month broadcasting course.

1967: Cornelius begins work at WVON radio.

1968: Cornelius starts work at WCIU-TV. His first on-camera job is on the series *A Black's View of the News*.

August 17, 1970: *Soul Train* premieres in Chicago on WCIU-TV, airing weekdays from 4:30 P.M. to 5:30 P.M. Cornelius quits his job at WVON.

1971: Johnson Products begins sponsorship of *Soul Train*, becoming the first black business to sponsor a television series.

August 13, 1971: King Curtis, who recorded *Soul Train*'s adopted theme song "Hot Potatoes," is murdered.

Summer-Fall 1971: Don Cornelius and Clinton Ghent establish production of *Soul Train* in Los Angeles.

October 2, 1971: The Los Angeles *Soul Train* enters national syndication. Meanwhile, the Chicago *Soul Train* continues to air weekdays on WCIU.

December 1972: Cornelius tours Washington, D.C.

1973: The telemarket record label Adam VIII begins selling compilation albums with the *Soul Train* name.

March-April 1973: Dick Clark's *Soul Unlimited* airs on ABC-TV. It is the first

show to compete against *Soul Train* by imitating it.

May 1973: Don Cornelius dances down the Soul Train Line for the first and only time in *Soul Train*'s run.

July 1973: The movie *Cleopatra Jones*, in which Cornelius makes a cameo appearance, is released.

August 4, 1973: Clinton Ghent is identified for the first time in the Chicago press as the host of WCIU's *Soul Train*.

August 16, 1973: Cornelius performs at "Soul at the Center '73" at the Lincoln Center in New York.

August 20, 1973: Cornelius presents a stage version of *Soul Train* at the Apollo Theater in New York.

October 27, 1973: The group Mother Father Sister Brother's song "TSOP — the Sound of Philadelphia" officially replaces "Hot Potatoes" as the syndicated *Soul Train*'s theme song. This episode introduces a new set with an image that becomes the show's trademark — a locomotive spewing psychedelic fire. The new animated opening sequence also features this image.

April 20, 1974: "TSOP" is the top song on the "Billboard 100" chart.

May 1974: Richard Pryor's album "That Nigger's Crazy," recorded at Don Cornelius' Soul Train Club, is released.

June 5, 1974: Don Cornelius and the Soul

Train Gang perform as part of Sly and the Family Stone's concert in Madison Square Garden, where Sly Stone marries Kathy Silva onstage.

August 1974: The Hues Corporation appears on WCIU's *Soul Train*.

October 11, 1974: The *New York Times* reports that the syndicated *Soul Train* is one of the two series most watched by African Americans.

Early 1975: WCIU reduces *Soul Train* from sixty to forty-five minutes and gives it the time slot of 4:15–5:00 P.M.

February 1975: Singer Gino Vannelli is the first white guest artist on the syndicated *Soul Train*.

May 1975: Cornelius hosts an episode of NBC's music variety series *The Midnight Special*.

September 1975: Cornelius and talent coordinator Dick Griffey launch Soul Train Records.

June 11, 1976: The five-day-a-week WCIU edition of *Soul Train* ends.

June 18, 1976: WCIU begins airing *Soul Train* only on Fridays.

Sept. 1976: WCIU begins airing *The Best of Soul Train* on Saturdays.

1977: WCIU's *The Best of Soul Train* ends.

1977: WCIU's *Soul Train* is reduced again to a half-hour, airing in the Friday 4:00–4:30 P.M. time slot.

September 1977: The syndicated *Soul Train* begins airing on WGN Channel 9 in Chicago.

March 1978: Soul Train Records is dissolved, and Griffey launches Solar Records.

October 1978: WGN becomes a satellite cable channel.

July 27, 1979: The Chicago edition of *Soul Train* airs for the last time on WCIU.

1980: The movie *Roadie*, in which Don Cornelius has the role of "Mohammed Johnson," is released.

September 1980: Kurtis Blow is *Soul Train's* first rap act.

1981: Black Entertainment Television launches *Video Soul*.

January 1983: Cornelius temporarily shuts down production on *Soul Train* for brain surgery.

September 1984: The situation comedy *The Cosby Show* premieres on NBC-TV.

1985: Tribune Entertainment begins syndicating *Soul Train* by satellite.

March 23, 1987: Soul Train Music Awards debuts.

1987: The Saturday morning television cartoon *Mighty Mouse: The New Adventures* parodies *Soul Train* as *Soul Caboose*.

1988: MTV launches the television series *Yo! MTV Raps*, which immediately surpasses *Soul Train* in the promotion of rap and hip-hop.

October 7, 1989: Dick Clark's *American Bandstand*, Cornelius' most durable competition, ends its run of twenty-two seasons.

June 24, 1990: Comedy variety series *In Living Color* parodies *Soul Train* as "Old Train" on FOX-TV.

September 1993: Cornelius steps down as host of *Soul Train*, installing a weekly guest-host format. The set, the theme song, and the opening animated sequence undergo major overhauls.

1994: Spike Lee's movie *Crooklyn*, which pays a nostalgic tribute to *Soul Train*, is released.

November 7, 1994: Cornelius guests on NBC's situation comedy *The Fresh Prince of Bel-Air* as himself.

August 6, 1995: *Soul Train Lady of Soul Awards* debuts.

March 29, 1996: Violence erupts at the Soul Train Music Awards between employees of Death Row Records and Bad Boy Records.

February 1997: The California legislature honors an entertainer for the first time — Don Cornelius.

March 1997: At a Los Angeles party in celebration of the 11th Annual Soul Train Music Awards, rapper Notorious B.I.G. is shot dead.

September 1997: Comedian Mystro Clark becomes the first permanent *Soul Train* host since Cornelius' retirement.

1998: The *Soul Train Christmas Starfest*— an annual celebration of the holiday via music and entertainers' cameos — debuts.

2000: Replacing Mystro Clark, Shemar Moore becomes the *Soul Train* host while continuing his acting role in the series *The Young and the Restless.*

2000: Compact disc series *Soul Train: The Dance Years,* which compiles popular urban radio songs from the 1970s and 1980s, is released.

2000: L'Oreal purchases Johnson Products.

August 2001: Cornelius and MTV quarrel over the network's pressure on Alicia Keys to appear only on MTV's Video Music Awards.

September 2003: The last annual *Lady of Soul Awards* ceremony airs.

October 11, 2003: Dorian Gregory, a star of the series *Charmed,* replaces Shemar Moore the *Soul Train* host.

February 2005: Cornelius receives a Grammy Award.

March 2005: Cornelius is honored at the TV Land Awards.

September 2005: Returning after a hiatus in 2004, the final *Lady of Soul Awards* is broadcast.

October 2005: Cable network VH1 agrees to rebroadcast Cornelius' specials of the 2005–06 season.

November 2005: The last *Christmas Starfest* airs.

March 25, 2006: The last new episode of the syndicated *Soul Train* airs. Reruns begin the following week.

December 2006: *The Best of Soul Train*— rebroadcasts of episodes spanning the years 1973 to 1988 — begins airing and replaces *Soul Train.*

March 10, 2007: The annual Soul Train Music Awards ceremony takes place, but many winners are absent.

Appendix D

Soul Train *Discography*

Adam VIII Compilations (1973–1974)

Soul Train: Hall of Fame
Soul Train: Hits That Made It Happen
Soul Train: Super Tracks

Soul Train Records (1975–1978)

Carrie Lucas: *Simply Carrie*
Produced by Dick Griffey

1. I Gotta Keep Dancin' (Keep Smiling)
2. Me For You
3. Play By Our Rule
4. Tender
5. Jammin' Tenderly (Tender Part II)
6. I Gotta Get Away From Your Love
7. I'll Close Love's Door
8. What's The Question
9. Men Kiss & Tell

Shalamar: *Uptown Festival*
Executive producers: Don Cornelius, Dick Griffey; Produced by Kevin Flaherty, Colleen Graven, Kirsten Kupper, Charles Levan, Terence P. Minogue, Cheryl Pawelski, Valerie Skard, Simon Soussan, Adam Varon

1. Inky Dinky Wang Dang Doo
2. Beautiful Night

3. Uptown Festival
4. High In Life
5. Ooh Baby Baby
6. You Know
7. Forever Came Today
8. Tossing Turning And Swinging
9. Shalamar Disco Gardens
10. Take That To The Bank
11. Stay Close To Love
12. Leave It All Up To Love
13. Lovely Lady
14. Cindy Cindy
15. Simon's Theme (Instrumental)

Soul Train Gang: *Don Cornelius Presents the Soul Train Gang*
Produced by Don Cornelius, Dick Griffey

1. Garbage Can
2. I Can Do It All Night
3. Soul Train '75
4. Music on My Mind
5. Fairy-tales

Soul Train Gang: *The Soul Train Gang*
Produced by Norman Harris

1. That Certain Way
2. Doh Cha
3. How Much Longer
4. All My Life (I Wanna Live with You)
5. Soul Train Theme
6. If It Takes All Night
7. Country Girl

The Whispers: *The Whispers*
Produced by Norman Harris

1. One for the Money
2. Living Together (In Sin)
3. Put Me in the News
4. You're Only as Good as You Think You Are
5. Sounds Like a Love Song
6. I've Got a Feeling
7. In My Heart

The Whispers: *Open Up Your Love*
Executive producers: Don Cornelius, Dick Griffey; Produced by Bernadette Fauver, Kevin Flaherty, Colleen Graven, Chance Johnson, Charles Levan, Terence P. Minogue, Cheryl Pawelski, Valerie Skard, Adam Varon, The Whispers

1. Make It with You
2. Chocolate Girl
3. Love Is a Dream
4. Open Up Your Love
5. I Fell in Love Last Night
6. You Are Number One
7. You Never Miss Your Water
8. I'm Gonna Make You My Wife

Capitol Records (1982–86)

O'Bryan: *Doin' Alright*
Produced by Don Cornelius

1. Right from the Start
2. Love Has Found Its Way
3. The Gigolo
4. It's Over
5. Doin' Alright
6. Can't Live Without Your Love
7. Mother Nature's Calling
8. Still Water (Love)

O'Bryan: *You and I*
Executive producer: Don Cornelius

1. I'm Freaky
2. Dazzlin' Lady
3. I'm In Love Again
4. Together Always

5. You and I
6. Shake
7. Soft Touch
8. Soul Train's A-Comin'

O'Bryan: *Be My Lover*
Executive producer: Don Cornelius

1. Lovelite
2. Be My Lover
3. You Gotta Use It
4. Go On and Cry
5. Breakin' Together
6. You're Always on My Mind
7. Too Hot
8. Lady I Love You

O'Bryan: *Surrender*
Executive producers: Don Cornelius, Wayne Edwards; Produced by Aaron Zigman, Jerry Knight

1. Tenderoni
2. Driving Force
3. Is This For Real
4. Surrender
5. What Goes Around
6. Maria
7. Dreamin' About You

Epic Records (1985–97)

Rosie Gaines: *Caring*
Produced by Don Cornelius and Rosie Gaines

1. Dance All Night Long
2. I've Gone Too Far
3. Skool-Ology (Ain't No Strain)
4. Caring
5. Frustration
6. Wake Up
7. Good Times
8. What Are We Coming To
9. Innocent Girl
10. Crazy
11. In a Jam

Soul Train Christmas Starfest (compilation of Christmas songs by R&B artists)

Rhino Records Compilations (1994–2000)

Soul Train 20th Anniversary Hall of Fame
Soul Train: The Dance Years (set of yearly compilations spanning 1970 to 1979)

MCA Records (1995)

Soul Train 25th Anniversary Hall of Fame (compilation)

Chapter Notes

Chapter 1

1. St. Clair Drake and Horace R. Cayton, *Black Metropolis: A Study of Negro Life in a Northern City* (New York: Harcourt, Brace, 1945), 438–439, 443–445, 454.

2. Alan B. Anderson and George W. Pickering, *Confronting the Color Line: The Broken Promise of the Civil Rights Movement in Chicago* (Athens: University of Georgia, 1986), 77.

3. Charles Reeves, "The Soul Train," *Philadelphia Tribune*, 30 June 1996, 17, magazine section.

4. Daniel Wolff, *You Send Me: The Life and Times of Sam Cooke* (New York: William Morrow, 1995), 84, 106, 108.

5. *Ibid.*, 108.

6. Taylor Bell, "Du Sable's Pain Endures," *Chicago Sun-Times*, 14 March 2004.

7. Clarence Petersen, "'Soul Train' Is a Hit in Spite of Itself," *Chicago Tribune*, 19 June 1971, 3, sec. C.

8. Allan Johnson, "Don Cornelius Is Still Rolling Along," *Chicago Tribune*, 26 September 1995, 5:1, sec. 5; Jae-Ha Kim, "TV Host Keeps 'Soul Train' on Fast Track," *Chicago Sun-Times*, 12 March 1991, 49, sec. 2.

9. James Bolden, "Soul Train Still on Track After 23 Years," *Los Angeles Sentinel*, 4 March 1993, 6, sec. B; Drake and Cayton, 462, 463.

10. Maurice Weaver, "'Soul Train' Awards Are a 1st for Black Music," *Chicago Tribune*, 23 March 1987, 3.

11. Al Raby, quoted in Henry Hampton and Steve Fayer, *Voices of Freedom: An Oral History of the Civil Rights Movement from the 1950s through the 1980s* (New York: Bantam, 1990), 309.

12. Gene Roberts and Hank Klibanoff, *The Race Beat: The Press, the Civil Rights Struggle, and the Awakening of a Nation* (New York: Alfred A. Knopf, 2007), 401.

13. Howard Saffold, quoted in Hampton and Fayer, 527–528.

14. Lucky Cordell, interview by author, 21 March 2007.

15. Cordell, interview; Priscilla English, "Don Cornelius: Man Who Engineers Soul Train," *Los Angeles Times Calendar*, 18 November 1973, 22.

16. Kim, 49, sec. 2; Bolden, 6, sec. B.

17. Ann Hodges, "Ladies of Soul," *Houston Chronicle*, 13 August 1995, 3.

18. Hillary Chura, "Cornelius Still on Track," *Advertising Age*, 7 March 2005, 12; Pervis Spann, *The 40 Year Spann of WVON* (Chicago: National Academy of Blues, 2003), 57; English, 22.

19. Chura, 12; English, 22.

20. Hodges, 3.

21. Earl Calloway, "The 'Good Guys' Made Chicago Fabulous Through WVON," *Chicago Defender*, 24 March 2003, 18; John Wirt, "E. Rodney Jones," *The Advocate*, 2 January 2004, Fun section; Brenda Warner Rotzoll, "E. Rodney Jones, 75 Disc Jockey," *Chicago Sun-Times*, 7 January 2004.

22. Wirt, Fun section; Rotzoll.

23. Wirt, Fun section; Rotzoll.

24. Lorenzo Clemons, letter to author, 20 March 2007.

25. Kim, 49, sec. 2.

26. "Black Radio: On a High Wire with No Net," *Broadcasting*, 31 August 1970, 45.

27. Taylor Branch, *At Canaan's Edge: America in the King Years, 1965–68* (New York: Simon & Schuster, 2006), 515, 524, 535; Linda Bryant Hall, quoted in Hampton and Fayer, 318.

28. Spann, 164.

29. Dave Hoekstra, "Electric Personality," *Chicago Sun-Times*, 29 October 1995, 3.

30. *Ibid.*

31. Chura, 12; Neil Strauss, "You Say 'Soul Train' Is How Old?" *New York Times*, 31 December 1995, 12:3; English, 22; Weaver, 3.

32. Cordell, interview.

33. George O'Hare, interview by author, March 2007.

34. O'Hare, interview; Spann, 99.
35. O'Hare, interview; Spann, 61.
36. O'Hare, interview; Spann, 61.
37. O'Hare, interview; Spann, 61.
38. Wolff, 289.
39. Spann, 57; English, 22.
40. "Black Radio," 49; Bolden, 6, sec. B.

Chapter 2

1. Hillary Chura, "Cornelius Still on Track," *Advertising Age*, 7 March 2005, 12.
2. Priscilla English, "Don Cornelius: Man Who Engineered Soul Train," *Los Angeles Times Calendar*, 18 November 1973, 22; Jae-Ha Kim, "TV Host Keeps 'Soul Train' on Fast Track," *Chicago Sun-Times*, 12 March 1991, 49, sec. 2.
3. "'Monkey Time' at Budland," *Chicago Defender*, 25 June 1963, 16; Dave Hoekstra, "Former TV Host of 'Soul Train' to Emcee 'Prom,'" *Chicago Sun-Times*, 30 January 1990, 29; Marshall Thompson, interview by author, 7 February 2007.
4. Hoekstra, 29.
5. Hoekstra, 29.
6. Don Cornelius, quoted in "Soul Conductor," interview with Tavis Smiley, *The Tavis Smiley Show*, 4 April 2002; Howard Shapiro, interview by author, 26 January 2007.
7. Crescendo Ward, interview by author, 22 February 2007; Lorenzo Clemons, letter to author, 20 March 2007; Art West, interview by author, 11 January 2007.
8. Allen Johnson, "Don Cornelius Is Still Rolling Along," *Chicago Tribune*, 26 September 1995, 5:1, sec. 5; Bobby Hutton, letter to author, March 2007.
9. Murray Schumach, "King Curtis, the Bandleader, Is Stabbed to Death," *New York Times*, 15 August 1971, 38.
10. *Ibid.*
11. Cash Michaels, "J.D. Lewis, Broadcast Pioneer, Dies at 87," *Wilmington Journal*, 24 February 2007; Jake Austen, *TV a-Go-Go: Rock on TV from* American Bandstand *to* American Idol (Chicago: Chicago Review, 2005), 97; Ward, interview.
12. Gregg Parker, interview by author, 30 January 2007; Hoekstra, 29; Garrick Anders, interview by author, 28 February 2007.
13. "Pervis Staples Leaves Group To Become Stax Representative," *Chicago Defender*, 20 August 1969, 13; Thompson, interview; The Dells, letter to author, 28 February 2007; Theresa Davis, letters to author, April 2007.
14. Davis, letters.
15. Clarice Kavanaugh, letter to author, 23 March 2007.
16. Parker, interview; Ward, interview.
17. Parker, interview; Andres, interview.
18. "Soul Train Hit With Teens," *Chicago Defender*, 21 September 1970, 13.
19. Hoekstra, 29.
20. Ward, interview.
21. Delwen Fields, interview by author, 26 February 2007; Kavanaugh, letter.
22. Shapiro, interview; Earl Calloway, "STAR Galaxy; Soul Train Dance Set Slated for Cultural Center at South Shore," *Chicago Defender*, 2 February 2002, 18; Davis, letters.
23. Pervis Spann, *The 40 Year Spann of WVON* (Chicago: National Academy of Blues, 2003), 164–165.
24. "On TV Show...," *Chicago Defender*, 13 January 1972, 2.
25. *Ibid.*; Henry Hampton and Steve Fayer, *Voices of Freedom: An Oral History of the Civil Rights Movement from the 1950s through the 1980s* (New York: Bantam, 1990), 523.
26. Earl Calloway, "The Auditions Dedicate New Disk to Soldiers," *Chicago Defender*, 7 March 1973, 10.
27. "Soul Train Has TV Guest Star Marc Copage as Guest," *Chicago Defender*, 24 July 1971, 35.
28. Anders, interview.
29. Clemons, letter; Kavanaugh, letter.
30. Thompson, interview.
31. Davis, letters.
32. "Pervis Staples Leaves Group To Become Stax Representative," 13.
33. *Ibid.*
34. Clemons, letter.
35. Thompson, interview; Gerri Hirshey, *Nowhere to Run: The Story of Soul Music* (New York: Times, 1984), 307–308.
36. Clemons, letter.
37. "Jerry Butler Kicks Off WCIU's Soul Train," *Chicago Defender*, 17 August 1970, 10.
38. *Ibid.*
39. George O'Hare, interview by author, March 2007.
40. Bill Jackson, interview by author, 31 January 2007.
41. Clayton Riley, "A 'Train' on the Soul Track," *New York Times*, 4 February 1973, 17:5, sec. II; Shapiro, interview; Anders, interview.
42. Riley, 17:5, sec. II.
43. Hampton and Fayer, *Voices of Freedom*, 523–524.
44. O'Hare, interview; Austen, 43, 97.
45. Cornelius, quoted in "Soul Conductor;"

Clarence Petersen, "'Soul Train' Is a Hit in Spite of Itself," *Chicago Tribune*, 19 June 1971, 3, sec. C.

46. O'Hare, interview.

47. O'Hare, interview.

48. O'Hare, interview.

49. Schumach, 38.

50. Marylin Bender, "Black Capitalist: Listing of His Concern on Amex Marks a 'First,'" *New York Times*, 24 January 1971, 2, sec. P.

51. "Johnson Products Trading on AMEX," *New York Times*, 15 January 1971, 32; Bender, "Black Capitalist," 2, sec. P.

52. Bender, "Black Capitalist," 2, sec. P; "Making Black Beautiful," *Time*, 7 December 1970.

53. "Making Black Beautiful," *Time*, 7 December 1970.

54. Christopher P. Lehman, *American Animated Cartoons of the Vietnam Era: A Study of Social Commentary in Films and Television Programs, 1961–1973* (Jefferson, N.C.: McFarland, 2006), 141.

55. Petersen, 3, sec. C.

56. "Soul Train Goes National on CBS," *Chicago Defender*, 23 October 1971, 22.

57. Kavanaugh, letter; Spann, 40–41, 51.

58. Kavanaugh, letter; Austen, 97.

59. Thompson, interview; Hal Erickson, *Syndicated Television: The First Forty Years, 1947–1987* (Jefferson, N.C.: McFarland, 1989), 252.

60. Dells, letter.

61. Riley, 17:5, sec. II; English, 22.

62. Dells, letter.

63. Petersen, 3, sec. C; Leah Davis, "*Soul Train*: We've Got Our Own," *Soul*, 14 February 1972, 12; "The Auditions Dedicate New Disk to Soldiers," 10; "Stars Honor Rodney Jones," *Chicago Defender*, 29 September 1973, 17.

64. "Guest...," *Chicago Defender*, 4 August 1973, 20; "Butler Considered for King Cole Story," *Chicago Defender*, 17 November 1973, 20.

65. Ward, interview; Kavanaugh, letter; Anders, interview.

66. Theresa Davis, letters; Fields, interview.

67. Ward, interview.

68. Ward, interview.

69. Ward, interview.

70. Jackson, interview.

71. "RCA's 'Rock the Boat' Party Welcomes Hues Corporation," *Chicago Defender*, 14 August 1974, 18.

72. Ward, interview.

73. Fields, interview.

74. Kavanaugh, letter; Ward, interview.

75. Kavanaugh, letter.

76. Fields, interview.

77. Shapiro, interview.

78. Shapiro, interview.

79. "Black of the Month," *Time*, 1 May 1972.

Chapter 3

1. Chris Pursell, "'Soul Train,' 'ET' Mark Milestones," *Electronic Media*, 4 January 2001, 31.

2. Dave Hoekstra, "Former TV Host of 'Soul Train' to Emcee 'Prom,'" *Chicago Sun-Times*, 30 January 1990, 29.

3. Priscilla English, "Don Cornelius: Man Who Engineers Soul Train," *Los Angeles Times Calendar*, 18 November 1973, 22; Garrick Anders, interview by author, 28 February 2007.

4. Leah Davis, "*Soul Train*: We've Got Our Own," *Soul*, 14 February 1972, 12.

5. Ron Bauchman, correspondence with author, May 2007.

6. Hal Erickson, *Syndicated Television: The First Forty Years, 1947–1987* (Jefferson, N.C.: McFarland, 1989), 184.

7. *Ibid.*, 146, 152.

8. "Don Cornelius Is a Businessman with Soul," *MSNBC Entertainment*, 8 March 2006, http://www.msnbc.msn.com; "Soul Train Story," *Don Cornelius Productions*, http://www.soul-train.com; Erickson, *Syndicated Television*, 252.

9. Angela Terrell, "Super Tall, Super Cool and Here," *Washington Post*, 13 December 1972, 15, sec. C.

10. Erickson, *Syndicated Television*, 183–185.

11. Terrell, "Super Tall, Super Cool and Here," 15, sec. C.

12. George O'Hare, interview with author, March 2007.

13. "Couples Dance for Scholarships," *Chicago Defender*, 13 May 1972, 4.

14. "'Soul Train' Is Great, Goes National," *Chicago Defender*, 1 November 1971, 10.

15. Davis, 12.

16. Marshall Thompson, interview by author, 7 February 2007; Bobby Hutton, letter to author, 18 May 2007.

17. Robert Pruter, *Chicago Soul* (Urbana: University of Illinois, 1992), 329, 339.

18. "A New Style," *Chicago Defender*, 23 September 1971, 19; Hutton, letter.

19. *Ibid.*; "Bobby Hutton Featured on 'Soul Train,'" *Chicago Defender*, 30 October 1971, 19; "'Soul Train' Goes National on CBS," *Chicago Defender*, 23 October 1971, 22.

20. Hutton, letter.

21. Hutton, letter.

22. Gerald Posner, *Motown: Music, Money,*

Sex, and Power (New York: Random House, 2002), 64, 168, 237.

23. Posner, 146, 149.

24. Pruter, 127–128.

25. Clayborne Carson, *In Struggle: SNCC and the Black Awakening of the 1960s* (Cambridge: Harvard University, 1981), 296.

26. Davis, 12–13.

27. Arhomuz, "Damita Jo, Resident Dance Diva," *Sentinel*, 10 November 1999, 6, sec. B.

28. Arhomuz, 6, sec. B; Jake Austen, *TV a-Go-Go: Rock on TV from* American Bandstand *to* American Idol (Chicago: Chicago Review Press, 2005), 258–259.

29. Paul Delaney, "Operation PUSH Opens a Black Expo in Chicago," *New York Times*, 28 September 1972, 28; Thomas A. Johnson, "Jesse Jackson Forms New Black Group for Economic and Political Action," *New York Times*, 19 December 1971, 44.

30. Paul Delaney, "Black Supporters of President Under Fire," *New York Times*, 17 October 1972, 29.

31. *Ibid.*

32. Hal Erickson, *"From Beautiful Downtown Burbank": A Critical History of* Rowan and Martin's Laugh-In, *1968–1973* (Jefferson, N.C.: McFarland, 2000), 186, 251.

33. Bauchman, correspondence.

34. Evan Marshall, "Drug Rip-Offs — Peace and Love Trip Is Over," *Los Angeles Times*, 4 December 1973, 1.

35. "'Soul Train' Is Great, Goes National," 10.

36. Christopher P. Lehman, *American Animated Cartoons of the Vietnam Era: A Study of Social Commentary in Films and Television Programs, 1961–1973* (Jefferson, N.C.: McFarland, 2006), 163.

37. Bauchman, correspondence.

38. Crescendo Ward, interview by author, 22 February 2007.

39. English, 22.

40. Mic Gillette, letter to author, 23 July 2007.

41. "Anthony Sabatino," *Variety*, 13 April 1993.

42. "Couples Dance for Scholarships," 4.

43. John A. Jackson, *American Bandstand: Dick Clark and the Making of a Rock 'n' Roll Empire* (New York: Oxford University, 1997), 258–259; Davis, 12.

Chapter 4

1. Leah Davis, "*Soul Train*: We've Got Our Own," *Soul*, 14 February 1972, 12–13.

2. Davis, 13.

3. Davis, 12.

4. Davis, 12–13.

5. "'Soul Train' Back for 2nd Season TV Series," *Chicago Defender*, 20 September 1972, 12.

6. Priscilla English, "Don Cornelius: Man Who Engineered Soul Train," *Los Angeles Times Calendar*, 18 November 1973, 96.

7. Angela Terrell, "Super Tall, Super Cool and Here," *Washington Post*, 13 December 1972, 15, sec. C.

8. "Don Cornelius Is Alive and Well," *Chicago Defender*, 26 February 1973, 9.

9. "'Soul Train' Back for 2nd Season TV Series," 12; Clayton Riley, "A 'Train' on the Soul Track," *New York Times*, 4 February 1973, 17.5, sec. II.

10. "Rising Complaints Shake Film Truce with Blacks," *New York Times*, 27 September 1972, 37.

11. "Don Cornelius Is Alive and Well," 9.

12. English, "Don Cornelius: Man Who Engineered Soul Train," 96.

13. Ben Fong-Torres, "'Soul Train' vs. Dick Clark: Battle of the Bandstands," *Rolling Stone*, 7 June 1973, 9–10.

14. Fong-Torres, 10.

15. Fong-Torres, 10.

16. Fong-Torres, 9–10; John A. Jackson, *American Bandstand: Dick Clark and the Making of a Rock 'n' Roll Empire* (New York: Oxford University, 1997), 57.

17. Fong-Torres, 10; Steve Holsey, "They Didn't Like It, But...," *Michigan Chronicle*, 30 November-6 December 2005, 1, sec. D.

18. Riley, 17.5, sec. II; English, 96.

19. William L. Van De Burg, *New Day in Babylon: The Black Power Movement and American Culture, 1965–1975* (Chicago: University of Chicago, 1992), 259.

20. George O'Hare, interview by author, March 2007.

21. English, 22.

22. English, 22, 96.

23. Hal Erickson, *"From Beautiful Downtown Burbank": A Critical History of* Rowan and Martin's Laugh-In, *1968–1973* (Jefferson, N.C.: McFarland, 2000), 210.

24. C. Gerald Fraser, "Soul '73 to Open Here Tomorrow," *New York Times*, 3 August 1973, 21.

25. Ian Dove, "TV's 'Soul Train' Moves to Apollo," *New York Times*, 22 August 1973, 45.1.

26. "Who Makes Music and Where," *New York Times*, 19 August 1973, 118.

27. English, "Don Cornelius: Man Who Engineered Soul Train," 96.

28. *Ibid.*

29. Martha Bayles, *Hole in Our Soul: the Loss*

of Beauty & Meaning in American Popular Music (Chicago: University of Chicago, 1994), 270.

30. James McPherson, "The New Comic Style of Richard Pryor," *New York Times*, 27 April 1975, 40.

31. *Ibid.*

32. Judith Cummings, "Sly of Rock Group Weds in the Garden," *New York Times*, 6 June 1974, 43; "People," *Time*, 17 June 1974, 62–64.

33. Earl Calloway, "Cornelius to MC NAACP Awards," *Chicago Defender*, 29 December 1973, 8.

34. R. Milton Clark, "The Dance Party as a Socialization Mechanism for Black Urban Pre-Adolescents and Adolescents," *Sociology and Sociological Research*, vol. 58, no. 2 (1974), 150.

35. John Laycock, Review: *The Wiz*, *New York Times*, 3 January 1975, 18.

36. Les Brown, "Blacks Watch More TV Than General Audiences," *New York Times*, 11 October 1974, 75.

37. John J. O'Connor, "TV: Don Kirshner Opens Rock Season," *New York Times*, 20 September 1974, 77.

38. Warren Foulkes, "Perspective on 'Soul Train,'" *Black World*, February 1975, 68, 71.

39. *Ibid.*, 70.

40. *Ibid.*, 68, 70.

Chapter 5

1. Stu Black, "She Took the Soul Train to Stardom," *Los Angeles Times*, 13 December 1987, 26.

2. *Ibid.*

3. *Ibid.*

4. "Soul Concert Gets an Energetic Lift from Betty Wright," *New York Times*, 1 April 1975, 28.

5. Barry Williams and Chris Kreski, *Growing Up Brady: I Was a Teenage Greg* (New York: Harper Perennial, 1992), 149.

6. Gerald Posner, *Motown: Music, Money, Sex and Power* (New York: Random House, 2002), 289.

7. Bruce W. Miller, letter to author, 12 April 2007.

8. Stephen Holden, "Solar could be the Motown of the 80's," *New York Times*, 23 March 1980, 25, sec. D.

9. Holden, 25, sec. D; "'Word Out' on Stewart," *Tri-State Defender*, 16 January 1985, 4.

10. Black, 26.

11. *Ibid.*

12. Holden, 25, sec. D.

13. Miller, letter.

14. Alan Niester, "POP Disco from Gary's Gang Leaves Audience Sitting," *Globe and Mail*, 11 March 1980, 16, sec. E; Andy Edelstein, "Disco Dancers Take a Fling at TV," *New York Times*, 31 December 1978, 17, sec. L.

15. Christa Lee, letter to author, 17 July 2007.

16. "Gino Vannelli Doesn't Like Comparisons," *Globe and Mail*, 12 March 1979, 15, sec. P.

17. Gino Vannelli, letter to author, 14 January 2007.

18. Vannelli, letter.

19. Vannelli, letter.

20. Vannelli, letter.

21. "Gino Vannelli Doesn't Like Comparisons," 15, sec. P.

22. Joe Vannelli, letter to author, 24 July 2007.

23. Robert Christgau, "David Bowie Discovers Rock and Roll," *Village Voice*, 5 August 1976.

24. Lee, letter.

25. Cameron Crowe, "David Bowie," *Playboy*, September 1976.

26. Vannelli, letter.

27. Lee, letter.

28. Larry Stammer, "Dymally-Curb Race Abounds in Charges," *Los Angeles Times*, 5 November 1978, 5, sec. II; Richard Bergholz, "Deukmejian and Justice Bird Victors; Props 5, 6 Go Down to Defeat," *Los Angeles Times*, 8 November 1978, 1.

29. Dick Clark with Fred Bronson, *Dick Clark's American Bandstand* (New York: Collins, 1997), 122; Arhomuz, "Damita Jo, Resident Dance Diva," *Sentinel*, 10 November 1999, 6, sec. B.

30. Lee, letter.

31. Lee, letter.

32. *Ibid.*

33. Lee, letter.

34. Lee, letter.

35. Lee, letter.

36. Lee, letter.

37. Lonnie Burr, "Diplomats of Dope Comedy," *Los Angeles Times*, 1 October 1978, 90, Calendar section.

38. Lee, letter.

39. Hal Erickson, *"From Beautiful Downtown Burbank": A Critical History of* Rowan & Martin's Laugh-In, *1968–1973* (Jefferson, N.C.: McFarland, 2000), 170–171; Burr, 91.

40. "Carney and Meat Loaf to Star in 'Roadie' Film," *New York Times*, 23 October 1979, 12, sec. C; Angela Terrell, "Super Tall, Super Cool and Here," *Washington Post*, 13 December 1972, 15, sec. C.

41. Phyllis Funke, "A Black Conductor Pushes the Cause of Music," *New York Times*, 30 No-

vember 1975, 142; Howard Thompson, "Going Out Guide," *New York Times*, 14 March 1979, 21, sec. C.

Chapter 6

1. Kevin Thomas, "Rudolph's 'Roadie': Sound of Music," *Los Angeles Times*, 14 June 1980, 2, sec. II; "*Roadie*," *Variety*, 11 June 1980.
2. Stephen Holden, "Solar Could Be the Motown of the 80's," *New York Times*, 23 March 1980, 25, sec. D.
3. Robert J. Dunphy, "Notes," *New York Times*, 2 December 1979, 7, sec. XX; "Super Bowl Notebook: Motown Area Adds Social Lilt to Its Beat," *New York Times*, 20 January 1982.
4. John A. Jackson, *American Bandstand: Dick Clark and the Making of a Rock 'N' Roll Empire* (New York: Oxford University, 1997), 270, 272; Andy Meisler, "The Beat Goes On for 'Soul Train' Conductor," *New York Times*, 7 August 1995, 7, sec. D.
5. Gerald Posner, *Motown: Music, Money, Sex, and Power* (New York: Random House, 2002), 307.
6. Vera Dunwoody, letter to author, 3 April 2007.
7. Lee Hildebrand, "Romance on the High Cs," *San Francisco Chronicle*, 9 February 1986, 40.
8. *Ibid.*
9. Bruce W. Miller, letter to author, 12 April 2007.
10. Mandalit del Barco, "Breakdancing, 'Present at the Creation,'" *Morning Edition*, National Public Radio, 14 October 2002.
11. LeeEllen Friedland, "Disco: Afro-American Vernacular Performance," *Dance Research Journal*, Spring 1983, 33.
12. Philip H. Dougherty, "Pony Plans Spot for Networks," *New York Times*, 22 February 1984.
13. Theresa Walker, "'Soul Train' Chugs into Echo Park Studio," *Los Angeles Times*, 26 December 1985, 1.
14. *Ibid.*
15. *Ibid.*
16. Denise Hamilton, "Storage Firm Buys Old Mack Sennett Studios," *Los Angeles Times*, 25 June 1987, 1.
17. David Bowman, quoted in "Proposed Sale of Sennett Studios," *Los Angeles Times*, 9 July 1987, 7.

18. James T. Jones IV and Retha Powers, "Dance Fever Kicks Up Again; The Young and Hip Get in Step," *USA Today*, 4 November 1988, 1, sec. D.
19. Jones and Powers, "Dance Fever Kicks Up Again," 1, sec. D; Mary Houlihan-Skilton, "High-Steppin' Teens Still Tune in to Dance Shows," *Chicago Sun-Times*, 18 March 1988, 69.
20. Jackson, 278–280.
21. Jake Austen, *TV a-Go-Go: Rock on TV from American Bandstand to American Idol* (Chicago: Chicago Review Press, 2005), 103.
22. Dunwoody, letter.
23. *Ibid.*
24. Vera Dunwoody, interview with author, 11 April 2007.
25. Jae-Ha Kim, "TV Host Keeps 'Soul Train' on Fast Track," *Chicago Sun-Times*, 12 March 1991, 49, sec. 2; Meisler, 7, sec. D.
26. Nick Ravo, "The '70s (Stayin' Alive) Won't Die (Stayin' Alive)," *New York Times*, 13 November 1991, 1, sec. C.
27. Steve Holsey, "'Soul Train' Rolls into Its 20th Season," *Michigan Chronicle*, 28 October 1989, 3, sec. B; Jones and Powers, "Dance Fever Kicks Up Again," 1, sec. D.
28. Richard Harrington, "Classy Soul Train Awards; Janet Jackson, Run-DMC Among Winners," *Washington Post*, 24 March 1987, 2, sec. C; "Train to Give Soul Awards," *Entertainment News Service*, 3 January 1987, 11.
29. Harrington, 2, sec. C.
30. Jeremy Lang, "Award Show Steams Into Second Year," *Sun Sentinel*, 27 May 1988, 4.
31. *Ibid.*
32. Harrington, 2, sec. C.
33. Stu Black, "She Took the Soul Train to Stardom," *Los Angeles Times*, 13 December 1987, 26.
34. *Ibid.*
35. *Ibid.*
36. Dunwoody, letter.
37. Dunwoody, interview.
38. *Ibid.*
39. Dunwoody, letter.
40. Lori Moody, "Peace, Love, and 'Soul Train,'" *Daily News*, 11 October 1995, 10, sec. L.
41. Dunwoody, letter.
42. Dunwoody, letter; Moody, 10, sec. L.
43. Dunwoody, interview.
44. *Ibid.*
45. Earl Calloway, "AFTRA Pickets 'Soul Train' Productions," *Chicago Defender*, 5 October 1989, 28; Walker, 1.

Chapter 7

1. "Anthony Sabatino," *Variety*, 13 April 1993.

2. *Ibid.*; "Anthony Sabatino," *Los Angeles Times*, 17 April 1993, 22.

3. Andy Meisler, "The Beat Goes On for 'Soul Train' Conductor," *New York Times*, 7 August 1995, 7, sec. D; Neil Strauss, "You Say 'Soul Train' Is How Old?" *New York Times*, 31 December 1995, 12:3, sec. 12.

4. Eric Deggans, "'Soul' Awards Honor Artists Often Ignored," *St. Petersburg Times*, 29 March 1996, 2, sec. B.

5. Strauss, 12:3, sec. 12.

6. Vera Dunwoody, interview with author, 11 April 2007; Jeff Lyon, "$oul Music '95," *Chicago Tribune*, 6 August 1995, 12.

7. Lori Moody, "Peace, Love, and 'Soul Train,'" *Daily News*, 11 October 1995, 10, sec. L.

8. Charles Reeves, "The Soul Train," *Philadelphia Tribune*, 30 June 1996, , 17, magazine section; Strauss, 12:3, sec. 12.

9. Carol U. Ozemhoya, "'Crooklyn' Is Heartwarming Family Entertainment," *Miami Times*, 19 May 1994, 1, sec. D.

10. Bryan Thompson, "A Look at Black Family Life During the '70s," *Recorder*, 14 May 1994, 1, sec. B.

11. Sheila Simmons, "'Soul Train' Hails Black Artists," *Plain Dealer*, 29 March 1996, 5, sec. E; Deggans, 2, sec. B.

12. Lyon, 12.

13. "Black Music Pioneer Saluted: Don Cornelius, Legendary Host of 'Soul Train,' To Be Honored By Legislature," *Sacramento Observer*, 4 June 1997.

14. Meisler, 7, sec. D.

15. Allan Johnson, "Soul Train Puts Black Comics on Track," *Chicago Tribune*, 13 August 1993, 4; Janis Da Silva, "'First Annual Soul Train Comedy Awards': A High Energy Experience," *Los Angeles Sentinel*, 25 August 1993, 3, sec. B.

16. Shauna Snow, "Comedy," *Los Angeles Times*, 1 June 1993, 2.

17. Da Silva, 3, sec. B.

18. "First Annual 'Soul Train Comedy Awards,'" *Los Angeles Sentinel*, 8 July 1993, 3, sec. B.

19. Johnson, "Soul Train Puts Black Comics on Track," 4.

20. Reeves, 17, magazine section.

21. Leah Cash, "Celebrity Showcase: Soul Train Awards," *Precinct Reporter*, 16 November 1995, 8, sec. A.

22. Steve Holsey, "The Hippest Trip in America," *Michigan Chronicle*, 30 August 1995, 1, sec. B.

23. Cash, 8, sec. A.

24. Reeves, 17, magazine section.

25. J. Freedom du Lac, "Rivalry & Rap East Coast-West Coast Marked by Harsh Words, Grudges," *Sacramento Bee*, 11 March 1997, 1, sec. E.

26. Todd S. Purdum, "Rapper Is Shot to Death in Echo of Killing 6 Months Ago," *New York Times*, 10 March 1997, 1, sec. A.

27. Cynthia Littleton, "Thesp Riding 'Soul Train,'" *Daily Variety*, 21 August 1997, 31.

28. Mystro Clark, letter to author, 28 May 2007.

29. Clark, letter.

30. Clark, letter.

31. "Shemar Moore — More Than a Pretty Face," *Jacksonville Free Press*, 25 April 2001, 11.

32. Carol Deegan, "Shemar Moore Calls Mom After Emmy," *AP Online*, 24 May 2000.

33. "Shemar Moore — More Than a Pretty Face," 11.

34. "Soul Train 30 Years Strong," *Los Angeles Sentinel*, 14 February 2001.

35. Gary Gentile, "'Soul Train' Creator Accuses MTV of Unfair Booking Policies," *Sentinel*, 23 August 2001, 3, sec. B.

36. Jeff Leeds, "MTV Is Subject of Antitrust Complaint," *Los Angeles Times*, 24 August 2001, 5, sec. C.

37. *Ibid.*

38. Neil Genzlinger, "TV Land Celebrates the Classics," *Naples Daily News*, 16 March 2005.

39. George Varga, "Meanwhile, at Grammys Other Shows," *Union-Tribune*, 20 February 2005.

40. "VH1's Got Soul," *Multichannel News*, 5 October 2005, www.multichannel.com.

41. "Hudson, Beyonce, T.I. Among BET Winners," *Time*, 27 June 2007, www.time.com.

42. John Medearis, "Dick Clark Turns 60 Hoping for a Hit," *San Francisco Chronicle*, 30 November 1989, 3, sec. E.

Bibliography

Books

Anderson, Alan B., and George W. Pickering. *Confronting the Color Line: The Broken Promise of the Civil Rights Movement in Chicago*. Athens: University of Georgia Press, 1986.

Austen, Jake. *TV a-Go-Go: Rock on TV from American Bandstand to American Idol*. Chicago: Chicago Review Press, 2005.

Bayles, Martha. *Hole in Our Soul: The Loss of Beauty & Meaning in American Popular Music*. Chicago: University of Chicago Press, 1994.

Branch, Taylor. *At Canaan's Edge: America in the King Years, 1965–68*. New York: Simon & Schuster, 2006.

Carson, Clayborne. *In Struggle: SNCC and the Black Awakening of the 1960s*. Cambridge: Harvard University Press, 1981.

Clark, Dick, with Fred Bronson. *Dick Clark's American Bandstand*. New York: Collins, 1997.

Erickson, Hal. *"From Beautiful Downtown Burbank": A Critical History of Rowan and Martin's Laugh-In, 1968–1973*. Jefferson, N.C.: McFarland, 2000.

_____. *Syndicated Television: The First Forty Years, 1947–1987*. Jefferson, N.C.: McFarland, 1989.

Hampton, Henry, and Steve Fayer. *Voice of Freedom: An Oral History of the Civil Rights Movement from the 1950s through the 1980s*. New York: Bantam, 1990.

Hirshey, Gerri. *Nowhere to Run: The Story of Soul Music*. New York: Times Books, 1984.

Jackson, John A. *American Bandstand: Dick Clark and the Making of a Rock 'N' Roll Empire*. New York: Oxford University Press, 1997.

Lehman, Christopher P. *American Animated Cartoons of the Vietnam Era: A Study of Social Commentary in Films and Television Programs, 1961–1973*. Jefferson, N.C.: McFarland, 2006.

Posner, Gerald. *Motown: Music, Money, Sex, and Power*. New York: Random House, 2002.

Pruter, Robert. *Chicago Soul*. Urbana: University of Illinois Press, 1991.

Roberts, Gene, and Hank Klibanoff. *The Race Beat: The Press, the Civil Rights Struggle, and the Awakening of a Nation*. New York: Alfred A. Knopf, 2007.

Spann, Pervis. *The 40 Year Spann of WVON*. Chicago: National Academy of Blues, 2003.

Van Deburg, William L. *New Day in Babylon: The Black Power Movement and American Culture, 1965–1975*. Chicago: University of Chicago Press, 1992.

Williams, Barry, and Chris Kreski. *Growing Up Brady: I Was a Teenage Greg*. New York: Harper Perennial, 1992.

Wilson, Mary. *Supreme Faith: Someday We'll Be Together*. New York: HarperCollins, 1990.

Wolff, Daniel. *You Send Me: The Life and Times of Sam Cooke*. New York: William Morrow, 1995.

Articles and Broadcasts

"A New Style." *Chicago Defender*, 23 September 1971, 19.

"Anthony Sabatino." *Los Angeles Times*, 17 April 1993, 22.

"Anthony Sabatino." *Variety*, 13 April 1993.

Arhomuz. "Damita Jo, Resident Dance Diva." *Sentinel*, 10 November 1999, 6, sec. B.

Bell, Taylor. "Du Sable's Pain Endures." *Chicago Sun-Times*, 24 March 2004.

Bender, Marilyn. "Black Capitalist: Listing of His Concern on Amex Marks a First." *New York Times*, 24 January 1971, 2, sec. P.

Bergholz, Richard. "Deukmejian and Justice Bird Victors; Props 5, 6 Go Down to Defeat." *Los Angeles Times*, 8 November 1978, 1.

"Black Music Pioneer Saluted: Don Cornelius, Legendary Host of 'Soul Train,' To Be Honored By Legislature." *Sacramento Observer*, 4 June 1997.

"Black of the Month." *Time*, 1 May 1972.

"Black Radio: On a High Wire with No Net." *Broadcasting*, 31 August 1970, 44–50.

Black, Stu. "She Took the Soul Train to Stardom." *Los Angeles Times*, 13 December 1987, 26.

"Bobby Hutton Featured on 'Soul Train.'" *Chicago Defender*, 30 October 1971, 19.

Bolden, James. "Soul Train Still on Track After 23 Years." *Los Angeles Sentinel*, 4 March 1993, 6, sec. B.

Brown, Les. "Blacks Watch More TV Than General Audiences." *New York Times*, 11 October 1974, 75.

Burr, Lonnie. "Diplomats of Dope Comedy." *Los Angeles Times*, 1 October 1978, 90, Calendar section.

"Butler Considered for King Cole Story." *Chicago Defender*, 17 November 1973, 20.

Calloway, Earl. "AFTRA Pickets 'Soul Train' Productions." *Chicago Defender*, 5 October 1989, 28.

_____. "Cornelius to MC NAACP Awards." *Chicago Defender*, 29 December 1973, 8.

_____. "STAR Galaxy; Soul Train Dance Set Slated for Cultural Center at South Shore." *Chicago Defender*, 2 February 2002, 18.

_____. "The Auditions Dedicates New Disk to Soldiers." *Chicago Defender*, 7 March 1973, 10.

_____. "The 'Good Guys' Made Chicago Fabulous Through WVON." *Chicago Defender*, 24 March 2003, 18.

"Carney and Meat Loaf to Star in 'Roadie' Film." *New York Times*, 23 October 1979, 12, sec. C.

Cash, Leah. "Celebrity Showcase: Soul Train Awards." *Precinct Reporter*, 16 November 1995, 8, sec. A.

Christgau, Robert. "David Bowie Discovers Rock and Roll." *Village Voice*, 5 August 1976.

Chura, Hillary. "Cornelius Still on Track." *Advertising Age*, 7 March 2005, 12.

"Clarification From Soul Train Music Awards Executive Producer Don Cornelius." *P.R. Newswire*, 12 March 1997.

Clark, R. Milton. "The Dance Party as a Socialization Mechanism for Black Urban Pre-Adolescents and Adolescents." *Sociology and Sociological Research*, vol. 58, no. 2, 1974.

Coleman, Larry G. "Black Comic Performance in the African Diaspora: A Comparison of the Comedy of Richard Pryor and Paul Keens-Douglas." *Journal of Black Studies*, vol. 15, no. 1 (September 1984), 67–78.

Cornelius, Don. "Soul Conductor." Interview with Tavis Smiley. *The Tavis Smiley Show*. National Public Radio, 4 April 2002.

"Couples Dance for Scholarships." *Chicago Defender*, 13 May 1972, 4.

Crowe, Cameron. "David Bowie." *Playboy*, September 1976.

Cummings, Judith. "Sly of Rock Group Weds in the Garden." *New York Times*, 6 June 1974, 43.

Da Silva, Janis. "'First Annual Soul Train Comedy Awards': A High Energy Experience." *Los Angeles Sentinel*, 25 August 1993, 3, sec. B.

Davis, Leah. "*Soul Train*: We've Got Our Own." *Soul*, 14 February 1972, 12–13.

DeArmond, Michelle. "Murders of Feuding Rappers Prompt Questions About Coastal Rivalry." *Associated Press*. 10 March 1997.

Deegan, Carol. "Shemar Moore Calls Mom after Emmy." *AP Online*, 24 May 2000.

Deggans, Eric. "'Soul' Awards Honor Artists Often Ignored." *St. Petersburg Times*, 29 March 1996, 2, sec. B.

Delaney, Paul. "Black Supporters of President Under Fire." *New York Times*, 17 October 1972, 29.

_____. "Operation PUSH Opens a Black Expo in Chicago." *New York Times*, 28 September 1972, 28.

del Barco, Mandalit. "Breakdancing, 'Present at the Creation.'" *Morning Edition*. National Public Radio, 14 October 2002.

"Don Cornelius Is a Businessman with Soul." *MSNBC Entertainment*, 8 March 2006, http://www.msnbc.msn.com.

"Don Cornelius Is Alive and Well." *Chicago Defender*, 26 February 1973, 9.

Dougherty, Philip H. "Pony Plans Spot for Networks." *New York Times*, 24 February 1984.

Dove, Ian. "TV's 'Soul Train' Moves to Apollo." *New York Times*, 22 August 1973, 45.1.

du Lac, J. Freedom. "Rivalry & Rap East Coast-West Coast Marked by Harsh Words, Grudges." *Sacramento Bee*, 11 March 1997, 1, sec. E.

Dunphy, Robert J. "Notes." *New York Times*, 2 December 1979, 7, sec. XX.

Edelstein, Andy. "Disco Dancers Take a Fling at TV." *New York Times*, 31 December 1978, 17, sec. L.

English, Priscilla. "Don Cornelius: Man Who Engineered Soul Train." *Los Angeles Times*, 18 November 1973, 22, 96, Calendar section.

"First Annual 'Soul Train Comedy Awards.'" *Los Angeles Sentinel*, 8 July 1993, 3, sec. B.

Fong-Torres, Ben. "'Soul Train' Vs. Dick Clark: Battle of the Bandstands." *Rolling Stone*, 7 June 1973, 9–10.

Foulkes, Warren. "Perspective on 'Soul Train.'" *Black World*, February 1975, 68–71.

Fraser, C. Gerald. "Soul '73 to Open Here Tomorrow." *New York Times*, 3 August 1973, 21.

Friedland, LeeEllen. "Disco: Afro-American Vernacular Performance." *Dance Research Journal*, vol. 15, no. 2 (Spring 1983), 27–35.

Funke, Phyllis. "A Black Conductor Pushes the Cause of Music." *New York Times*, 30 November 1975, 142.

Gentile, Gary. "'Soul Train' Creator Accuses MTV of Unfair Booking Policies." *Sentinel*, 23 August 2001, 3, sec. B.

Genzlinger, Neil. "TV Land Celebrates the Classics." *Naples Daily News*, 16 March 2005.

"Gino Vannelli Doesn't Like Comparisons." *Globe and Mail*, 12 March 1979, 15, sec. P.

"Guest..." *Chicago Defender*, 4 August 1973, 20.

Hamilton, Denise. "Storage Firm Buys Old Mack Sennett Studios." *Los Angeles Times*, 25 June 1987, 1.

Harrington, Richard. "Classy Soul Train Awards; Janet Jackson, Run-DMC Among Winners." *Washington Post*, 24 March 1987, 2, sec. C.

Hazzard-Gordon, Katrina. "Afro-American Core Culture Social Dance: An Examination of Four Aspects of Meaning." *Dance Research Journal*, vol. 15, no. 2 (Spring 1983), 21–26.

Hodges, Ann. "Ladies of Soul." *Houston Chronicle*, 13 August 1995, 3.

Hoekstra, Dave. "Electric Personality." *Chicago Sun-Times*, 29 October 1995, 3.

_____. "Former TV Host of 'Soul Train' to Emcee 'Prom.'" *Chicago Sun-Times*, 30 January 1990, 29.

Holden, Stephen. "Solar Could be the Motown of the 80's." *New York Times*, 23 March 1980, 25, sec. D.

Holsey, Steve. "'Soul Train' Rolls into 20th Season." *Michigan Chronicle*, 28 October 1989, 3, sec. B.

_____. "The Hippest Trip in America."

Michigan Chronicle, 30 August 1995, 1, sec. B.

_____. "They Didn't Like It, But..." *Michigan Chronicle*, 30 November–6 December 2005, 1, sec. D.

Houlihan-Skilton, Mary. "High-Steppin' Teens Still Tune in to Dance Shows." *Chicago Sun-Times*, 18 March 1988, 69.

"Hudson, Beyonce, T.I. Among BET Winners." *Time*, 27 June 2007, www.time.com.

"Jerry Butler Kicks Off WCIU's Soul Train." *Chicago Defender*, 17 August 1970, 10.

Johnson, Allan. "Soul Train Puts Black Comics on Track." *Chicago Tribune*, 13 August 1993, 4.

_____. "Don Cornelius Is Still Rolling Along." *Chicago Tribune*, 26 September 1995, 5:1, sec. 5.

"Johnson Products Trading on AMEX." *New York Times*, 15 January 1971, 32.

Johnson, Thomas A. "Jesse Jackson Forms New Black Group for Economic and Political Action." *New York Times*, 19 December 1971, 44.

Jones, James T., IV, and Retha Powers. "Dance Fever Kicks Up Again; The Young and Hip Get in Step." *USA Today*, 4 November 1988, 1, sec. D.

Katz, Ian. "Death Wish." *Guardian Unlimited*. 20 September 1996.

Kim, Jae-Han. "TV Host Keeps 'Soul Train' on Fast Track." *Chicago Sun-Times*, 12 March 1991, 49, sec. 2.

Lang, Jeremy. "Award Show Steams Into Second Year." *Sun Sentinel*, 27 May 1988, 4.

Laycock, John. Review: *The Wiz. New York Times*, 3 January 1975, 18.

Leeds, Jeff. "MTV Is Subject of Antitrust Complaint." *Los Angeles Times*, 24 August 2001, 5, sec. C.

Littleton, Cynthia. "Thesp Riding 'Soul Train.'" *Daily Variety*, 21 August 1997, 31.

Lott, Eric. "The Aesthetic Ante: Pleasure, Pop Culture, and the Middle Passage." *Callaloo*, vol. 17, no. 2 (Spring 1994), 545–555.

Lyon, Jeff. "$oul Music '95." *Chicago Tribune*, 6 August 1995, 12.

"Making Black Beautiful." *Time*, 7 December 1970.

Marshall, Evan. "Drug Rip-Offs — Peace and Love Trip Is Over." *Los Angeles Times*, 4 December 1973, 1.

McMichael, Robert K. "'We Insist — Freedom Now!': Black Moral Authority, Jazz, and the Changeable Shape of Whiteness." *American Music*, vol. 16, no. 4 (Winter 1998), 375–416.

McPherson, James. "The New Comic Style of Richard Pryor." *New York Times*, 27 April 1975, 20, 22, 34, 40.

Medearis, John. "Dick Clark Turns 60 Hoping for a Hit." *San Francisco Chronicle*, 30 November 1989, 3, sec. E.

Meisler, Andy. "The Beat Goes On for 'Soul Train' Conductor." *New York Times*, 7 August 1995, 7, sec. D.

Michaels, Cash. "J.D. Lewis, Broadcast Pioneer, Dies at 87." *Wilmington Journal*, 24 February 2007.

"'Monkey Time' at Budland." *Chicago Defender*, 25 June 1963, 16.

Moody, Lori. "Peace, Love, and 'Soul Train.'" *Daily News*, 11 October 1995, 10, sec. L.

"Motown Area Adds Social Lilt to Its Beat." *New York Times*, 20 January 1982.

Myers, Brenda T. "An Afternoon with Dick Griffey: His Philosophy and Thoughts on Business, with Reflections." *African American Review*, vol. 29, no. 2 (Summer 1995), 341–346.

Niester, Alan. "POP Disco from Gary's Gang Leaves Audience Sitting." *Globe and Mail*, 11 March 1980, 16, sec. E.

O'Connor, John J. "TV: Don Kirshner Opens Rock Season." *New York Times*, 20 September 1974, 77.

"On TV Show..." *Chicago Defender*, 13 January 1972, 2.

Ozemhoya, Carol U. "'Crooklyn' Is Heartwarming Family Entertainment." *Miami Times*, 19 May 1994, 1, sec. D.

"People." *Time*, 17 June 1974, 62–65.

"Pervis Staples Leaves Group to Become Stax Representative." *Chicago Defender*, 20 August 1969, 13.

Petersen, Clarence. "'Soul Train' Is a Hit in Spite of Itself." *Chicago Tribune*, 19 June 1971, 3, sec. C.

"Proposed Sale of Sennett Studios." *Los Angeles Times*, 9 July 1987, 7.

Purdum, Todd S. "Rapper Is Shot to Death in Echo of Killing 6 Months Ago." *New York Times*, 10 March 1997, 1, sec. A.

Pursell, Chris. "'Soul Train,' 'ET' Mark Milestones." *Electronic Media*, 4 January 2001, 31.

Ravo, Nick. "The 70's (Stayin' Alive) Won't Die (Stayin' Alive)." *New York Times*, 13 November 1991, 1, sec. C.

"RCA's 'Rock the Boat' Party Welcomes Hues Corporation." *Chicago Defender*, 14 August 1974, 18.

Reeves, Charles. "The Soul Train." *Philadelphia Tribune*, 30 June 1996, 17, magazine section.

Riley, Clayton. "A 'Train' on the Soul Track." *New York Times*, 4 February 1973, 17.5, sec. II.

"Rising Complaints Shake Film Truce with Blacks." *New York Times*, 27 September 1972, 37.

"*Roadie*." *Variety*, 11 June 1980.

Rotzoll, Brenda Warner. "E. Rodney Jones, 75, Disc Jockey." *Chicago Sun-Times*, 7 January 2004.

Schumach, Murray. "King Curtis, the Bandleader, Is Stabbed to Death." *New York Times*, 15 August 1971, 38.

"Shemar Moore — More Than a Pretty Face." *Jacksonville Free Press*, 25 April 2001, 11.

Simmons, Sheila. "'Soul Train' Hails Black Artists." *Plain Dealer*, 29 March 1996, 5, sec. E.

"Sly and the Family Stone." Advertisement. *New York Times*, 2 June 1974, 120.

Snow, Shauna. "Comedy." *Los Angeles Times*, 1 June 1993, 2.

"Soul at the Center '73." Advertisement. *New York Times*, 15 July 1973, 102.

"Soul Concert Gets an Energetic Lift from Betty Wright." *New York Times*, 1 April 1975, 28.

"'Soul Train' Back for 2nd Season TV Series." *Chicago Defender*, 20 September 1972, 12.

"'Soul Train' Goes National on CBS."

Chicago Defender, 23 October 1971, 22.

"Soul Train Has TV Guest Star Marc Copage As Guest." *Chicago Defender*, 24 July 1971, 35.

"Soul Train Hit With Teens." *Chicago Defender*, 21 September 1970, 13.

"'Soul Train' Is Great, Goes National." *Chicago Defender*, 1 November 1971, 10.

"Soul Train Story." *Don Cornelius Productions*. http://www.soultrain.com.

"Soul Train 30 Years Strong." *Los Angeles Sentinel*, 14 February 2001.

Stammer, Larry. "Dymally-Curb Race Abounds in Charges." *Los Angeles Times*, 5 November 1978, 5, sec. II.

"Stars Honor Rodney Jones." *Chicago Defender*, 29 September 1973, 17.

Strauss, Neil. "You Say 'Soul Train' Is How Old?" *New York Times*, 31 December 1995, 12.3, sec. 12.

Terrell, Angela. "Super Tall, Super Cool and Here." *Washington Post*, 13 December 1972, 15, sec. C.

Thomas, Kevin. "Rudolph's 'Roadie': Sound of Music." *New York Times*, 14 June 1980, 2, sec. II.

Thompson, Bryan. "A Look at Black Family Life During the '70s." *Recorder*, 14 May 1994, 1, sec. B.

Thompson, Howard. "Going Out Guide." *New York Times*, 14 March 1979, 21, sec. C.

Varga, George. "Meanwhile, at Grammys Other Shows," *Union-Tribune*, 20 February 2005.

"VH1's Got Soul." *Multichannel News*, 5 October 2005, www.multichannel.com.

Walker, Theresa. "'Soul Train' Chugs into Echo Park Studio." *Los Angeles Times*, 26 December 1985, 1.

Weaver, Maurice. "'Soul Train' Awards Are a 1st for Black Music." *Chicago Tribune*, 23 March 1987, 3.

"Who Makes Music and Where." *New York Times*, 19 August 1973, 118.

Wirt, John. "E. Rodney Jones." *The Advocate*, 3 January 2004, Fun section.

"'Word Out' on Stewart." *Tri-State Defender*, 16 January 1985, 4.

Interviews with and Letters to Author

Anders, Garrick. Interview. 28 February 2007.

Bauchman, Ron. Correspondence. May 2007.

Clark, Mystro. Letter. 28 May 2007.

Clemons, Lorenzo. Letter. 20 March 2007.

Cordell, Lucky. Interview. 21 March 2007.

Davis, Theresa. Letters. April 2007.

Dells, The. Letter. 28 February 2007.

Dunwoody, Vera. Letter. 3 April 2007.

_____. Interview. 11 April 2007.

Fields, Delwen. Interview. 26 February 2007.

Gillette, Mic. Letter. 23 July 2007.

Hutton, Bobby. Letter. March 2007.

Jackson, Bill. Letter. 31 January 2007.

Kavanaugh, Clarice. Letters. March-April 2007.

Lee, Christa. Letter. 17 July 2007.

Miller, Bruce W. Letter. 12 April 2007.

O'Hare, George. Interview. March 2007.

Parker, Gregg. Interview. 30 January 2007.

Shapiro, Howard. Interview. 26 January 2007.

Thompson, Marshall. Interview. 7 February 2007.

Vannelli, Gino. Letter. 14 January 2007.

Vannelli, Joe. Letter. 24 July 2007.

Ward, Crescendo. Interview. 22 February 2007.

West, Art. Interview. 11 January 2007.

Web sites

us.imdb.com

www.soultrain.com

www.tv.com

Index